7/23

A Summer
of
British Wildlife

100 GREAT DAYS OUT WATCHING WILDLIFE

JAMES LOWEN

Bradt

A ged three, standing in a leafy Devon lane, **James Lowen** confidently identified a common buzzard that his dad had dismissed as a crow. Ever since, James has been immersed in all aspects of natural history. He is now a well-established wildlife and travel writer, editor, photographer and guide (see http://jameslowen.com). James's travels and writing commissions have led him to live and work all over the world, but he retains a vibrant fondness for the nature of his home country, the UK. This book – along with its predecessor for Bradt Travel Guides, *52 Wildlife Weekends: A Year of British Wildlife-Watching Breaks* – is the result.

A member of the British Guild of Travel Writers, James has written one further book for Bradt (*Pantanal Wildlife: A Visitor's Guide to Brazil's Great Wetland*), plus two other books: *Badgers* and *Antarctic Wildlife: A Visitor's Guide to the Wildlife of the Beagle Channel, Drake Passage and Antarctic Peninsula*. James writes regularly for magazines such as *BBC Wildlife*, *The Countryman* and *Bird Watching*, and his photography is represented by FLPA Images.

Acknowledgements

A notable rabble furnished information or inspiration that found an outlet in *A Summer of British Wildlife*. I thank Mike Alibone, Richard Allison, Steve Babbs, Patrick Barkham, Dave Bent, Karen Bulsara, Stuart Butchart (BirdLife International), Andy Butler, Simon Close, Mark Cocker, Sean Cole, Colin Davies, John Dixon, Steve Elliott, Neil Forbes (National Trust), Martin Fowlie, Seth Gibson, Matt Gooch, James Hanlon, Ian Haworth, Marc Heath, Jan Hein, Andrew Hodgson, Mark Hows, James Hunter, Terence Ilott, Hannah Jones (Marine Discovery Penzance), Josh Jones (Birdguides), Martin Kitching (Northern Experience Wildlife Tours), Sophie Lake, Andy Lawson, Iain Leach, Jono Leadley (Yorkshire Wildlife Trust), Ben Lewis (RSPB), Durwyn Liley, Dougal McNeil (Natural England), Peter Moore, Rich Moores, Andy Musgrove (BTO), David Newland, Jonathan Newman, Rob Petley-Jones (Natural England), Ben Porter, Phil Rhodes, Alick Simmons, Will Soar (Rare Bird Alert), Allan Spencer, Steven Stansfield, Trevor Strudwick (RSPB), Adam Taylor, Mark Telfer, Chris Townend (Wise Birding Tours), Mike Unwin, Howard Vaughan (RSPB), Mike Waller and Simon West. My apologies to anyone inadvertently omitted.

Iain Leach and Oliver Smart were excellent primary photographic collaborators – and I widen my gratitude to all those photographer-friends who submitted images (see page 256). From Bradt Travel Guides, I thank Hugh Collins, Rachel Fielding, Deborah Gerrard, Janet Mears, Anna Moores, Adrian Phillips; Laura Pidgley, Ian Spick and Marianne Taylor for editing and advice,

Photograph

management and marketing. Donald Greig's kind words about publishing *52 Wildlife Weekends* served as encouragement for me to pitch this follow-up.

A gaggle of magazine editors have commissioned work from me over recent years and warrant in-print gratitude: David Callahan, Martin Fowlie, Sheena Harvey, Matt Havercroft, Ben Hoare, Angharad Moran, Matt Merritt, Ben Ross, Matt Swaine and Mark Whitley. Matt Merritt kindly allowed me to adapt for this book several columns written for *Bird Watching* magazine. The writings of Patrick Barkham, Simon Barnes, Mark Cocker and Rob Macfarlane constantly excite me. I have occasionally quoted from their books, and from publications written by Mark Avery, Michael Easterbrook, Charlie Elder, Simon Harrap, Sophie Lake, Durwyn Liley, Peter Marren and George Peterken.

Maya and Sharon Lowen accompanied me on many a 'research' trip, often carefully disguised under the cloak of a fun family day out. Maya's excitement levels were a key determinant in the 'child-friendliness' parameter ascribed to each day out.

FEEDBACK REQUEST

Why not write and tell us about your experiences using this guide? Post reviews to 🖳 www.bradtguides.com or Amazon. You can send in updates on out-of-date information or suggestions for your own recommended wildlife-watching days to 📞 01753 893444 or e info@bradtguides.com. Any contributors will be thanked by James Lowen in future editions. We may also post 'one-off updates' at 🖳 www.bradtupdates.com/britwild.

Introduction

What will be your summer wildlife highlight? Lying in a meadow of orchids and ox-eye daisies, accompanied by the surround sound of an orchestra of grasshoppers and bees? A dawn chorus that combines the birds of meadows and mires, woodland and heathland? A boat trip to an offshore island where puffins peer curiously at you, barely an arm's-length away, while Arctic terns scud overhead? Or a dune tiger-beetle, scurrying along a coastal sand dune beneath the bluest of summer skies?

Your summer of British wildlife could feature them all – and much, much more besides. Summer is, after all, our richest season. There is so much to seek, to watch and to explore. With this book, I aim to celebrate the bounty and variety of British nature. I do so through showcasing 100 of what I believe to be the finest wildlife-watching experiences, each carefully timed for a suitable date between mid-May and late August.

I seek to inspire you to venture out to places new and old, from Cornish clifftops to Shetland lochs. I encourage you to experience familiar sights with fresh eyes, whether by donning a wetsuit to snorkel in the Western Isles or by lacing up walking boots to scramble up chalk escarpments in Sussex. Whether you are a paid-up member of a county wildlife trust or the parent of a nature-loving child, I hope that you will tread novel paths looking for previously

The Somerset Levels, featured on *June 25.* (AS)

4

unimaginable creatures. If you are a birdwatcher, I seek to make you a botanist. If you already love dragonflies and butterflies, may your horizons expand into creatures that have no wings.

Above all, I hope that my suggestions and personal experiences frame your own 100 days with British wildlife (which social media afficionados might convert into the hashtag #100dayswild (see page 16). As you travel this brilliant country, laud the diversity of British fauna and flora, and honour those who strive to safeguard nature's future. Enjoy your summer of British wildlife!

A Summer of British Wildlife

Coloured circles identify the location of each day. Each circle contains the number of the day (ie: 1 = Day 1: May 15). The colour of the circle varies with month, following the colour scheme used in the guide.

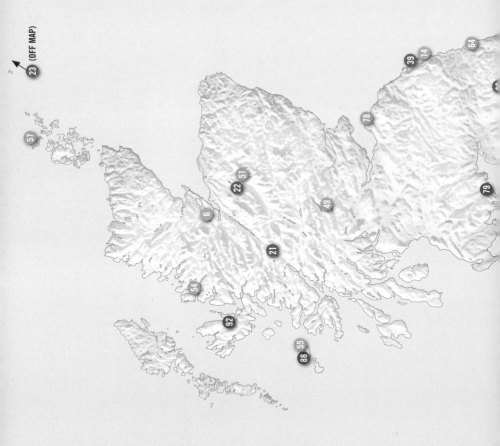

23 (OFF MAP)

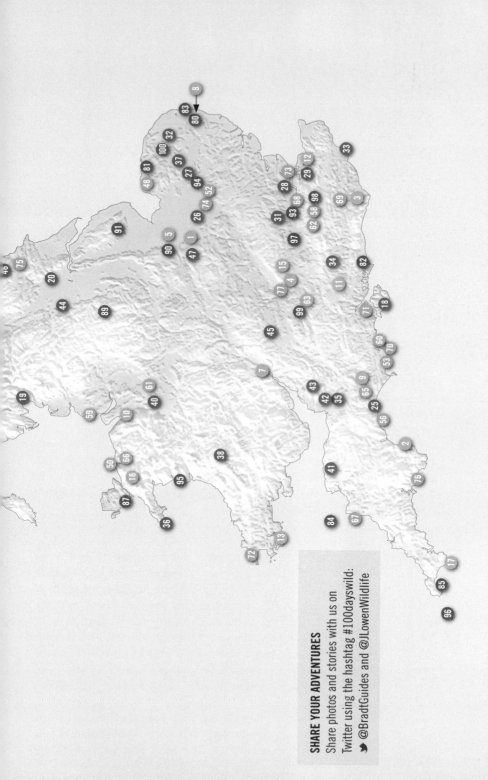

SHARE YOUR ADVENTURES
Share photos and stories with us on
Twitter using the hashtag #100dayswild:
@BradtGuides and @JLowenWildlife

Many of the days out are designed to appeal to children – these girls are admiring a fly orchid. (JL)

How to use this book

In this book, I suggest an itinerary for each of 100 days of summer wildlife-watching between 15 May and 22 August. The locations cover Great Britain *sensu strictu* (England, Scotland and Wales), and stretch from Cornwall to Shetland. I choose days that enable you to see the very best of British wildlife, with a focus on the special, the rare and the spectacular. To help you focus your attention, I suggest up to five wildlife 'targets' for each day.

About the 100 days

Each entry covers two pages. The main text walks you through the day, bringing to life the sites, the scenery, the target species and the experience. I offer a subjective take on the **child-friendliness** and **accessibility** of each day. For the former, I have used my young daughter as a barometer: how much would the day excite her? For the latter, I have thought about accessibility for a wheelchair-using friend: how easy or tough would the day be for him? A score of 1 means the experience is not particularly child-friendly or accessible; 5 means very child-friendly or accessible.

Practicalities

Each entry finishes with a box on practical considerations. *Where to go* summarises access details, including grid references based on Ordnance Survey mapping (which you can key into an internet map provider such as ● www.streetmap.co.uk). I reference websites of reserves which typically offer further information on accessibility and travel by public transport.

Each date is carefully chosen to reflect the seasonality of special creatures: there's no point hoping to hear a nightingale sing in August, or expecting to see flowering autumn lady's-tresses in May. But what if summer comes late or you can't make the specific date suggested? A section on *Flexibility* summarises your room for manoeuvre.

Some days involve quite a journey; realistically you would only visit the locations suggested as part of a longer trip. *Make it a weekend* suggests how you might expand the day into a short break of wildlife-watching, or a couple of nature-focused days in a longer holiday with broader interests (perfect for families!). Finally, *Alternative locations* does what it says on the tin – it suggests alternative sites for seeing the wildlife targets.

What's in a name?
Where no confusion is possible, I have used the names for species that are commonly used, rather than the formal taxonomic moniker. Hence badger rather than Eurasian badger, for example; but also common redshank to differentiate that shorebird from spotted redshank. Scientific names for target species (only) appear in the *Index of target species* (pages 250–5) alongside each species' vernacular name.

Further information
A Summer of British Wildlife is neither an identification guide nor an ecological handbook. It is neither a comprehensive site guide nor a gazeteer of nature reserves. For such publications, see *Further information*, pages 244–5.

Missing species
I am intentionally silent on particular species or sites that some readers might expect to appear in a book about Britain's special summer wildlife. This heeds guidance from conservationists and land managers, whose view is that increased visitation would risk harming the species concerned. Red helleborine, spiny seahorse and most black grouse sites are notable examples. Should viewing arrangements change, I may be able to incorporate such experiences in future editions of the book.

▶ Each day out is rated for ease of accessibility. (JL)

WILDLIFE-WATCHERS CODES OF CONDUCT

Responsible enjoyment of wildlife is essential. The guiding principle is that the welfare and conservation of the species comes before our enjoyment of them. All readers of this book must respect legislative constraints (eg: it is illegal to disturb certain Nationally Scarce species) and, additionally, I strongly encourage all to abide by a series of codes of conduct, including those specified below.

Countryside Code 🖱 tinyurl.com/CountrysideCodeNE
Butterflies 🖱 www.purple-emperor.co.uk/page42.htm
Moths 🖱 tinyurl.com/MothsCode
Plants 🖱 www.bsbi.org.uk/Code_of_Conduct.pdf
Birds 🖱 tinyurl.com/crny831
Seashore 🖱 explorethecoast.org/pageresources/seashorecode.pdf
Dragonflies 🖱 tinyurl.com/dragonflycode
Bird Photography 🖱 tinyurl.com/BirdPhotoCode

Contents

▶ Brown long-eared bat (Hugh Clark/FLPA)

▶ Great skua, aka bonxie (OS)

▶ Small pearl-bordered fritillary (IHL)

FOLLOW US
Use the hashtag #100dayswild to share your adventures using this guide with us and to make your own suggestions – we'd love to hear from you.

f www.facebook.com/BradtTravelGuides
🐦 @BradtGuides and @JLowenWildlife (#100dayswild)
📷 @bradtguides (#100dayswild)
𝓅 pinterest.com/bradtguides

Grey seals feature in several days out. (RC)

Male black grouse displaying at a lek. (IHL.)

May

Bluebell – nightingale – Eurasian beaver – pasqueflower
dawn chorus – common bottlenose dolphin – Duke of Burgundy
emperor moth – black grouse – mayflies – club-tailed dragonfly
military orchid – puffin – spiny spider crab – monkey orchid
Snowdon lily – twin-headed clover

Purple haze

WHERE Northamptonshire
TARGETS Britain's best bluebell wood, nightingale & Goldilocks buttercup
ACCESSIBILITY ④
CHILD-FRIENDLINESS ④

What finer way to commence your summer of British wildlife than combining one of the country's most spectacular sights with one of our best-loved sounds? For this sensory treat – bluebells and nightingales, respectively – visit surviving fragments of the medieval royal hunting forest of Rockingham.

Bluebells routinely crest polls of Britain's favourite flowers, and for just reason. In deciduous woodlands countrywide, May's purple haze is eagerly awaited – and rarely disappoints. The Woodland Trust has identified some 1,500 forests worth visiting to see bluebells, so you have no need to travel far to experience them. But botanist Simon Harrap (author of *Harrap's Wild Flowers*) rates Short Wood as Britain's very best bluebell display – and who am I to dissent?

> **❝Can Britain really be in danger of losing two such iconic natural experiences?❞**

Under assiduously coppiced elms and hazels, the carpet of nodding 'bells hovers six inches above ground. Although delicately tubular in close-up, these flowers are best appreciated as a collective, a mauve wash sluicing the understorey. Half close your eyes to intensify the lilac shimmer, then indulge another sense by inhaling the mineral coolness of the bluebells' perfume.

Take your time to admire Short Wood's other sylvan flora. Dog's mercury, wood speedwell and wood sorrel are all comparatively common. Goldilocks buttercup may be harder to track down; if you fail, console yourself with orange-tip, that classic May butterfly, as it strims sun-thawed glades.

Then relocate a country mile to Glapthorn Cow Pastures. Despite the site name, livestock were removed last century, enabling blackthorn to infiltrate. The dense scrub that now complements Glapthorn's oak-based woodland hosts a handful of nightingale pairs, here nudging the northwestern edge of their shrinking range. Males arrive mid-April and immediately

◀ Will fortune favour you with such a good view of a nightingale? (IHL)

Bluebell woods are quintessential Britain. (BT)

advertise their existence through inimitable, unparalleled song. Optimum serenades take place early morning or on a calm evening. Enter Glapthorn at its southeast corner, turn immediately left, walk 100m, and listen. Should you feel the need to see as well as hear, good luck! Nightingales are renowned skulkers, pouring forth vocally while remaining demurely concealed. But with patience and guile, you should succeed.

Savour your hours with both bluebells and nightingales. Both may be quintessentially British and quintessentially May, but both are also threatened. Our native bluebells comprise half the world's population, yet face competition from a naturalised interloper. The Spanish bluebell has spurned householders' efforts to restrict it to gardens, escaping into the wider environment, there to wreck our native plant's gene pool through vigorous interbreeding. Nightingales face no such contamination, but Britain's population has – for currently unfathomed reasons – declined by 90% in just 40 years. Can Britain really be in danger of losing two such iconic natural experiences?

WHERE TO GO Access Short Wood west along a footpath from the Oundle–Southwick road, 1km north of Glapthorn (◉ TL022914 ▸ tinyurl.com/ShortWood2). Enter Glapthorn Cow Pastures from Green Lane, 1.5km west of Glapthorn (◉ TL006902 ▸ tinyurl.com/GCowP).
FLEXIBILITY Bluebell flowering varies, but is typically late April to late May. Nightingales sing mid-April to early June.
MAKE IT A WEEKEND Barnack Hills and Holes for pasqueflower and man orchid (*May 19*).
ALTERNATIVE LOCATIONS For numerous bluebell woodlands see ▸ tinyurl.com/bluebellwoodlands. Nightingale: Abbot's Wood (*May 17*), Minsmere (*May 22*), Brampton Wood (Cambridgeshire) and Pulborough Brooks (Sussex). Goldilocks buttercup: Whitbarrow (Cumbria).

Cuddly fish?

WHERE Devon
TARGETS common cuttlefish, spiny spider crab & Eurasian beaver
ACCESSIBILITY ①
CHILD-FRIENDLINESS ①

Can there be a cuter, crazier inhabitant of British coasts? The common cuttlefish floats serenely on undulating fins, as adept at rippling backwards or sideways as it is at forward motion. With a mouthpiece that evokes both an elephant's trunk and waving seaweed, zebra-striped flanks and squinting eyes, this foot-long beast is a creature worth spending time with. Time to head to Devon and don wetsuit.

Each spring, cuttlefish throng to the sheltered, picturesque cove of Babbacombe, where – with a modicum of underwater effort – you can gawp at males performing their graceful courtship display or at females laying eggs, zealously guarded by their protective partners. As Babbacombe Bay is protected by wooded cliffs to its north and west and rarely descends deeper than 6m, you need not be a divemaster to watch marine marvels. Provided visibility enables you to make out the sandy bed, you could conceivably snorkel to the gently swaying kelp gardens at the midpoint of the bay where these sub-aqua hovercrafts tend to hang out.

The common cuttlefish may be a mollusc, but it sure is an odd one. Unlike a mussel, say, the cuttlefish has internalised its shell. Cuttlefish are cephalopods, a

❝Snorkel to gently swaying kelp gardens where these sub-aqua hovercrafts hang out❞

Common cuttlefish are stunning, rippling creatures. (Steve Trewhella/FLPA)

Beavers released in Devon have been marked with ear tags. (JD)

tongue-twister of a grouping that also includes octopus and squid. We have long eaten those more familiar cephalopods (if only on Mediterranean holidays), but now cuttlefish also feature on menus and dining tables. As a consequence, local divers fear that Babbacombe's population is under threat from fishermen, who snare the molluscs in pots to sate our appetite for marine foodstuffs.

As you search, take time out to watch other life under the waves. Snakelocks anemones wave in greeting as the hint of a current alters their mood. Ballan wrasse gather around the breakwater, and scorpionfish sport a seaweed wig. Spiny spider crabs cower under rocks, their spindly legs and teardrop-shaped body lending them an inadvertently comical demeanour.

Once you return to shore, throttle east past the Exe Estuary to the tranquil River Otter. Your quest is not the aquatic mammal of the river's name – though you may glimpse that too – but Eurasian beaver, which is re-establishing itself in Britain after a 200-year absence. The Otter's beavers have been reintroduced within the philosophy of 'rewilding' Britain (the manifesto for which is George Monbiot's book *Feral*).

Seeing the beavers is tricky, but spring is the optimum season. These are mobile creatures that may relocate territory should conditions change or disturbance rise. Try the well-vegetated stretch of river northeast of Budleigh Salterton or the quieter areas north of Tipton St John. Arrive an hour before dusk, and prepare for these nocturnal creatures to awake... and emerge.

WHERE TO GO Babbacombe Bay (www.babbacombebeach.com) lies northeast of Torquay. From the A379, either take the funicular or drive along Hampton Avenue then descend Cliffside Road to Oddicombe Beach car park (SX926657). Try the River Otter northeast of Budleigh Salterton (park by road bridge at SY075830, then walk north) or Tipton St John (SY090918; park in the village then walk north).
FLEXIBILITY Cuttlefish visit Babbacombe for a few weeks in April and May; timing varies between years. Beavers are resident, but best seen in spring. Crab: May–June.
MAKE IT A WEEKEND View the guillemot colony on cliffs at Berry Head, south of Torquay, or visit RSPB Labrador Bay for cirl bunting.
ALTERNATIVE LOCATIONS None really for common cuttlefish. Eurasian beaver: Knapdale (Argyll & Bute) and Aigas (Highland). Crab: Stackpole Quay (*May 27*).

String of pearls

WHERE Sussex
TARGETS pearl-bordered fritillary, nightingale, two-banded longhorn beetle, burnt orchid & early spider orchid
ACCESSIBILITY ①
CHILD-FRIENDLINESS ②

I n *The Butterfly Isles*, Patrick Barkham's enchanting tale of his quest to observe Britain's 59 butterfly species in a single summer, Barkham admits to peering at a pearl-bordered fritillary 'with childish wonder.' An octet of fritillaries grace Britain, all similarly attired: a dichotomy of the delicate (a spider's web of wing-markings) and dynamic (the upperwing's fiery glow). But no British fritillary has endured as catastrophic a decline as the pearl-bordered, its population plummeting by three-quarters in nary 40 years. Wonder, childish or otherwise, is warranted.

In consequence, seeing pearl-bordered fritillaries has become as much a challenge for us as surviving is for the butterflies themselves. Fortunately, Butterfly Conservation – guardians of British lepidoptera – are imaginatively resisting extinction of the 'PBF'. Its 'Fritillaries for the Future' project, for example, is reintroducing captive-bred butterflies to improved woodland habitats in Sussex.

> **"Arrive early morning, before the fritillaries have awoken and while nightingales are still serenading"**

One of the county's reintroduction sites is a football-pitch-sized clearing in Abbot's Wood. Visit when the sky is clear and the day promises warmth. Arrive early morning, before the fritillaries have awoken and while nightingales are still serenading. Pause a moment – go on, indulge yourself – to marvel at the complexity, volume and vibrancy of the nightingale's score.

Then start searching for the string of pearls. Scrutinise the lilac blooms of violets, bluebells and borage on dead leaf-litter along the clearing's sheltered southern flank. These form the pearl-bordered fritillary's favoured nectar sources.

By late morning, the fritillaries typically attain an irrepressible sugar high, zipping between nectar sources,

◀ Conservationists are striving to turn round the fortunes of pearl-bordered fritillaries. (IHL)

the incorrigible males displaying to any lingering female. Should you find that close approach has become impossible, look for other flying creatures. Among butterflies, the diminutive and finely patterned grizzled skipper excels. Day-flying moths include speckled yellow, common swift and lesser treble-bar, while other winged insects include the striking two-banded longhorn beetle.

Then depart for two floral delights. Southeast of Lewes, take a deep lungful then hike up the south-facing chalk escarpment of Mount Caburn. Reaching the Bronze Age hillfort, scour the dry valley to the northwest for burnt orchid, a burgundy-toasted bonsai delight. Barely the height of your little finger, this orchid baffles by flowering in two distinct periods, the other coming in July. Caburn's population is of the 'early-flowering' form.

Early spider orchid (JL)

If time and energy remain unsapped, head south to Castle Hill, east of Brighton. This chalk downland holds numerous early spider orchids, although they are not always easy to track down. For reasons unknown, Castle Hill's scattered groups flower weeks later than elsewhere in England, thus are still going strong this late in spring.

WHERE TO GO Abbot's Wood (🚶 www.forestry.gov.uk/abbotswood) is 3km southwest of Hailsham. Park at Oak Tree pub (📍 TQ558078). Walk southeast then northeast to reach the clearing (📍 TQ569085). For Mount Caburn (📍 TQ444091 🚶 tinyurl.com/EastSussexOrchids), follow the footpath 1.5km west from Glynde. For Castle Hill (📍 TQ371070 🚶 tinyurl.com/CastleHill2015), park on the B2123 north of Woodingdean (📍 TQ356063); walk northeast.

FLEXIBILITY Pearl-bordered fritillaries fly late April to early June. Burnt orchid flowers early May to early June, early spider orchid (here) throughout May. Nightingales sing mid-April to early June. Beetle: April–June.

MAKE IT A WEEKEND Watch dragonflies, including white-legged damselfly and club-tailed dragonfly, at New Bridge, West Sussex (📍 TQ069260).

ALTERNATIVE LOCATIONS Pearl-bordered fritillary: Wyre Forest (Worcestershire), Dartmoor (Devon) and Eyarth Rocks (Denbighshire). Early-flowering burnt orchid: Clearbury Down (Wiltshire) and Knocking Hoe (Bedfordshire). Early spider orchid: Samphire Hoe (Kent) and Dancing Ledge (Dorset). Nightingale: see *May 15*. Beetle: widespread.

Day 4: **May 18**

Metamorphosis

WHERE Oxfordshire
TARGETS club-tailed dragonfly, monkey orchid & lady orchid
ACCESSIBILITY ④ (Goring), ① (Hartslock)
CHILD-FRIENDLINESS ④

In Franz Kafka's novella, travelling salesman Gregor Samsa is transformed into a gargantuan bug. Such fundamental changes are a routine – if seminal – stage in an insect's life cycle. One of the most spectacular conversions, arguably the equal of caterpillars becoming butterflies, occurs with dragonflies. Today's trip to Oxfordshire should enable you to witness this invertebrate 'coming of age.'

The River Thames at Goring is bloated and languid: a river indulging itself in mid-life spread. Make your way to the railway bridge that casts a shadow over the water, making the scene feel even more sedate. Directly below the bridge is Britain's finest location for watching one of our most localised dragonflies shift its abode from one element (water) to another (air). During fine spring weather, from mid-morning until early afternoon, 'clubtail' larvae crawl upwards from the silty river bed, scaling the concrete bank.

> **The River Thames is bloated and languid: a river indulging itself in mid-life spread**

Clubtail larvae are squat, flattened and spider-like, rather recalling an extra-terrestrial. Halfway up its ascent, the larva stops and – emphasising the alien impression – the adult inside starts to break free of its former self. After an hour or so, the clubtail has emerged into recognisable dragonfly form. It will not move for another hour or two, until body and wings have hardened up sufficiently to attempt a maiden flight. Once departed, only the larval casing ('exuvia') remains, an eerie reminder of an earlier life stage.

Come early afternoon, walk eastwards along the Thames. *En route*, you may encounter adult clubtails that emerged in previous days, although these may be tricky to spot as they perch high in trees. Easier to see will be banded demoiselles, stunningly

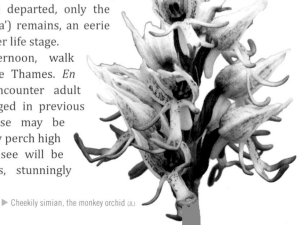

▶ Cheekily simian, the monkey orchid (JL)

delicate damselflies with wine-bottle colouration and black-spotted wings, and brown mayflies dancing above the water.

After a kilometre ascend the steep chalk bank to enter Hartslock reserve for a botanical treat. Monkey orchids grow at only three sites in Britain, this being one. Roped-off areas guide your access; an orchid this rare is vulnerable to inadvertent trampling. Look closely at the flowers to decipher the head, slender arms and curved legs of the spider monkey-like form.

Here too are lady orchids, at one of their two sites outside Kent/Sussex. These beautiful flowers are garbed in a burgundy bonnet and pink-flecked petticoat. The sharpest-eyed observer may discern hybrids between the two species, their jumbled features suggesting a metamorphosis every bit as intriguing as that of club-tailed dragonflies or, indeed, Gregor Samsa.

WHERE TO GO Park near Goring & Streatley railway station, 11km northwest of Reading. Walk along the River Thames to the railway bridge (♀ SU606796). Hartslock reserve is 1km southeast (♀ SU617797 🖳 tinyurl.com/hartslock).
FLEXIBILITY Club-tailed dragonfly, lady orchid: early May to early June; monkey orchid: mid-May to early June.
MAKE IT A WEEKEND See military orchids at Homefield Wood, Bucks (*May 29*).
ALTERNATIVE LOCATIONS Club-tailed dragonfly: Arun Valley (Sussex); lady orchid: Bonsai Bank (Kent); monkey orchid: Park Gate Down (Kent).

Hills and holes

riting in *The Englishman's flora* 60 years ago, Geoffrey Grigson considered that the pasqueflower had 'a fair claim to be the most dramatically and exotically beautiful of all English plants.'

'Fair,' in my view, is an understatement. In appearance, pasqueflowers are stunning: deep purple with a central yellow orb, they flood across chalk hillsides. In rarity, pasqueflowers are alluring: nationally threatened with only 18 scattered populations remaining. In cultural resonance, pasqueflowers are rich; legend tells that they bloom from the blood of Vikings, festooning the barrows that house warriors' graves. In Britain's floral kingdom, I believe, pasqueflowers are peerless.

> **66** **Man orchid florets really do resemble tiny, hooded human figures** **99**

The pasqueflower's name is a nod to its flowering time (*pasque*; Easter), but the blooms persist from April into late May. The county flower of Cambridgeshire, it is particularly numerous at Barnack Hills and Holes, an idyllic National Nature Reserve scant minutes east of the hectic A1.

The 'holes' of this limestone grassland are medieval quarries. Formerly furnishing stone used to bring into being both Peterborough and Ely cathedrals, the 'holes' are now wrapped in short turf. As you follow the waymarked Limestone Trail, the pasqueflowers are easy to find: the biggest groups are typically roped off to minimise inadvertent trampling and harmful enrichment of the soil from dog poo (if you've brought a mutt, don't fail to bag and bin!).

◀ Stunning, alluring and culturally rich: the pasqueflower (JL)

Somewhat harder to track down is another nationally
threatened plant: man orchid. The southwest quadrant
of the reserve tends to be best, and diligent searching
should reveal scores of slender yellow-green spikes
resolutely thrusting skywards.

Drop down to your knees to appreciate the aptness
of this orchid's English name. The florets really do
resemble tiny, hooded human figures – leggy mannikins
with dangling arms, a demure 'face' and russet stripes
on the bonnet. Look too for the magenta of early purple
orchids, standing proud.

As you beaver around looking at plants, don't
ignore Barnack's butterflies. Green hairstreaks can be
particularly common. Initially, this classic May insect
may be hard to spot, blending in with the vegetation.
Once you have your eye in, however, its luminosity
sears your eyeballs – and you may be baffled by how you
ever overlooked it. More subdued in colouration are
brown argus (titchy, too!) and dingy skipper. Close-up,
however, their intricate patterns enthral.

Finally, spend some time admiring the eternal architects
of this particular limestone grassland: yellow meadow ants.
Numerous mounds constructed over decades by generations
of ants create a series of hummocks, which bubble-wrap Barnack's
hills – and its holes. Every bit as impressive as the shire's spires.

▶ Man orchid: two 'legs' and two 'arms' (IHL)

Common bottlenose dolphins are frequently extroverts. (PM)

Black Isle bottlenose

WHERE Highland
TARGETS common bottlenose dolphin, harbour seal & long-tailed skua
ACCESSIBILITY ④
CHILD-FRIENDLINESS ⑤

With a frantic shimmy, a large fish wriggles itself clear of the sea. Dotted flanks reveal it to be a sea trout – and its airborne leap heralds the arrival of the pinnacle of the Moray Firth foodchain. And there it is! Powering out of the water, muscled sleekness in silver armour, is a common bottlenose dolphin. Then another, and another. For ten glorious minutes the sea surface freeze-frames a confusion of snouts and dorsal fins as a pod of dolphins feasts on salmon and trout that the returning tide is funnelling along a deep-water trench.

> **The sea surface freeze-frames a confusion of snouts and dorsal fins as dolphins feast**

There are two main ways to enjoy the world's northernmost bottlenose population. You can join a boat trip from Cromarty to get close views while bobbing in the swell. Alternatively, landlubbers can position themselves at the tip of the pebbly spit kneeling below Chanonry Point lighthouse and look eastwards offshore. If daylight permits, why not dedicate one approach to each of the day's two high tides?

There may be as many as 200 dolphins inhabiting the Moray Firth and environs, yet researchers from Aberdeen University can recognise individual animals by dint of their uniquely shaped dorsal fin. 'Jigsaw' is a mature female with a section missing from her fin; 'Mischief' has a slash at the base of his fin. Unique recognition allows the scientists to piece together life histories. Some Moray animals have even been spotted as far south as Yorkshire.

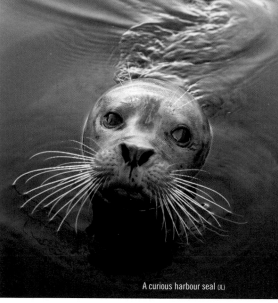
A curious harbour seal (JL)

Views from Chanonry Point are often very close indeed, and photographers may find themselves toting lenses with shorter focal lengths than they anticipated. The wildlife paparazzi can be rather numerous here, but they fill local coffers to the tune of £4 million each year.

As well as dolphins, the transitory abundance of fish attracts other piscivorous mammals. Harbour porpoises are regularly seen, although they are as undemonstrative as the dolphins are exhibitionist. Both grey and harbour seals occur; if you don't see the latter here, you can often spot them hauled out on roadside rocks flanking nearby Cromarty Firth.

Visiting in May also offers prospects of a particularly unusual encounter. Birdwatchers have recently discovered that migrating skuas – piratical seabirds breeding from northern Scotland into the Arctic – sometimes sneak an overland shortcut along the Great Glen. By following this channel northeastwards to enter the North Sea, the skuas often emerge on the Moray Firth. Arctic skuas are most regular, but the real prizes are flocks of the delicate, foppish long-tailed skua or the brutish, spoon-tailed pomarine skua.

WHERE TO GO Chanonry Point lighthouse (NH749557) is 2.5km southeast of Fortrose. Boat trips depart from Cromarty (www.ecoventures.co.uk). The Moray Firth dolphin population can also be seen from nearby locations including North Kessock, Burghead and Spey Bay.
FLEXIBILITY Dolphins and seals: year-round but May–September is best. Skuas: May.
MAKE IT A WEEKEND In an early spring, try for chequered skipper around Fort William (*June 4*), with a fallback of pine marten and otter.
ALTERNATIVE LOCATIONS Common bottlenose dolphin: Inner Hebrides, Cardigan Bay (*July 25*) and Durlston (*July 23*). Passage skuas: Balranald (North Uist, Western Isles). Harbour seal: Blakeney Point (*August 3*).

Dukes, without hazard

WHERE Gloucestershire
TARGETS Duke of Burgundy, Adonis blue, sword-leaved helleborine & pasqueflower
ACCESSIBILITY ②
CHILD-FRIENDLINESS ②

As you contour the limestone downland escarpment, there is a spring in your step. The trampoline of the plant-rich sward counteracts your footfall with upwards momentum, as if trying its best to fling you skywards. Not that you may need much persuasion: steep chalk-related escarpments such as Rodborough Common, as landscape-writer Robert Macfarlane argues in *Old Ways*, somehow instill walkers with a 'forceful... dream of flight.'

On this grassland, wildlife also reaches heady heights. Rodborough is the seat of nobility, for the Duke of Burgundy – one of Britain's rarest butterflies – resides here. 'His Grace' congregates in a handful of colonies smattering the common's western slopes and the lower reaches of Swellshill Bank, 1km southeast. Microclimate influences each group's timetable, with

> **The Duke is pugnacious, males attacking pretty much any butterfly that gatecrashes their territory**

those in exposed locations upslope starting adult life a week later than those claiming sheltered, sunny spots. This chequered 'metalmark' is a pugnacious creature, males attacking pretty much any butterfly that gatecrashes their territory: Rodborough's dingy skippers and brown arguses are frequent targets.

An utterly different butterfly should be your other personal target today. In appearance, Adonis blue lives up to its Greek-god namesake. The male is a stunner, extravagantly sky-blue in colour. There are two generations each year, the first of which emerges around this time. To see them, try the steep west-facing slope between Rodborough Manor Spur and Little London,

Sword-leaved helleborine (IHL)

▶ Male Adonis blues are every bit as beautiful as their name suggests. (OS)

the incline of Butterrow Hill or Swellshill Bank. Day-flying moths can be fun here, with the inky-emerald foresters locally abundant.

Enjoy Rodborough's plants as well. The turf is stippled with cowslips, a regular if suboptimal foodstuff for His Grace. A scattering of intense lilac above the road by Rodborough Manor Spur draws your eye to the final flourish of pasqueflowers. Taller plants with a magenta hue are early purple orchid. Rodborough is blessed with a further dozen types of orchid. Some will only be starting to contemplate emerging from the nutrient-poor, alkaline soil: plan a return trip in a month's time to see musk, frog and chalk fragrant orchids. One speciality, however, should be reaching its peak. The Nationally Scarce sword-leaved helleborine, a slender orchid with distinct poise, grows on the upper fringe of the wood overlooking a road called Bear Hill.

After all the effort of ascending and descending slopes, pause to admire the view over Stroud, surveying the terrain onwards towards the Severn Estuary and yet further to the Welsh Mountains. His Grace would undoubtedly approve.

◀ The male Duke of Burgundy is feisty as well as delicately patterned. (IHL)

WHERE TO GO Rodborough Common is immediately southeast of Stroud. From the A46 in Rodborough, take Walkley Hill to the National Trust car park (♥ SO850035). Follow the Trust's suggested 'butterfly walk' (🖰 tinyurl.com/NTRodborough). For Swellshill Bank, park on Bownham Park (♥ SO859024) then walk downhill.

FLEXIBILITY Duke of Burgundy: end April to early June. Adonis blue: mid-May to mid-June, and mid-August to mid-September. Sword-leaved helleborine: mid-May to early June. Pasqueflower: mid-April to early June.

MAKE IT A WEEKEND There are more dukes and Adonis blues at Prestbury Hill (🖰 tinyurl.com/BCPrestburyHill), or try Forest of Dean for wild boar on quiet tracks around Cinderford (🖰 http://forestofdeanblog.com).

ALTERNATIVE LOCATIONS Duke of Burgundy: Heyshott Escarpment (West Sussex), Noar Hill (Hampshire), Cerne Abbas (*May 23*) and Bison Hill (Bedfordshire). Sword-leaved helleborine: Chappetts Copse, East Sussex. Adonis blue: Cerne Giant Hill (*May* 23), Denbies Hillside (*Aug 20*). Pasqueflower: Barnack Hills and Holes (*May 19*) and Therfield Heath (Hertfordshire).

Day 8: **May 22**

The Emperor's dawn

WHERE Suffolk
TARGETS the dawn chorus, stone-curlew, woodlark & emperor moth
ACCESSIBILITY ⑤
CHILD-FRIENDLINESS ④

It would not be a proper summer of wildlife without experiencing a dawn chorus. All components are integral. The hardship that comes with forsaking a snug duvet at silly o'clock. The uncertainty of the evaporating darkness – which birds will sing? And which won't? – that intensifies into the gratification of a private audience with an avian choir. And the hearty, celebratory and richly deserved breakfast that feels timed for lunch.

The joy of a dawn chorus is its accessibility. You can hear versions of the vocal outpouring pretty much anywhere, even in your local woodland, park or garden. But for the greatest range of troubadors, nowhere trumps Minsmere with its trio of privileged habitats: wetland, woodland and heathland. Try to wander amidst this landscape mosaic either side of first light.

> **❝For the most varied choir, nowhere trumps Minsmere with its wetlands, woodlands and heathlands❞**

Near the reedbeds, listen for great bitterns 'booming' – a profound, airy exhalation – while sedge warblers chide and reed warblers rasp. On the lagoons, avocets pipe, nervously guarding their first teetering chicks. At the scrubby segue between reed and carr, Cetti's warblers explode with a song that nature-writer Simon Barnes transcribes as 'Me? Cetti's? If you don't like it – f*ck off!'

In woodland, all manner of warblers serenade potential suitors: try to discern the conversational melody of a garden warbler. The density of blackbirds, song thrushes and robins swells their songs together – yet, near the canopy hide, a nightingale still manages to cut through; an unstoppable chorister.

On sandy heathland north of Minsmere's car park, a stone-curlew wails, banshee-like; this camouflaged oddity stands tall on stony

◀ Female emperor moths are active on sunny, warm spring days. (IHL)

Goggle-eyed and long-legged, stone-curlews are unlike any other British wader. (DT)

terrain. North towards Dunwich Heath, punk-haired Dartford warblers churr, scratchily, and a woodlark's viscous lullaby drips down from the sky.

When the serenades have become subdued, explore the reserve for as long as your growling stomach grants. The 'Scrape' buzzes with life – northbound shorebirds such as dunlins and black-tailed godwits, fellow transients such as little gulls, and local breeders such as Mediterranean gull and Sandwich tern. Female great bitterns flap over reedbeds at Island Mere and North Wall, diligently provisioning their offspring. The former location excels for viewing marsh harrier, hobby and otter, the latter for bearded tit. Although more readily seen earlier in spring, the odd adder still basks, slovenly, between Bittern Hide and Island Mere.

Finally, if the air is calm and warm, return to Dunwich Heath. With luck you will encounter the emperor, one of Britain's largest and most gorgeous moths, each wing blessed with a staring eyespot. Males fly rapidly as they scent pheromones released by females eager to breed. By this point in the day, you will be in awe of their energy levels. Time for that breakfast.

WHERE TO GO Both sites are signposted from the A12 and accessed from Westleton. For Dunwich Heath (♀ TM475683 🖱 www.nationaltrust.org.uk/dunwich-heath) take Minsmere Road for 1.5km to the National Trust car park. For RSPB Minsmere (♀ TM473672; 🖱 tinyurl.com/RSPBMinsmere) leave Westleton east and follow signs.
FLEXIBILITY International Dawn Chorus Day (🖱 www.idcd.info) happens in early May: in Britain, this coincides with peak song. By end May, fewer birds sing. Emperor moth: mid-April for five to six weeks. Stone-curlew: end March to late September. Woodlark: resident.
MAKE IT A WEEKEND There's enough at Minsmere and Dunwich for a full weekend; repeating your footfall won't replicate the experience!
ALTERNATIVE LOCATIONS For dawn chorus events, see 🖱 www.idcd.info. Stodmarsh (Kent) combines woodland and wetland habitats, but lacks Minsmere's heathland element. Emperor moths occur widely. Stone-curlew: Weeting Heath (Norfolk), Cavenham Heath (*August 16*). Woodlark: New Forest (Hampshire), Stoborough Heath (*July 6*), Ashdown Forest (*July 22*).

Fertility rites

WHERE Dorset
TARGETS marsh fritillary, Adonis blue, Duke of Burgundy
& grizzled skipper
ACCESSIBILITY ②
CHILD-FRIENDLINESS ③

Nobody knows how long the Cerne Giant has titillated the chalk escarpment rising above Dorset's picture-postcard village, Cerne Abbas. Some claim 400 years; others argue 4,000. But what is certain is that many couples have made the pilgrimage to this gargantuan chalk carving, harbouring the faith that his raised club and erect penis will bring them children.

It is not merely humans whose fertility rites are associated with Cerne Giant Hill. The downland has long been grazed, and the resulting flower-rich slopes provide ample foodplants and fabulous breeding grounds for a joyous profusion of butterflies.

First among equals is marsh fritillary. As its name infers, this butterfly typically occupies low-lying wetlands – except at occasional locations such as Cerne Giant Hill. On

> **Cerne swarms with marsh fritillaries, flying stained-glass windows in orange, brown, black and cream**

this dry grassland, the proliferation of devil's-bit scabious, the caterpillars' mauve, fabulously named foodplant, nourishes a considerable population. On sunny days, Cerne's hillside swarms with adult fritillaries, flying stained-glass windows in orange, brown, black and cream. As you enjoy the spectacle, bear in mind that marsh fritillary is nationally threatened: its vulnerability renders the experience even more special.

The Cerne Giant is more than 50m high. (JL)

WHERE TO GO At Cerne Giant Hill (👆 www.nationaltrust.org.uk/cerne-giant/; the viewpoint car park is at 📍 ST662016; the picnic area car park 📍 ST664015) is off the A352 immediately north of Cerne Abbas. From the picnic area cross Kettle Bridge then follow footpaths left then right onto and around the hill.

FLEXIBILITY Marsh fritillary: early May to end June; Duke of Burgundy: mid-April to end May; Adonis blue: mid-May to mid-June; mid-August to mid-September. Grizzled skipper: April–June.

MAKE IT A WEEKEND Visit Blandford Forum (Dorset) for peri-urban otters then Martin Down (Hampshire) for butterflies similar to Cerne Abbas (minus marsh fritillary) plus burnt orchid.

ALTERNATIVE LOCATIONS Marsh fritillary: Bentley Wood (Wiltshire), Caeau Ffos Fach (Camarthenshire) and Powerstock Common (Dorset). Adonis blue: Rodborough Common (*May 21*), Denbies Hillside (*August 20*). Duke of Burgundy: Bonsai Bank (*May 26*), Gait Barrow (*June 2*) and sites mentioned under Rodborough Common (*May 21*). Grizzled skipper: Abbot's Wood (*May 17*), Bonsai Bank (*May 26*).

Similarly rare is the Duke of Burgundy. After 20 years of being rarely seen at Cerne Giant Hill, this metalmark – described by Charlie Elder in *Few and far between* as a 'flyweight champion... you don't mess with the Duke' – has bounced back since 2012. You may easily find a score around cowslips along the lower western escarpment. Next on the list is Adonis blue, the handsome males of which readily cause jaws to drop: these over-Photoshopped tropical-sky-blue butterflies nectar on horseshoe vetch, its flowers the colour of sun.

Equivalently vibrant in tone but more retiring in demeanour is green hairstreak. Somehow proficient at concealing its luminosity on even the sparsest vegetation, this species measures your alertness. See lots, and you know you're not missing *anything*. See few, however, and...

... you can bet your bottom dollar that you are overlooking Cerne Giant Hill's quartet of small, dapper butterflies. The smartest is brown argus, its chocolate upperwings studded amber. The smallest is small blue. The remaining duo are grizzled skipper (a flying chessboard) and dingy skipper (less mundane than its name suggests).

Then there is a butterfly rainbow comprising widespread species such as brimstone (yellow, green), common blue (erm, blue), red admiral (red, black, white), small tortoiseshell (orange, blue, white), wall (orange, brown), and peacock (a full spectrum in itself) for a day replete with colour and form. Then throw in day-flying moths such as cinnabar and five-spot burnet (crimson, charcoal), forester (inky-green), and ruby tiger (chestnut, rose). Whether or not he endowed us with offspring, we all have much for which to thank the Cerne Giant.

▶ Grizzled skipper is one of Britain's smallest butterflies. (Marek R. Swadzba/S)

Seeing displaying black grouse demands an early (and often chilly) start. (OS)

The early bird...

WHERE Denbighshire, Powys & Ceredigion
TARGETS black grouse, common redstart & lesser twayblade
ACCESSIBILITY ④
CHILD-FRIENDLINESS ④

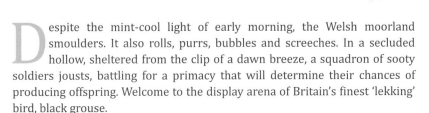

Despite the mint-cool light of early morning, the Welsh moorland smoulders. It also rolls, purrs, bubbles and screeches. In a secluded hollow, sheltered from the clip of a dawn breeze, a squadron of sooty soldiers jousts, battling for a primacy that will determine their chances of producing offspring. Welcome to the display arena of Britain's finest 'lekking' bird, black grouse.

The word 'lek' may be derived from the Swedish *leka* (to play), but fun is not the purpose of this gamebird's hormone-fuelled strutting and squabbling. Procreation is serious business: only the supremely fit are permitted market entry. To showcase their wares, male black grouse puff themselves up, accentuating the contrast between black and white feathering. Females compare offerings at Nature's singles bar, select 'Mr Right' – typically the highest-ranking male – and mate.

The best way to enjoy a black grouse lek is to join a RSPB event at a Coed Llandegla Forest's purpose-built hide. This avoids risking disturbance to a highly sensitive species. The alternative is to drive slowly between Minera and World's End, scanning slopes for gatherings of black footballs. If you do this, *stay in your car*. It takes disconcertingly little interference for grouse to abandon leks and for populations to shrink as a consequence.

Lesser twayblade (JL)

Lekking activity dissipates by 8.00am, so head westwards to another Welsh moorland for a tiny, elusive but beautiful plant. Lesser twayblade is a scarlet orchid that flowers demurely under heather. Being smaller than you can possibly imagine, finding it requires patience, sharp eyes and, usually, crawling. But once you spot one... Wow! What a stunner!

Lake Vyrnwy is the destination of choice. Here the RSPB operates under a long-term tenancy to supervise Wales's largest organic farm and maximise wildlife benefit. Enquire at the visitor centre for the best location to see lesser twayblade. Alternatively, a good area to search is along the minor road leading to Bala from the lake's northwest tip. Once you leave the pine plantations and enter open moorland, search below mature heather.

While ambling around the reserve, look for mature downy birch trees. Welsh clearwing is one of a spectacular group of wasp-mimicking moths. Males sometimes sunbathe on birch trunks and, if you are suitably equipped, may be attracted with pheromone lures.

After today's early start, gather your remaining energy resources to explore another RSPB reserve, Ynys-hir. Choose from trails leading through woodland, peat bogs, wetlands, and saltmarshes. The reserve's most treasured feathered visitors inhabit the oaks of the first-named trail. Common redstarts quiver their russet tails, pied flycatchers flash black and white, and wood warblers shiver with their trilling song. Enchanting.

> **" Female black grouse compare offerings at Nature's singles bar, select 'Mr Right' – and mate "**

WHERE TO GO At Llandegla Forest (Denbighshire) RSPB black grouse events (tinyurl.com/RSPBEvents) start from the visitor centre (♀ SJ240524) off the B5430, 5km west of Minera. At World's End take the B5426 south from Minera then the minor road west for 8km over Esclusham Mountain. Stay in your car. RSPB Lake Vyrnwy (Powys ♀ SJ016192 🐾 tinyurl.com/RSPBVyrnwy) is off the B4393 Llanfyllin–Llanwddyn road. RSPB Ynys-hir (Ceredigion ♀ SN682961 🐾 tinyurl.com/RSPBYnysHir) is signposted west from the A487 at Eglwys-Fach.
FLEXIBILITY Black grouse lek March–early June. Lesser twayblade: mid-May–early July. Common redstart: May–July.
MAKE IT A WEEKEND Gilfach Farm (Powys) has brook lamprey, otter and woodland birds or try Stackpole Quay for spiny spider crab (*May 27*) or Snowdonia (*May 30*).
ALTERNATIVE LOCATIONS Black grouse safari: RSPB Corrimony (Highland). Lesser twayblade: RSPB Abernethy (*June 5*) and Cliburn Moss (Cumbria). Redstart: Cheddar Gorge (*June 26*), Pensychnant (*July 19*), Ashdown Forest (*July 22*).

Ephemera

WHERE Hampshire
TARGETS mayflies, brown trout & bullhead
ACCESSIBILITY ⑤
CHILD-FRIENDLINESS ⑤

*E*phemera n., pl. -eras or -erae 1. a mayfly, esp. one of the genus Ephemera. 2. something transitory or short-lived.

Is any creature more poignantly named than this delicately beautiful riverfly? Mayflies mark the month in which they most readily attract our attention, but their adult lives are often over within a single day. These fragile winged mites evoke balmy, airless afternoons when clouds hatch en masse and billow over the shiny curtain of a river surface.

> **❝Of just 200 chalk rivers worldwide, Britain is privileged to host an amazing 85%❞**

A drake mackerel mayfly at rest (JL)

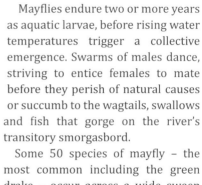

Mayflies endure two or more years as aquatic larvae, before rising water temperatures trigger a collective emergence. Swarms of males dance, striving to entice females to mate before they perish of natural causes or succumb to the wagtails, swallows and fish that gorge on the river's transitory smorgasbord.

Some 50 species of mayfly – the most common including the green drake – occur across a wide sweep of Britain. Wherever you live, you should be able to marvel at their condensed lifespan close to home. But mayflies are intrinsically associated with one landscape above all others so seeing them in that iconic domain is the standout experience. Of just 200 chalk rivers worldwide, Britain is privileged to host an amazing 85%. Their number includes Hampshire's stunning River Itchen, which can be enjoyed near the village of Ovington.

Sophie Lake and Durwyn Liley, in their majestic guide, *Britain's Habitats*, describe chalk rivers as 'particularly serene and equable watercourses' – idyllic settings for wildlife-watching.

Brown trout, a keen predator of mayflies (JL)

The Itchen's low banks are stratified with tall herbs and reed-grasses. Its waters are transparent and sedate in flow, characteristics that result from ribbons of aquatic plantlife such as the white-flowered water-crowfoot.

Ovington's unfettered gravel riverbed provides breeding grounds for brown trout, bullhead and Atlantic salmon. During mayfly season, these fish are easily seen from banks and bridges as they congregate close to the surface, eager to snaffle up for lunch. Look attentively and you may even spot brook lamprey, an eel-like fish with a sucker for a mouth and an adult life not much longer than that of the riverflies.

By scanning riverside vegetation, you should find mayflies perched, spent. Up close, these are stunning insects, with lacy wings held aloft above a curved body that culminates in three tails. Their beauty rivals that of another winged wonder, the banded demoiselle, a compact gleaming damselfly that twirls in dotted hordes behind The Bush Inn. Longer-lived than Ovington's mayflies, for sure, but never forget that beauty is unfailingly ephemeral.

WHERE TO GO The River Itchen at Ovington (♀ SU561319) lies 3km west of New Alresford (Hampshire). From the A31 roundabout, take the B3047 north towards Itchen Stoke then west to Ovington. Park at The Bush Inn, then walk north to the river. Follow paths along the banks.

FLEXIBILITY Late May to early June is the peak emergence for many species of mayfly, but timing depends on weather conditions. Fish: April–June best.

MAKE IT A WEEKEND Chappetts Copse (♀ SU654230), 13km west of Petersfield, has sword-leaved helleborine, bird's-nest orchid and fly orchid.

ALTERNATIVE LOCATIONS Other fine chalk rivers include the Wensum (Norfolk; try the bridge at Great Ryburgh ♀ TF963273) and the Frome (Dorset; try between Wareham and Stoborough ♀ SY922870). Fish: widespread.

Ladies and gentlemen

WHERE Kent
TARGETS lady orchid, man orchid & monkey orchid
ACCESSIBILITY ②
CHILD-FRIENDLINESS ③

L adies and gentlemen, roll up, roll up! Welcome to the North Downs of Kent! Today, for your eyes only, we have on show ladies and gentlemen... or, rather, lady orchids and man orchids. I'll even throw in a fellow primate: monkey orchid.

This orchid trio is nationally threatened, and Britain's southeasternmost county holds the lion's share of two (lady and man) plus one of just three populations nationwide of the third. Conveniently, the trio flower at broadly the same time, so marrying them into a single trip is eminently feasible.

All three orchids derive names from their appearance. The man orchid flowerhead takes a delicate human form, and is coloured pale green and burnt crimson. Lady orchid has a frilled 'skirt' topped by a burgundy bonnet. The monkey orchid has elongated and curled magenta 'arms' and 'legs', plus a stump of a tail.

> **Seven thousand man orchids flourish at Darland Banks – more than anywhere else**

Double delight: a Duke of Burgundy perches on the bonnet of a lady orchid. (HHL)

Today's outing takes in Britain's standout location for each species. Start on the steep, south-facing chalk escarpment of Darland Banks, which rims a dense series of Medway towns. Some 7,000 man orchids flourish here – more than anywhere else. Darland is halved by a small wood that is itself dissected by a restricted byway called Star Lane. The West Meadow offers both the finest views and weightiest orchid population.

Other floral contributors to Darland's tonal spectrum include lesser bird's-foot trefoil (yellow), sainfoin (candy pink), salad burnet (crimson), and common vetch (pinkish-purple). If the day is stoked by sun, three blue butterflies should wing between nectar sources. Common blue is the most abundant, but look too for Adonis and small blues. Later in the summer, there is chalkhill blue too.

Next stop is Denge Wood in east Kent. Once you have traversed the wood, the etymology of Bonsai Bank reserve makes sense. This wee suntrap, perched on a chalky incline, is an orchid haven. Lady orchid abounds: expect to see several hundred stately spikes, including ghostly all-white variants. Greater butterfly orchids grace the lower slopes, early purple orchids daub colour and inconspicuous common twayblades morph into their background.

If the day remains sunny, there should be ample butterfly action. Dingy and grizzled skippers bask on unvegetated ground, and green hairstreaks sidle along hawthorn sprigs. Duke of Burgundy occurs, although it is now rather late in the flight season to be sure of seeing this feisty flyweight.

For a final flurry, visit Park Gate Down, inland from Dover's famous white cliffs. May's botanical highlight is monkey orchid, which can otherwise be seen only in the Chilterns (*May 18*); the first of the Down's three steep meadows tends to be best. So, ladies and gentlemen, did you enjoy the show?

▶ In Britain, lady orchid is largely confined to Kent. (JL)

Spider(crab)man and Batman

WHERE Pembrokeshire
TARGETS spiny spider crab, otter, greater horseshoe bat & chough
ACCESSIBILITY ②
CHILD-FRIENDLINESS ③

With steep limestone cliffs as your bodyguard, wade through knee-high water and between fishing boats to exit the tiny harbour at Stackpole Quay. Snugly encased in a wetsuit, and with head adorned with mask and snorkel, you are prepared for one of Britain's finest underwater experiences. Each spring, a normally oceanic crustacean, the spiny spider crab, scuttles leggily towards the shallow waters of Pembrokeshire's coastline, there to mate.

Facing southeast and sheltered by those cliffs, Stackpole's coastal waters are clear and calm: visibility excels. A gentle stony slope cedes to a sandy bottom with a smattering of rocks. Snorkelling north, you spot a hairy rock scampering from your approach: spider crab! Males possess

> **A clifftop walk reveals a chough family, ragged and red-billed, floating in the breeze**

exceedingly long limbs, and both sexes have triangular bodies armored with spines and decorated with seaweed fronds. Get your eye in, and you should spy hordes trampling one another in a libidinal frenzy.

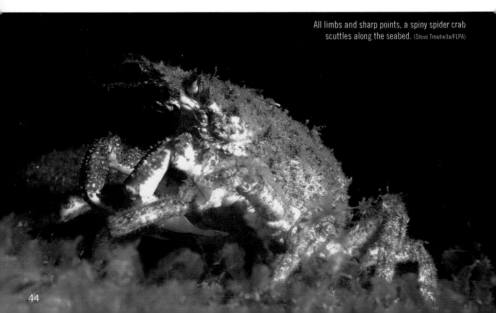

All limbs and sharp points, a spiny spider crab scuttles along the seabed. (Steve Trewhella/FLPA)

Then decipher other inhabitants of these marine shallows. Dragonets rest on the sand, masters of camouflage among fish. Dogfish flee surreptitiously at your approach, their nerves belying their size. Snakelocks anemones wave green tentacles. Sea hares and nudibranchs – aliens of the sea – ripple in slow motion.

When the tide turns, retreat to land. You now face a conundrum. At Stackpole, the National Trust manages an absolute gem of a site. You could spend a full week exploring – and still want more. So which of Stackpole's many natural attractions should you now target?

Wooded valleys bristle with ferns, and throb mauve with bluebells or magenta with early purple orchids. A clifftop walk around Stackpole Head, its turf flecked lilac by spring squill, reveals a chough family, ragged and red-billed, floating in the breeze. Guillemots hasten back to precarious breeding ledges from feeding grounds far offshore. Check the thinnest soils for the remarkable scrambled-egg lichen (which looks just like you think it might).

Visit Mere Pool Valley, with its flower-rich dunes, behind Broadhaven Beach. Or Bosherston Lakes, stippled with lily pads and the haunt of electric-blue kingfishers, which blur past if disturbed. An evening visit may produce otter, which are best seen from Nine Arches Bridge: they thrive on a fishy diet of pike and perch, roach and tench.

Whatever you do, arrive at Stackpole Court's former stable block (now courtyard flats) for dusk to see greater horseshoe bats from Wales's largest colony emerge to seize insects as large as cockchafers (aka 'maybugs'). This makes you Batman; after the morning's Spider(crab)man, this makes for a super(hero of a) day.

WHERE TO GO Stackpole is 6km south of Pembroke (🖥 www.nationaltrust.org.uk/stackpole). Park at Stackpole Quay (♀ SR993957) for snorkelling or diving; a high tide is best. Park here or at Broadhaven beach (♀ SR976937) for Stackpole Head and dunes. For Bosherston Lakes, park at ♀ SR967948; Nine Arches Bridge is at ♀ SR977956. For Stackpole Court, park just west of Stackpole (♀ SR979965), walk downhill, cross the bridge to your left then walk uphill to the Courtyard Flats. Respect residents' privacy.
FLEXIBILITY Spider crabs: May–June. Chough, otter: resident. Greater horseshoe bats: May–September.
MAKE IT A WEEKEND Explore the rest of the Stackpole estate!
ALTERNATIVE LOCATIONS Greater horseshoe bat: Buckfastleigh (Devon). Chough: many west coast locations, including South Stack (Anglesey) and Bardsey (*June 19*). Otter: widespread (try *June 25*). Crab: Babbacombe Bay (*May 16*).

Puffin without the huffin'

WHERE Northumberland
TARGETS Amble Puffin Festival & roseate tern
ACCESSIBILITY ④
CHILD-FRIENDLINESS ⑤

There is a compelling rationale for placing the puffin centre-stage on this book's front cover. It is an avian superstar, right here in Britain. Puffins are instantly recognisable and smartly attired: proper pin-ups. With clown-like bill, but wistful eyes, puffins are both comical and endearing – who doesn't want to mother one?

Little wonder that no species has featured more frequently on the front cover of the RSPB members' magazine. Little wonder that the puffin reached the Top 10 in the 2015 vote for the UK's national bird. And little wonder that the Northumberland town of Amble dedicates its spring festivities to its most famous resident.

For a week or more each spring, centered on the Whitsun school half-term, this routinely sleepy seaside town awakes – and how! First held in 2013, the rapid success of the 'Amble Puffin Festival' has enshrined it as a firm fixture on the county calendar. Including exhibitions, children's events, live music and watersports, the festival is ideal for a family outing.

> **❝Several thousand puffin pairs breed on Coquet, making it England's second-largest colony❞**

To see puffins breeding on Coquet Island, a RSPB reserve offshore, take a Puffin Cruise. Boat trips operate once or twice daily, with timings decreed by tide times. Landing on the island is not permitted, so boats bob gently beside Coquet's rocky shoreline, enabling fine views.

Several thousand puffin pairs breed here, making Coquet England's second-largest colony. This is exciting stuff, but poignant too. As well as numerous RSPB magazines, the puffin graces the front cover of the 2015 *European Red List for*

Unmistakable, much-loved but now globally threatened: the puffin. (OS)

Roseate tern (front, with Arctic tern behind) is another globally threatened seabird. (RC)

Birds, published by BirdLife International. At a European level, the Puffin – formally the Atlantic Puffin – is officially endangered. This means that it is at considerable risk of extinction within our lifetimes. Sobering stuff.

Coquet protects much else besides puffins. Among several thousand nesting pairs of Sandwich, Arctic and common terns which make a blizzard around the island, filling the air with noise and wings, there are more than 90% of Britain's roseate terns, which reached 100 pairs in summer 2015. Let's take time out to reflect on that. Nine in every ten pairs of this graceful, globally threatened seabird breeding in Britain do so on this single island. Coquet is some lump of rock.

Before the boat returns to the mainland, the skipper may circumnavigate Coquet to show you grey seals that hang out along the island's eastern face. And then it's back to Amble harbour, with common eiders – another threatened species at the European level, no less – bubbling a welcome.

WHERE TO GO RSPB Coquet Island (♀ NU293045 📱 tinyurl.com/RSPBCoquet) lies offshore from Amble (♀ NU267047), which is off the A1068 southeast of Alnwick. Dave Gray operates trips (📱 www.puffincruises.co.uk), or phone Amble Tourist Information Centre (☎ 01665 712313) for sailing times. The Amble Puffin Festival (📱 www.amblepuffinfest.com) runs annually each spring; check website for dates.
FLEXIBILITY Puffins are on Coquet from March to August, roseate terns from May to July. The festival lasts one to two weeks.
MAKE IT A WEEKEND Take a boat trip to the Farne Islands for a different type of seabird experience (*June 22*).
ALTERNATIVE LOCATIONS Puffin: Farne Islands, Bempton Cliffs (*June 3*), South Stack (Anglesey), Sumburgh Head (Shetland) and Skomer (Pembrokeshire). Roseate tern: nearby Hauxley or Cemlyn Bay (Anglesey).

Butter-coloured flies

Like many readers, I imagine, butterflies featured prominently in my childhood. Small tortoiseshells lent vibrancy to our garden and 'cabbage' whites deposited eggs on our allotment cabbages. The lemon lacework of a swallowtail illuminated a family holiday in Norfolk – but somehow failed to spark wider interest.

Thus I remained primarily a birdwatcher until the day when I stumbled across an unfamiliar, massive glowing ember of a butterfly. Shortly afterwards, at a wedding, an expert from Butterfly Conservation confirmed my tentative identification of Large Tortoiseshell, a former breeder but now only a vagrant. Within a year, I was hooked: butterflies even became the theme for my own wedding.

Seeing Britain's butterflies is both easy and tricky. A manageable number of species – 60 or so – breed in Britain. A score are widespread and common. Many others frequent well-known sites at well-defined times of the year – so you can easily organise seeing them.

> **"Pursuing butterflies demands that you visit Britain's most beautiful locations..."**

The tricky bit relates to changes wrought by declining populations (largely due to habitat damage) and erratic weather conditions, meaning variable hatching dates and unnaturally brief adult lives. Warm springs typically advance flight times by weeks whilst damp summers are catastrophic for procreation.

Should their varied beauty be insufficient to elicit your enthusiasm, pursuing butterflies demands that you visit Britain's most beautiful locations and best-preserved landscapes. Chalk downlands for Adonis blue, sheltered glens for chequered skipper, lilac heathlands for silver-studded blue, and ancient woodlands for purple emperor. What a hardship!

Entrancing differences in ecology keep the fascination flowing throughout summer. Orange-tips fly through April into May, but rarely beyond. Don't even think about looking for brown hairstreaks until school is out for summer. The painted lady slurping nectar from your garden buddleia may have hatched in Africa, whereas black hairstreaks spend their entire life cycle – from egg to adult – within a few square metres. Then there is even the allure of the rare, such as the long-tailed blues that hint at colonising Britain.

The subspecies of swallowtail breeding in the Norfolk
Broads occurs only in Britain. uu

Military bearing

WHERE Buckinghamshire
TARGETS military orchid, fly orchid, greater butterfly orchid & bird's-nest orchid
ACCESSIBILITY ⑤
CHILD-FRIENDLINESS ③

'The military orchid,' botanist Simon Harrap opines in *Orchids of Britain and Ireland*, 'combines two qualities which make orchids so alluring; great rarity and great beauty.' This ivory and pink orchid's name reflects the soldier-like form of its flowers, which cap a robust stem standing to attention. Each two-armed, two-legged figure appears to wear both buttoned tunic and coal-scuttle helmet. A stunner indeed.

Military orchid was not always scarce. In the 19th century, it flourished widely, sometimes abundantly, across the Chilterns. Come 1929, however, the plant was presumed extinct – a fate surmised to be due to a devastating combination of rampant grazing by rabbits, surreptitious collecting of plants for gardens, and chalk downland falling under the plough.

Within two years of World War II ending, the military orchid was rediscovered, a fact kept secret by the finder for fear of collectors. The news was eventually publicised in 1975, and visitors have been welcomed to Homefield Wood near Marlow since the late 1980s. Given the rarity of the species – it grows at just two other sites across Britain – such open access is a treasured privilege.

Appropriately, Homefield feels special. As a roe deer ushers you through the beech glades, you exit the trees and reach an unexpected meadow. Your spirits soar. Throughout the sheltered, sun-blessed green are splashes of pink, violet, magenta, lemon and snow-white. Grant yourself the time to investigate every single one.

Clearly, the battalion of military orchids is your primary quarry. But the supporting cast (reserves?) is impressive too. Greater butterfly orchid is languid and graceful, with bridal white flowers floating in mid-air like angels. A few grow at the far side of the enclosure. Bird's-nest

▶ Military orchid grows at only three sites in Britain, with Homefield Wood being the easiest to visit. (IHL)

orchid is a queer one: a translucent honey-brown orchid that looks half-dead but is actually full of life. Lacking chlorophyll, it depends on a fungal partner to provide sustenance. As Simon Harrap writes, 'spotting a bird's-nest orchid in the woodland gloom is somehow very reassuring; it is a sign that you are in a special place.'

Common twayblade is a lemon-green, spindly and undemonstrative orchid that makes you look twice to check that it is indeed an orchid. Once you have your eye in, you may spot dozens. Look too for shorter lime-green needles topped with tiny claret and sky-blue flowers. These West Ham United fans are fly orchids, beguiling plants that demand repeated inspection. They belong to a genus (*Ophrys*) renowned for fooling insects into assisting the plant's pollination.

'Fly orchid' is actually a misnomer: the flowers have evolved to resemble female digger wasps. The orchid emits a pheromone that lures male digger wasps to visit. Once at the plant, the male attempts to copulate with the 'female' and departs with the orchid's pollinia attached to its head. It wouldn't happen in the military.

▶ The flowers on a fly orchid mimic a female digger wasp. (IHL)

WHERE TO GO Homefield Wood (♀ SU814867 ☎ tinyurl.com/HomefieldWood) is 4km west of Marlow (Buckinghamshire). On the A4155 west of Marlow, turn right at the Dog and Badger pub. At the T-junction, turn right then left. After 500m park at the bottom of the hill. Walk 50m through the wood to the meadow.

FLEXIBILITY Military orchid: mid-May to end June. Fly orchid: late April to end June, but mainly late May to mid-June. Greater butterfly orchid: late May to July. Bird's-nest orchid: May–June.

MAKE IT A WEEKEND Goring and Hartslock (*May 18*) have club-tailed dragonfly and monkey orchid.

ALTERNATIVE LOCATIONS The only other accessible site for military orchid is Rex Graham reserve, near Mildenhall (Suffolk). Greater butterfly orchid: Bonsai Bank (*May 26*), Upper Teesdale (*June 13*), Aberdaron (*June 19*), Vicarage Meadows (*June 21*). Fly orchid: Chappetts Copse (Hampshire). Bird's-nest orchid: Chappetts Copse and Grays (*July 21*).

Snowdonia, in black and white

WHERE Snowdonia
TARGETS Snowdon lily, moss campion, starry saxifrage & raven
ACCESSIBILITY ①
CHILD-FRIENDLINESS ②

When a site is revered by botanists *and* climbers, by walkers *and* geologists, you know it has to be special. With a rock ampitheatre soaring above a montane lake of unfettered clarity, Cwm Idwal is one such location. To hike around the *llyn* is to enter a physical geography textbook – and to reach a botanist's nirvana. The dark, dank, north-facing walls of Devil's Kitchen rim the corrie's southern sweep. Here, and on banks and flushes descending *llyn*-wards, grows Wales's best collation of arctic-alpine flora.

Snowdon lily is one of Britain's most quixotic plants.
(Jean-Paul Chatagnon/FLPA)

Among commoner plants, thyme levitates in pink mats on the lake banks; roseroot gleams yellow on scree; and butterwort – a deep purple carnivorous plant – adores soaked ground. The Nationally Scarce mountain avens has anemone-like yellow and white flowers; Snowdonia is among just three non-Scottish sites where it grows. Likewise moss campion, which forms lush green cushions starred with rose-pink flowers.

Look for mountain sorrel and starry saxifrage on damp, stony stream banks. The latter's flower comprises a stellar quintet of delicate white petals, each with a red or yellow dot. Mossy saxifrage lies supine as cream mats on scree beneath Devil's Kitchen. Saxifrage means 'stonebreaker', marking the association between its representatives and rocky terrain.

▲ Moss campion forms dense green cushions, starred with pink flowers. (Bill Coster/FLPA)

Cwm Idwal's most precious plant is a glacial relic, a species hailing from the last Ice Age. Snowdon lily is among Britain's rarest flora, and spotting one is challenging. Only 100 or so plants remain, most on ledges inaccessible without a rope, and only a fifth of the population flowers each year. Best to first scan upwards with binoculars, looking for the grass-like leaves or delicate white flowers cheekily protruding from fissures in the rock.

> **❝Mossy saxifrage lies supine as cream mats on scree beneath Devil's Kitchen❞**

Should you see one, rejoice – and reflect. Although Snowdon lily is *rarissimo* in Britain, it abounds in North American meadows and Mongolian mountains. Thinking globally, should we worry if climate change forces its extinction in Britain given such populations elsewhere? Or are we right to care – and conserve – precisely because of the message this lily-cum-pit-canary hollers about our maltreatment of Planet Earth?

As you ponder, your ear catches a muffled cronk and your eye discerns a hefty dark form huddling on the cliff. As this raven is reminding you, there are birds here as well as plants. The raven is rugged and sooty, the lily delicate and ivory – yet both are superbly adapted to Cwm Idwal's cold, shady rigours. They *are* Snowdonia, in black and white.

WHERE TO GO In Snowdonia (🍎 www.snowdoniatourism.co.uk), Cwm Idwal is off the A5 between Bethesda and Capel Curig. Use Ogwen car park (📍 SH648604). Follow the footpath southeast then southwest to Llyn Idwal. Tread carefully around the lake to avoid trampling plants; Devil's Kitchen forms the corrie's southwestern wall.
FLEXIBILITY May–June for target plants. Raven: resident.
MAKE IT A WEEKEND Look for feral goat at Padarn Country Park near Llanberis or Craflwyn near Beddgelert. Or Coed Llandegla for black grouse (*May 24*).
ALTERNATIVE LOCATIONS None for Snowdon lily but good sites for arctic-alpine flora generally include the Cairngorms (*July 4*) and Ben Lawers (*July 2*). Raven: Lizard Peninsula (*May 31*), Bardsey (*June 19*), Newborough Warren (*August 9*).

Ma'n Lesard goz dinerby

WHERE Cornwall
TARGETS twin-headed clover, thyme broomrape, heath spotted orchid, thrift clearwing & red-veined darter
ACCESSIBILITY ②
CHILD-FRIENDLINESS ④

'Welcome to the Lizard!' The 150-km-long peninsula of Cornwall is England's outstretched lower leg, tentatively reaching into the churning Atlantic. This makes the Lizard Peninsula – England's southernmost extremity – its heel. Geologically unique and botanically heterogenic, the Lizard ranks amongst Britain's top four floral regions. The segue from May into June is the richest time to visit.

> **Geologically unique and botanically heterogenic, the Lizard ranks amongst Britain's top four floral regions**

So bounteous is the Lizard that choosing a single day's itinerary is tricky. On balance, spend most hours along or near the South West Coast Path, for it is the dramatic sea-cliffs and environs that particularly excel in early summer.

Kynance Cove car park is the place to start. Growing near here are spring squill (sublime, blue), kidney vetch (extrovert, yellow), spring sandwort (slender-petalled, white), tree mallow (towering, pink) and bloody cranesbill (starburst-leaved, crimson-pink). Wherever you find wild thyme, look for thyme broomrape, a reddish plant that parasitises the roots of its namesake.

The Lizard: one of the finest sites for plants in the whole of Britain. (AS)

A young red-veined darter: the pale blue underside to the eyes is diagnostic. (JL)

Climb valley slopes to examine outcrops of magnesium-rich serpentine, rising above schists and Devonian slate, which host condensed rock-garden plant communities. Sought-after rarities include twin-headed clover, fringed rupturewort and dwarf rush.

The track descending to the cove passes clumps of Babbington's leek and royal fern. Reaching the coastal footpath, candy-pink thrift washes the cliffs. This is the domain of a tiny, wasp-imitating moth: thrift clearwing. Rummage among the flower bases or entice a libidinal male with a vial infused with a pheromone lure. The Lizard is a brilliant place for moths overall. You may flush grass wave from tussocks, and if you stay overnight and run a moth trap, expect to catch Brussels lace and chamomile shark.

The Cove's awkward boulders are matted with hairy greenweed, a rare relative of the pea. Heading along the cliffs, heath spotted orchids shelter under western gorse. Keep a non-botanist ear out for birds. The chough's carefree call is commonplace now that this unkempt crow has returned to Cornwall. A raven's gruff bark may indicate that a local peregrine is prowling.

When you reach Caerthillian Cove, duck inland, up-valley. The conservation charity Plantlife considers this Britain's 'richest spot for clovers.' Searching diligently – which means crawling – may reveal western, rough, knotted, subterranean, upright, twin-headed and long-headed clovers. Good luck differentiating them all...

After lunch, retire to Windmill Farm reserve. Heath spotted orchids offer colour before Cornish heath is even considering flowering. Marsh fritillary should be flickering across damp grasslands and adders may bask on the airfield approach road. Check shallow, muddy-fringed ponds for red-veined darter, a largely Continental dragonfly that regularly breeds here. The Lizard welcomes allcomers.

WHERE TO GO Access Lizard Peninsula (📱 tinyurl.com/NELizardPeninsula & www.the-lizard.org) via the A3083 and B3293 south of Helston. West of Lizard village, use the National Trust car park for Kynance Cove (♀ SW688132 📱 tinyurl.com/NTKynanceCove). Walk down-valley then southeast to Caerthillian Cove (♀ SW694125). Windmill Farm (♀ SW693152 📱 tinyurl.com/WindmillFarmNR) is 1km west of the A3083, 3.5km south of Penhale.
FLEXIBILITY Mid-May to end June is best for the first flush of flowers and both non-floral targets.
MAKE IT A WEEKEND Kennack Sands has great rockpooling (♀ SW734165). Visit Boscregan Farm at Nanquidno (♀ SW362297) for Britain's only colony of purple viper's-bugloss.
ALTERNATIVE LOCATIONS Nowhere else has the Lizard Peninsula's floral assemblage. Red-veined darter: Sandwich Bay (Kent), Spurn Point (East Yorkshire). Thrift clearwing: Bardsey (*June 19*).

Britain's red squirrel population has reduced as a result of habitat
destruction and virus. Seeing one has become a treat. (IHL)

June

Glanville fritillary – lady's slipper orchid – pine marten
red squirrel – red-necked phalarope – black hairstreak
cliff tiger-beetle – elephant hawkmoth – swallowtail
bee orchid – large blue – Manx shearwater – Arctic tern
proliferous pink – white-faced darter – purple emperor

The Wight stuff

WHERE Isle of Wight
TARGETS Glanville fritillary, small blue, common wall lizard, Dartford warbler & red squirrel
ACCESSIBILITY ③
CHILD-FRIENDLINESS ⑤

O f Britain's eight species of fritillary, amber-coloured butterflies with embroidery for wings, the most special is Glanville fritillary. Granted, it is not the *rarest*: high brown and pearl-bordered fritillaries dispute that dubious honour. Nor is it the most *dramatic*: the majestic silver-washed fritillary merits that superlative, wings down. But there are dimensions to the Glanville that set it apart.

The first is its etymology, and, through that, its history: the butterfly is named after its discoverer, Eleanor Glanville, whose relatives successfully contested her sizeable will on grounds that pursuit of butterflies signalled insanity. The second is the Glanville fritillary's current distribution, sadly now a smidgeon of its

> **"Compton's soft-cliff landslip – the classic site for Glanville fritillary – is rich in other critters too"**

former range. Unless you visit a trio of sites on the English mainland, where Glanvilles have been illicitly released by lepidopterists seeking to play God, you must travel to the Isle of Wight to see this butterfly in Britain.

Even once you have crossed the Solent on to what Patrick Barkham, in *Coastlines,* considers this 'splendidly curmudgeonly island,' you don't simply bump into Glanvilles. These rapid fliers favour warm, sheltered undercliffs carpeted with thrift and common birdsfoot trefoil along the 'Back of the Wight', its southern and southeastern coastline. Good locations are Culver Down, Tennyson Down and Compton Bay.

Compton's soft-cliff landslip – the classic site for Glanville – is rich in other critters too. Another butterfly, small blue, can be common. Cliff tiger-beetles scurry across the friable clay on solar-fuelled legs. On the grassy clifftop above, a colony of bee orchids enthrals, whilst hoary stock and wild cabbage add botanical interest.

For the remainder of the day, three options stand out. At Tennyson Down, wait

▲ Glanville fritillary: a butterfly with history (IHL)

respectfully by coastal gorse patches for a Dartford warbler to emerge. Visit Ventnor – either the botanical gardens or La Falaise car park – checking the sheltered, sunny base of low walls for the sun-addicted common wall lizard. Although introduced on mainland England, the Isle of Wight animals may well be native.

Finally, head deep into Wight's peaceful interior. Alverstone Mead is famed for particularly confiding red squirrels. For wildlife-watchers who associate this scarce mammal with remote Scottish pine forests, feeding 'Tufty' by hand in a southern deciduous woodland feels dreamlike.

Alverstone Mead's red squirrels are so tame they can even be fed by hand. (JL)

Wherever you explore Wight, expect to succumb to the island's unique enchantment. Flowery meadows, sunny villages and a laidback attitude to life impart a sense of an island community living happily in the 1950s. Nowhere else in Britain has such garlic farms, such tomatoes bursting with flavour or such a special fritillary. Here's to Eleanor Glanville.

WHERE TO GO Compton Bay is off the A3055, 2km southeast of Freshwater. Park at Compton Chine (♥ SZ371851) or Shippards Chine (♥ SZ378840); walk between them (♣ tinyurl.com/ComptonWalk). Tennyson Down (car park ♥ SZ325856) is 2km southwest of Totland. Ventnor Botanical Gardens is on the A3055 (♥ SZ547769 ♣ www.botanic.co.uk); La Falaise car park is 1.5km east (♥ SZ558773). Park in Alverstone for Alverstone Mead (♥ SZ580852 ♣ tinyurl.com/Alverstone). South of the bridge, follow the footpath east.
FLEXIBILITY Glanville fritillary: mid-May to end June. Small blue: May–June. Red squirrel: resident. Common wall lizard: March–September. Dartford warbler: resident.
MAKE IT A WEEKEND Try all three options suggested, or join PTES to explore Briddlesford Woods for hazel dormouse (♣ tinyurl.com/PTESBriddlesford).
ALTERNATIVE LOCATIONS Glanville fritillary: Hutchinson's Bank (Surrey). Common wall lizards: Winspit (Dorset) or Dover Castle (Kent). Red squirrel: widespread. Dartford warbler: Dunwich Heath (*May 22*), Stoborough Heath (*July 6*), Thursley Common (*July 15*), Ashdown Forest (*July 22*). Small blue: Cerne Abbas (*May 23*), Darland Banks (*May 26*).

Day 19: June 2

Does the Lady's slipper fit?

WHERE Cumbria
TARGETS lady's slipper orchid, lily-of-the-valley, white-spotted sable & pearl-bordered fritillary
ACCESSIBILITY ③
CHILD-FRIENDLINESS ⑤

Sheltering beside chunks of Cumbrian limestone or beneath long-lived juniper trees, a dissonant fusion of the comical and the tropical glows incongruously. The presence of lady's slipper orchids at Gait Barrows is no quirk, but instead the result of diligent intent. This remarkable plant – with its twisted burgundy sepals and bulbous yellow 'slipper' – is Britain's rarest. After decades of over-avid collecting, just two native individuals remain, both at secret sites across the Pennines in Yorkshire (and one only discovered in 2015!).

Let's pause a moment to take that in. A glorious and formerly widespread species, stolen from the wild to sate a craze for garden-based show-and-not-tell. How oddly and obtusely destructive human obsessions can be.

Fortunately, an alliance of botanists and conservationists has managed to salvage the lady's slipper from national extinction. Using seeds gathered from a Yorkshire plant, then sown and pollinated by hand at the Royal Botanic Gardens, Kew, lady's slippers have been introduced to a sprinkling of clandestine sites across northern England. Gait Barrows is the public face of the reintroduction project; here, and only here, visiting orchid-admirers are welcomed.

From the car park, follow arrows along the Yew Trail to an open area of limestone pavement, that mainstay of school geography field trips. The groups of lady's slippers are obvious and striking. Kneel to appreciate them fully, but

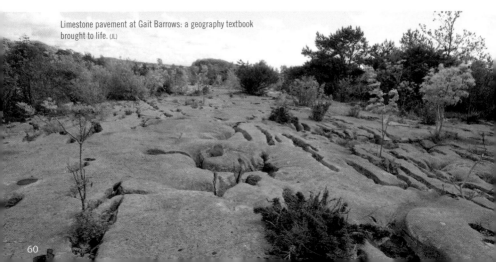

Limestone pavement at Gait Barrows: a geography textbook brought to life. (JL)

> **"An alliance of botanists and conservationists has salvaged the lady's slipper orchid from extinction"**

avoid trampling plants or disturbing the unnaturally glaucous, slug-deterring pellets.

Take time to explore the adjacent pavement. Lily-of-the-valley, with its drooping bell-like blooms, abounds. White-spotted sable, a delicate and sumptuous micro-moth that occurs only very locally, flutters when the sun shines. Look for this winged waif around the base of common juniper and goldenrod.

Then peer deep into the pavement's grikes. In his ode to natural Britain, *The Wild Places*, Robert Macfarlane celebrates the world of life inhabiting each and every one of these miniature chasms. Mosses, lichens and grasses flourish; so too the very rare rigid buckler fern and scarce hart's-tongue. You may even discern the first sproutings of two further botanical specialities: dark red helleborine and angular Solomon's seal.

If, somehow, this world is not enough, continue to wander the Yew and Limestone trails. Northern marsh orchids pockmark damp areas with magenta. In sheltered glades, Duke of Burgundy and pearl-bordered fritillary – two declining butterflies – may rest in the sun, consolidating after a hectic day of feeding, territorial defence and mating. Before departing, return to those lady's slippers, to honour the foresight and know-how of the green-fingered conservationists who have spared this stunning plant from national extinction.

▶ There is a no more exotic-looking orchid in Britain than the lady's slipper. (JL)

WHERE TO GO Gait Barrows National Nature Reserve
(♀ SD478776 📱 tinyurl.com/gaitbarrows) is 3km southeast of Arnside. Take Black Dyke Road south then east to the car park south of the road, typically signed with a photo of a lady's slipper. Follow the waymarked Yew and Limestone Trails.
FLEXIBILITY Lady's slipper: mid-May to late June. White-spotted sable: late May to July. Duke of Burgundy: May. Pearl-bordered fritillary: May–June. Lily-of-the-valley: May–June. Sable: mid-May to mid-June.
MAKE IT A WEEKEND Visit Walney for gulls and rare plants (*June 7*), or explore dune slacks at Sandscale Haws (♀ SD189750 📱 www.nationaltrust.org.uk/sandscale-haws) for coralroot orchid and natterjack toad. Check locations with the rangers (📞 01229 462855).
ALTERNATIVE LOCATIONS None for lady's slipper orchid. Pearl-bordered fritillary, *May 17*. Lily-of-the-valley: Congham Heath Woods (Norfolk), Warton Crag (Lancashire). Sable: scattered limestone regions, including Warton Crag.

Mating tansy beetles are a welcome sight for conservationists; but will they survive summer floods? (JL)

Beetlejuice

WHERE North & East Yorkshire
TARGETS tansy beetle, gannet & puffin
ACCESSIBILITY ⑤
CHILD-FRIENDLINESS ⑤

Along the floodplains of the River Ouse as it meanders in and around York, a jewel of an insect clings physically on to a fern-like plant – and metaphorically on to survival. A globally threatened creature that has vanished from much of its European range, tansy beetle is teetering on the riverbank of extinction within Britain.

A mere centimetre in length, tansy beetles are vibrantly coloured copper and green. No more than a few thousand of these stunners remain along a 30km stretch of the Ouse. Other than a surprising rediscovery and an incipient reintroduction programme, both in fenland Cambridgeshire in 2014, tansy beetles occur nowhere else in Britain. 'God's Own Beetle' is a source of local pride for Yorkshire folk – an invertebrate celebrity with pin-up looks.

Along the Ouse, tansy beetles feed solely on tansy, a perennial herb with clusters of yellow flowerheads that flourishes in dense swards. During spring and summer, seeing beetles is straightforward at several sites around York. At Fulford Ings the Parish Council celebrates

> **❝The globally threatened tansy beetle is teetering on the riverbank of extinction within Britain❞**

▶ Britain's largest seabird is
the gannet. (IHL)

the beetle's presence with an
informative display board.
Other locations include
the newly designated
Site of Special Scientific
Interest at Clifton Ings and Rawcliffe
Meadows, and even central York itself (near Millennium
Bridge). My personal favourite rendezvous lies between
Bishopthorpe and Acaster Malbis: peruse the tansy under the
lone ash tree immediately southwest of Naburn Bridge.

Unfortunately, York's tansy and its namesake invertebrate are both in
trouble. The plant is being outcompeted by invasive aliens such as Himalayan
balsam, uprooted through agricultural intensification or munched by cattle.

Worse still, this beetle is often drowned during summer floods. With its
forewings ('elytra' in entomologist-speak) fused together, it is incapable of
flight. Escaping floods or colonising new clumps of tansy away from floodplains
is possible only by six-legged foot (or human hand). Thank heavens for the
efforts of the Tansy Beetle Action Group, a consortium of conservation bodies
including Natural England, Buglife and the Yorkshire Wildlife Trust, which is
surveying and saving beetles.

For the remainder of the day, head coastwards to visit Yorkshire's seabird
city at Bempton Cliffs. Britain hosts Europe's finest seabird colonies – and they
are justly celebrated in this book. From the RSPB's carefully sited lookouts,
insinuate yourself into the soap opera that aggregates the lives of thousands
of gannets, kittiwakes, razorbills, guillemots and puffins. You will see loving
and courtship, foraging and feeding, bickering and chuntering. The sun should
now be shining from the south or west, rendering photography a dream. A
wall of sound and a feast for the eyes: superb!

WHERE TO GO From Bishopthorpe (immediately south of York) take Acaster Lane
south towards Acaster Malbis. Park by the bridge over the road, walk to the River
Ouse then south for 50m to a lone ash tree (♀ SE597464). RSPB Bempton Cliffs
(♀ TA197738 ☷ tinyurl.com/RSPBBempton) is signposted 1.5km north of Bempton,
off the B1229 between Filey and Flamborough.
FLEXIBILITY Adult tansy beetles are active April–June and August–September.
Bempton's seabirds are present March–September.
MAKE IT A WEEKEND Spend a full day at Bempton, combine with Fen Bog (*June
29*) or scan skies above Wykeham Forest (North Yorkshire) for honey-buzzard and
goshawk.
ALTERNATIVE LOCATIONS None for tansy beetle. Other seabird colonies include the
Farne Islands (*June 22*) and Bass Rock (*July 31*).

Day 21: June 4
Skip, skip, skip to the Loy

WHERE Highland
TARGETS chequered skipper, pearl-bordered fritillary, argent and sable, & pine marten
ACCESSIBILITY ⑤
CHILD-FRIENDLINESS ④

N ear the Northamptonshire market town of Oundle lies a picturesque thatched country pub called The Chequered Skipper. It is the sole remaining hint that the butterfly of the same name ever occurred in the county, or – indeed – ever occurred *anywhere* in England.

Early in the Swinging Sixties, the Midlands' chequered skipper populations were in fine fettle. Yet by the time Abba topped the British charts with 'Dancing Queen' in summer 1976, this dappled butterfly was extinct. Gone, disappeared, vanished – inexplicably, mysteriously, disconcertingly. Forty years on, its sole British populations survive on sheltered slopes in western Scotland, most below open deciduous woodland bordering rivers or lochs, and all within an hour's drive of Fort William.

> **"Chequered skipper times its emergence for the flowering of bluebells, which flexes with the severity of spring"**

For most readers, visiting the gateway to Ben Nevis will require quite some road trip. Getting there is only half the battle, for the skipper is hardly straightforward to find. This butterfly times its emergence for the flowering of bluebells, which flexes with the severity of spring – so it is risky to plan far in advance. Worse, skippers fly only in sun – yet the Scottish Highlands are better known for rain.

Now prepped for the challenge, head to Glen Loy. A wee road soldiers up-valley for 6km, traversing dappled woodland and fringing fern-clad inclines. Skipper colonies are scattered along the valley and may vary in usage between years. Search wherever you see bluebells, where bracken-lined burns flow south into the River Loy, where bog-myrtle

◀ Once widespread in Britain, chequered skipper is now confined to a small area of western Scotland. (IHL)

A privileged daytime view of a pine marten in the garden at Glenloy Lodge. (JJ)

flushes sage and scarlet amidst purple moor grass, and where sunny banks adjoin dry ditches.

In *The Butterfly Isles*, Patrick Barkham ascribes 'a formidable personality' to chequered skippers, citing as evidence their heavy-clubbed antennae, disproportionately chunky and furry body, and unrelentingly pugnacious nature. Once tracked down, these butterflies are a joy to watch – which may make dragging oneself away somewhat tricky.

But away you must, for Glen Loy volunteers more. Pearl-bordered fritillaries – that ever rarer butterfly – are reaching the conclusion of their flight period, to be supplanted by small pearl-bordered fritillaries. Green hairstreaks dazzle, whilst black-and-white moths flitting around bog-myrtle and birch should be the Nationally Scarce argent and sable.

Finally, retire to the area's standout accommodation offering: Glenloy Lodge. Site yourself in the conservatory by 5.00pm, and watch owners (and wildlife guides) Jon and Angela Mercer place miniature jam sandwiches on the terrace. The spread is not for you, but for a pine marten that dwells nearby – and visits every day. There is *nowhere* better in Britain to see this notoriously reclusive mammal, in broad daylight and within touching distance. That calls for a pint, if not at The Chequered Skipper.

WHERE TO GO Glen Loy is 11km north of Fort William, between Banavie and Gairlochy. From the B8004, follow the single-track road for 6km to the Forestry Commission car park (♀ NN113839), then wander along the north bank of the River Loy (♀ NN104845 to ♀ NN113837). Try also around ♀ NN108846 and ♀ NN125832. Glenloy Lodge guesthouse is at the foot of the valley (🖱 www.glenloywildlife.co.uk; see ad, page 243). **FLEXIBILITY** Chequered skipper: late May to late June, but timing varies. Pearl-bordered fritillary: May. Argent and sable: late May to July. Pine marten: resident. **MAKE IT A WEEKEND** A little further north, Allt Mhuic is a Butterfly Conservation reserve that holds chequered skipper, lesser twayblade and azure hawker. **ALTERNATIVE LOCATIONS** Chequered skipper: Glasdrum Wood (Argyll & Bute). Pearl-bordered fritillary, see *May 17*. Argent and sable: Avalon Marshes (*June 25*). Pine marten: Ardnamurchan Peninsula (Argyll), Rothiemurchus Forest (*June 5*).

Day 22: June 5

Whiteface

WHERE Highland
TARGETS white-faced darter, lesser twayblade, red squirrel & osprey
ACCESSIBILITY ⑤
CHILD-FRIENDLINESS ⑤

In a boggy clearing luxuriating in golden sphagnum moss, amidst springy, heathery Caledonian pine forest, you squat at the culmination of a short boardwalk. There may be crested tits purring from a nearby tree, but your attention is focused on the gloopy tar-black pool just beyond your toes. Checking the vegetation protruding from the mire and straining towards the sky, you come to a halt. Clinging to the sedge stem and warming its glistening, gradually unfurling silvery wings is a white-faced darter.

This stunning dragonfly has become very rare and localised in Britain. It has vanished from more than half of its 20 or so English sites within the last 50 years, and climate change is likely to threaten it wherever it currently survives. In Scotland, fortunately, the white-faced darter is doing better. Abernethy Forest remains a stronghold, and this particular bog-mire is a well-known site to observe this attractive insect.

The white frons (face) is unique among British dragonflies, as is the largely black body studded with either red (males) or yellow (females and immatures). Leather-clad, face-painted and blood-splashed, this is a rock star of an insect. For those used to seeing the relatively robust common darter, the diminutive size of the 'small whiteface' (as it is alternatively monikered) may surprise.

Early morning in Abernethy Forest: still and verdant (JL)

"Leather-clad, face-painted and blood-splashed, white-faced darter is a rock star of an insect"

A freshly emerged white-faced darter at Abernethy (JL)

On a nearby roadside a similarly petite plant beckons you. The lesser twayblade – a crimson orchid with star-like flowers – will take some finding, however. Its needle-thin spikes are tricky to decipher from the gingery backdrop of moss above which they poke. Nobody I know who has seen one has ever expected them to be quite so titchy – or quite so exquisite. Well worth the effort.

From crimson to chestnut, as you head a few minutes west to the visitor centre at Loch Garten. Your initial quarry is red squirrel. You should have no problems connecting with Tufty Flufftail, emblem of the Royal Society for the Prevention of Accidents. Feeders crammed with peanuts conveniently entice the squirrels to descend from pine canopy to eye-level.

Then onto Loch Garten's famous osprey observation hide. Whilst the piscivorous raptor's eyrie is further from the viewpoint than the summer's 35,000 visitors anticipate, the wonder that is CCTV provides real-time, intimate footage of osprey family life. It is easy to spend an hour or two watching the comings and goings of this avian 'whiteface', and being entertained by the window box feeders that attract coal tits, chaffinches and even bank voles.

WHERE TO GO All sites are in RSPB Abernethy Forest (tinyurl.com/RSPBAbernethy). Loch Garten Osprey Centre (♀ NH978183) lies 5km east of Boat of Garten, off the B970. White-faced darter pool (♀ NH982175) is 1.2km east, 100m before the turn to Tulloch. Lesser twayblades grow along the roadside, c250m west of the sandy parking area at ♀ NH992179.

FLEXIBILITY White-faced darter: end May to end July. Osprey: April–August. Red squirrel: resident. Lesser twayblade: mid-May to mid-July.

MAKE IT A WEEKEND Lots of options. For northern damselfly go just west of Loch Garten (♀ NH966192). Cairn Gorm for dotterel, ptarmigan and alpine flowers (*July 4*), or pine marten at the Speyside Wildlife hide in Rothiemurchus Forest.

ALTERNATIVE LOCATIONS White-faced darter: Whixall Moss (*June 23*). Lesser twayblade: Lake Vrynwy (*May 24*). Red squirrel: Alverstone Meads (*June 1*). Osprey: Rutland Water (*August 12*), Cors Dyfi (*August 17*).

Rain goose

WHERE Shetland
TARGETS red-throated diver, red-necked phalarope & whimbrel
ACCESSIBILITY ⑤
CHILD-FRIENDLINESS ③

I f you have invested considerable effort in reaching the island of Fetlar in the Shetland Islands, almost as far north as you can get in Britain, you have earned the right to recuperate for a full day at a single wildlife-rich location. Spend it at Loch Funzie, Britain's best site to watch a trio of our rarest breeding birds.

Fetlar, nicknamed 'The Garden of Shetland' on account of its greenness, is inhabited by just 80 people. Low, rolling hills lend Fetlar a less rugged, less wild feel than much of its archipelago. Less *wild*, perhaps, but absolutely not less wild*life*.

> **"Beauty, rarity and culture coalesce in a single feathered bundle: the red-throated diver"**

Park yourself on the loch shore and scan for a long-necked, low-slung form swimming sinuously – a bird almost reptilian in outline. With its bill inflected upwards, the red-throated diver imparts an inquisitive demeanour, but your eye may equally be caught by its elegant garb: a silver-grey head with pin-striped hind neck, fiery red eye and flaming throat.

This scarce waterbird is Shetland's 'rain goose', an old moniker that hints at the reverence with which indigenous tribes across the crown of the world, from Siberia to Alaska, hold this diver. It is a harbinger of rain and more. Beauty, rarity and culture coalesce in a single feathered bundle.

▼ The red-throated diver is known as 'rain goose' in Shetland. (RN)

Equally stunning and rare is the red-necked phalarope. This tiny, delicate wader breeds near the RSPB hide at Mires of Funzie, but regularly visits the loch's shoreline to forage in shallow, peaty waters. For four varied reasons the phalarope merits the accolade 'exceptional'.

First, it is astonishingly confiding – a bird at no risk of stage fright. Second, the phalarope's typical feeding behaviour is enchanting: it swims buoyantly and spins constantly, like some demented clockwork toy. Third, phalarope parental roles are reversed:

Loch Funzie's red-necked phalaropes allow very close approach. (IHL)

males assume sole responsibility for raising offspring, leaving females to seduce multiple mates. Finally, this is the only bird to breed in Scotland yet winter in the Pacific Ocean off Peru – an epic 25,000km round trip, discovered by satellite-tracking in 2014!

A more recognisable wader is the whimbrel. Its familiarity is slightly deceptive, however, because it stems from resemblance to the better-known curlew. Both are long-legged brown birds with a long, decurved bill, but only the whimbrel possesses a distinctively striped head. Look for whimbrels feeding along the roadside between Funzie and Aith, or in crofts around the Mires. Like the diver and phalarope, this is a strictly protected species so back away should you sense it is alarmed; vulnerable chicks may be nearby. Like your well-travelled self, these birds need time and space to recuperate.

WHERE TO GO Reach Shetland by sea (from Aberdeen) or air. Take inter-island ferries from Toft (Mainland) via Yell to Hamarsness (Fetlar). RSPB Loch Funzie (♀ HU655900 📱 tinyurl.com/RSPBFunzie) is 10km east. Use the car park west of the loch, then walk around the loch or visit Mires hide, 400m away.
FLEXIBILITY Late May to late June for all three species.
MAKE IT A WEEKEND Keen of Hamar (Unst) has Arctic sandwort, northern rock-cress and the endemic Shetland mouse-ear. You could easily spend a fortnight exploring Shetland, if you can survive the 'simmer dim' (summer's eternal twilight)!
ALTERNATIVE LOCATIONS The trio's protected status while breeding means no other locations are recommended. You can, however, see wintering divers off many coastlines, plus whimbrel and (rarely) phalaropes on passage.

Day 24: June 7
Gull able
not gullible

WHERE Cumbria
TARGETS lesser black-backed gull, herring gull, 'Walney pink',
coralroot orchid & natterjack toad
ACCESSIBILITY ⑤
CHILD-FRIENDLINESS ④

G ulls have long had a bad press. And relationships between bird and human appear to be worsening. In coastal communities and the 'red-top' press, 'seagulls' are vilified for allegedly stealing chips, dive-bombing pensioners and attacking small pets. During 2015, British Prime Minister David Cameron weighed in, blowing the tizz out of sane proportion by suggesting that a 'big conversation' be held about how to deal with 'marauding' gulls.

Time, then, for some positive PR. Or, as the RSPB argues, time to be 'gull able not gullible.' So let's visit the exhilarating colony of herring and lesser black-backed gulls inhabiting England's eighth-largest island. Ten times longer than it is wide, Walney is an elongated crescent moon-face with a furrowed brow, pursed lips and bulging chin.

More than 10,000 pairs of the two gull species breed at South Walney Nature Reserve. The fact that herring gull – the species behind the archetypal 'seagull' – now features on Britain's 'Red List' of threatened species renders Walney significant in European terms.

Various trails web the coastal shingle. The sight, sound and smell of this incessantly active avian colony make a dramatic impression. Thousands

'Walney pink', the exclusive local form of bloody cranesbill (RP-J)

of gulls may be airborne simultaneously, with hundreds abluting in the shallows or feeding chicks on the stony ground. This is feathered chaos, acoustic bedlam, unrelenting excitement.

> **"This gull colony is feathered chaos, acoustic bedlam, unrelenting excitement"**

Gulls are proud parents, suspicious of any intrusion of their breeding domain. Understandably, they sometimes consider attack as the best form of defence, harrying human visitors. If Wildlife Trust wardens offer you a hard hat and stick, it pays to accept so you can delight in the experience without concern.

Once you have enjoyed the gulls and watched common eiders bubble along the shoreline, head to the opposite tip of the island at North Walney National Nature Reserve. In grassy dunes, slacks and heathland, look for a suite of special plants. Coralroot orchid grows as a tiny but stocky spike. Whilst hard to spot, it pays to persevere as the mahogany stem rises to subtly enchanting yellowish-green flowers. More likely, you will encounter clumps of a local variant of bloody cranesbill that grows nowhere else on Earth. The 'Walney pink' or 'Walney geranium' blushes rose and is veined crimson. Sublime.

▼ Lesser black-backed gulls are proud parents. (IHL)

End the day by taking a seat by one of the fenced-off dune pools. The encroaching gloaming is the conductor's baton for an amphibian orchestra. The territorial chuntering of natterjack toads rings in your ears long after you have returned to the Cumbrian mainland.

WHERE TO GO From Barrow-in-Furness, follow the A590 west to Walney Island. Across Jubilee Bridge, follow brown signs to South Walney reserve (♥ SD225620 📱 tinyurl.com/SouthWalney), 1km beyond South End caravan site. Or head 2km northwest for North Walney reserve; park at Earnse Point (♥ SD170700 📱 tinyurl.com/NorthWalney) and walk 1.5km north.

FLEXIBILITY Gulls nest April to August. Coralroot orchid: mid-May to mid-June. 'Walney pink': June–August. Natterjack toad April to August.

MAKE IT A WEEKEND 5km north of Barrow-in-Furness, Sandscale Hawes (for details, see *June 2*) holds Britain's biggest coralroot orchid population plus natterjacks.

ALTERNATIVE LOCATIONS Nowhere for 'Walney pink'. No other similar-sized colony of large gulls. Sandscale Haws and Spey Bay (Moray) for coralroot orchid. Sandscale and Winterton Dunes (Norfolk) for natterjacks.

Day 25: June 8
Eype of the tiger

WHERE Dorset & Devon
TARGETS cliff tiger-beetle & wood white
ACCESSIBILITY ②
CHILD-FRIENDLINESS ④

It may share a name with a different species of cat, but the cliff tiger-beetle is the cheetah among British insects. Sprinting fast on unfeasibly long legs, this dusty green ground-beetle spots moving prey with its massive eyes and grabs its victim with uncompromising, sickle-shaped jaws. Make no mistake: it may be only a centimetre long, but the cliff tiger-beetle is a *supreme* predator. It is also a rare creature – and one confined to a special British habitat that was overlooked by conservationists for far too long: soft cliffs.

Soft-rock cliffs may appear an oxymoron. Surely the point of cliffs is that they stand tall, firm and resolute, defying all that the vagaries of weather can throw at them? Coastal soft cliffs are composed of rocks that poorly resist the natural processes of erosion that shape our coasts. They are formed of easily friable rocks such as clays, and fray or slump frequently thanks to the combined action of the sea (from below) and rain (from above).

> **❝It may be only a centimetre long, but the cliff tiger-beetle is a supreme predator❞**

Best-known as fossil-hunting grounds, the maritime soft cliffs west of Eype Mouth in Dorset laze down to the English Channel. These south-facing, sun-baked landslip systems are among Britain's most important locations for invertebrates. The incessant restlessness of the terrain provides perpetually evolving conditions. The resulting mosaic of micro-habitats is prime real estate for ecological pioneers such as colt's-foot and wild carrot.

In turn these provide nectar, pollen and living space for species of mining-bee (*Lasioglossum angusticepsi*) and ground-beetle (*Drypta dentata*) that are so rare that they lack a common name. Choose a sunny day, tread carefully and heavily in deep-sea-diver boots that are an occupational hazard of walking on clay, and prepare for muddy knees as you lower your eyes to beetle level.

◀ A cliff tiger-beetle, scurrying across slumping clays.
(Steve Trewhella/FLPA)

The subtly beautiful wood white is as delicate as they come. (IHL)

Once sated, head west into east Devon. Your destination is another south-facing coastal cliff: the scrubby, sheltered slopes of Branscombe. Your aim is to see Britain's daintiest butterfly, wood white, with its characteristically floppy flight. Starting at Branscombe Mouth, walk the beach in each direction as far as the final chalets and scan the hillside vegetation.

Wood white is a strange butterfly. This localised species typically occurs in woodland rides, so its choice of habitat here bewilders lepidopterists. One fascinating conceit is that Branscombe's butterflies might actually be a separate species known as cryptic wood white. This Irish butterfly prefers open areas, but the only way to tell it apart would be to examine minute details of its genitalia! If Branscombe's wood whites were actually cryptic wood white, what a turn-up that would be for such an overlooked habitat as soft cliffs.

WHERE TO GO Eype Mouth (♀ SY447910) is off the A35, 2km southwest of Bridport (Dorset). Use the clifftop car park, descend to the beach and walk either direction. Branscombe Mouth (♀ SY207882 ☻ www.nationaltrust.org.uk/branscombe) is 40 minutes' drive west, 4km southwest of Seaton (Devon) along minor roads from the A3052. Use the village car park and walk along undercliff.

FLEXIBILITY Adult cliff tiger-beetles: May–September, particularly June–July. Wood white: May to late June, often again mid-July to late August.

MAKE IT A WEEKEND At Branscombe, bait mini-pitfall traps (eg: a plastic container) and bury them in the shingle overnight. The next morning, check for scaly cricket, a real rarity.

ALTERNATIVE LOCATIONS Wood white: Oaken Wood (Surrey), Powerstock Common (Dorset). Cliff tiger-beetle: Compton Bay (*May 31*).

Six-belted clearwing is one of several harmless moths that mimic wasps. (IHL)

Streaky

WHERE Cambridgeshire
TARGETS black hairstreak, six-belted clearwing, glowworm
& moon carrot
ACCESSIBILITY ③
CHILD-FRIENDLINESS ④

Ancient woodlands have a unique allure. No summer of British wildlife would be replete without exploring one. The Midlands' best-preserved example of ash–oak woodland keeps its own counsel in northwest Cambridgeshire. A National Nature Reserve for more than 60 years, Monks Wood is an isolated haven – a reminder of what much of England looked like in centuries past.

"Monks Wood remains one of the finest places to see this small, localised butterfly"

The reserve is conveniently cross-hatched by rides, all so deserted that you are more likely to encounter a Reeve's muntjac (Britain's smallest deer) stumbling along their length than a fellow *Homo sapiens*. Turn right or left at will to investigate ample sylvan treats. As well as ash and oak, field maple trees abound and the scarce wild service tree is frequent, whilst Monks Wood's understorey richly mixes hazel, blackthorn, dogwood and sallow. The sheltered rides, abundant sun and rich flowering shrubs should hum with hoverflies.

Today's visit is about a very special butterfly. Britain's first-ever black hairstreak was discovered at Monks Wood in 1828 – and the site remains one of the finest places to see this small, localised butterfly. Black hairstreak is the

A female glowworm brightening a dark night. (BL)

second of Britain's five hairstreaks to emerge; the first fortnight of June is the classic time to find it.

Your initial encounter is often with a butterfly bobbing around high up in an ash tree. Be patient and it may descend to sup nectar from privet flowers, or settle on leaves to slurp aphid honeydew. Once pinned down, black hairstreaks appear to welcome very close scrutiny, enabling you to see black spots dotting the inner edge of the orange band on the hindwing (the key feature differentiating this species from white-letter hairstreak).

Wood explored, hairstreak enjoyed, mission complete. With evening dropping hints, depart eastwards to the county town of Cambridge. At Cherry Hinton, two derelict chalk quarries nudge urbanity. They once furnished construction material for university buildings; now Nature has reasserted dominance.

Backed by East Pit's sheer walls, flowers such as milkwort, harebell and kidney vetch now thrive. Wild thyme and pyramidal orchids turn the ground pink. Check common birdsfoot trefoil for six-belted clearwing, a titchy wasp-mimic moth (or use a pheromone lure to entice males to visit).

Remarkably, the very rare moon carrot survives here both inside the pit and on its western fringe of Limekiln Road, at the southwestern apex of the pit. The only other British locations are in Sussex and Bedfordshire. Look for its distinctive cauliflower-headed form, said to gleam at night. Should you remain until dark, and if the air is muggy and mild, female glowworms will certainly illuminate the pit's obscurity with green. Are these Christmas lights in mid-summer?

WHERE TO GO Monks Wood is 1.5km northeast of the A1/A14 junction (♀ TL198792 ☏ tinyurl.com/MonksWood2). Park at the junction of the B1090 and turnoff to Wood Walton. Walk west into the wood. The best area is the first ride to left. Cherry Hinton chalk pits (♀ TL486561 ☏ www.wildlifebcn.org/reserves/cherry-hinton) are immediately east of Cambridge, at the junction of Cherry Hinton Road and Queen Edith's Way. Park in the layby opposite Robin Hood pub on Fulbourn Road.
FLEXIBILITY Black hairstreak: early to mid-June. Glowworm: May–August, especially June–September. Six-belted clearwing: June–July. Moon carrot best July to early September.
MAKE IT A WEEKEND Spend time at Lakenheath (*June 10*) or Breckland (*June 20*).
ALTERNATIVE LOCATIONS Black hairstreak: Glapthorn Cow Pastures (*May 15*), Whitecross Green Wood (Buckinghamshire/Oxfordshire) and Woodwalton Fen (Cambridgeshire). Six-belted clearwing: widespread, including Devil's Dyke (*July 5*). Moon carrot: only Knocking Hoe (Bedfordshire) and Beachy Head (Sussex). Glowworm: widespread in England.

Day 27: June 10
Water into wine

WHERE Suffolk
TARGETS great bittern, common crane, golden-bloomed grey
longhorn beetle, elephant hawkmoth & reed dagger
ACCESSIBILITY ⑤
CHILD-FRIENDLINESS ③

In a mere 20 years since the RSPB purchased an unremarkable arable plot in mid-Suffolk, the conservation organisation has performed a miracle. The ecological equivalent of transforming water into wine has seen the recreation of a sizeable wetland blending vast reedbeds with grazing marshes. Lakenheath Fen is a watery wonderland that teems and hums with wildlife.

Layered between the River Little Ouse and Ely–Norwich railway line, paths traverse fenland, flank poplar woodland and culminate in viewpoints over meres. On a typical day, you should be able to enjoy birds and mammals, beetles and dragonflies, moths and plants – a proper 'pan-species' visit.

If the visitor centre is open, enquire whether any moths were trapped overnight. If so, the catch may include fen specialities such as reed dagger and Fenland pearl as well as crowd-pleasers such as eyed, poplar and elephant hawkmoths. If you really luck out, the actinic lights might have attracted a stunning goat moth.

> **"Lakenheath Fen is a wetland wonderland that drips and hums with wildlife"**

Leaving the centre, linger by the feeding station: finches and tits are omnipresent, and great spotted woodpeckers may undulate in. Tramping trails westwards, keep an eye on pathside vegetation for insects. Damselflies should wisp up from nettlebeds. Aim to discern the localised variable damselfly from the widespread azure. Posing no such identification conundrum, their larger relatives such as banded demoiselle helicopter upwards, and scarce chasers flaunt themselves on sunny posts.

Peruse the immodestly flowered vegetation to spot various beetles, including the golden-bloomed grey longhorn – every bit as spectacular as its name suggests. You may also discern nursery-web spiders biding their time, waiting for freshly emerged, eerily translucent damselflies to make an errant

▶ My daughter's favourite animal: the candy-pink elephant hawkmoth (JL)

▲ Lakenheath has a booming population of great bitterns. (DT)

move. Crawling along the paths may be caterpillars of various moths: emperor, garden tiger and more.

Then on to larger fare. Kingfishers add strident colour in front of the viewpoints. Bitterns may be flying around, these 'fen tigers' seeking out frogs and fish to nourish their growing young. Reed and sedge warblers may break off from feeding their offspring to indulge in a token chuntering songburst.

Common cranes first bred at Lakenheath in 2007, returning to the Fens after a 400-year absence. They stride imperiously around the reserve; listen for their evocative bugle as a precursor to seeing them. Look up too, for hobbies arc through the skies: the whoosh of wings a death-knell for dragonflies.

Finally, mammals. Stoats are regularly seen, particularly near Joist Fen. Water voles and otters swim the channels, particularly on New Fen. Now that wouldn't have happened 20 years ago... 'Build it,' seems to be the RSPB motto, 'and the wildlife will come.'

WHERE TO GO RSPB Lakenheath Fen (♥ TL722864 📱 tinyurl.com/RSPBLakenheath) is signposted from Station Road by Lakenheath station on the B1112, 4km north of Lakenheath. Trails lead through the best areas.
FLEXIBILITY Bittern and crane: resident. Moths and beetles are best June–July.
MAKE IT A WEEKEND Look for sand catchfly, other Breckland plants and scarce moths such as powdered grass-veneer at Maidscross Hill local nature reserve in Lakenheath (♥ TL728822 📱 tinyurl.com/MaidscrossHill). Military orchids are at Rex Graham reserve, Mildenhall Woods (Suffolk ♥ TL738745). Alternatively combine with Broadland (*June 15*) or Breckland (*June 20*) itineraries.
ALTERNATIVE LOCATIONS Woodwalton Fen (Cambridgeshire) or Strumpshaw Fen (*June 20*) for fenland moths. Bittern: Minsmere (*May 22*). Common crane: Hickling Broad (*June 20*) or Slimbridge (Gloucestershire). Beetle: widespread but local in central and eastern England.

Day 28: June 11

Flitting fritillaries

WHERE Essex
TARGETS heath fritillary, shrill carder bee, horehound longhorn & slowworm
ACCESSIBILITY ④
CHILD-FRIENDLINESS ④

The muddy path winds through shady woodland and prises apart lofty shrubs. Whilst the vegetation falls short of inducing claustrophobia, it is certainly highly *present*: literally in your face. Then, without warning, it is absent. The pressure is unexpectedly released, freeing light scrub punctuated by tree stumps to bask in sun-warmed air. This coppiced clearing at Little Haven Woods in southern Essex is perfect for the twisted lemon flowers of common cow-wheat – and thus similarly optimal for one of Britain's rarest butterflies: heath fritillary.

There it is! A small chocolate-orange form glides gently just above ground. It perches, halts and opens its chequered wings – solar panels powering flight. Very few populations survive in Britain; all have conservationists to thank. Here in Essex, as across the Thames in Kent, heath fritillary – 'woodman's follower' in country-speak – inhabits painstakingly managed woodlands. In years of plenty, when conditions come good, this fritillary's localised colonies may hold thousands of individuals: a blessedly far cry from the nadir of 1980, when extinction was widely predicted. Savour what you could so easily have missed.

Spend the afternoon at a reserve bordering the Thames Estuary: either Wat Tyler Country Park, honouring the best-known leader of the 1381 Peasants' Revolt, or the recently developed Thurrock Thamesside Nature Park. Both are inspirational developments on brownfield sites: formerly naval depot and landfill site respectively. Both are brilliantly designed for family activities, and boast decent cafés within modernist visitor centres.

Shrill carder bee occurs at several brownfield sites along the Thames Estuary. (JL)

▶ Slowworm: a snake-like lizard (JL)

The wildlife highlights are principally small but stunning insects, all greatly prized by entomologists. They offer a reminder that one in every seven of Britain's nationally rare and scarce invertebrates inhabit brownfield sites – which thus routinely become battlegrounds between developers and conservationists. How appropriate that Wat Tyler's revolt started at Fobbing, a stone's throw from the reserve now bearing his name.

The star insect is the shrill carder bee, one of Britain's rarest bumbles, for which Thameside flowering scrub is a national stronghold. June is early days in its life cycle, so you may have better fortune with brown-banded carder bee, a slightly commoner buzzer. The third rarity is a shimmering rainbow of a micro-moth with preposterously lengthy antennae: horehound longhorn. Find the moth's foodplant, black horehound, then look for two incessantly twitching appendages.

❝When conditions come good, heath fritillary's localised colonies may hold thousands of individuals❞

Should you fancy seeing something larger, seek permission from a warden to turn over some of the felt squares scattered across the grassland. These provide warmth and concealment for reptiles, such as common lizard, slowworm and grass snake. The kids would love discovering them...

WHERE TO GO Little Haven (♀ TQ808890 🖱 tinyurl.com/LittleHaven) lies south of the A127, 1km east of Thundersley. Park at junction of Daws Heath Road and Western Road. Follow the footpath north into the reserve. Thurrock Thameside Nature Park (♀ TQ696806 🖱 tinyurl.com/ThurrockReserve) and Wat Tyler Country Park (♀ TQ738864 🖱 www.wattylercountrypark.org.uk) are signposted south from the A13 at Stanford-le-Hope and Pitsea respectively.
FLEXIBILITY Heath fritillary: early June to early July. Carder bees: June–September, but best August–September. Horehound longhorn: June–July. Slowworm: April–September.
MAKE IT A WEEKEND RSPB Rainham Marshes (*August 15*), further west along the A13 towards London, is a fine day out – for adults and families alike.
ALTERNATIVE LOCATIONS Heath fritillary: Hockley Woods (Essex), East Blean Woods (Kent) and Lydford Old Railway (Devon; where it flies from late May). Bee and longhorn: Rainham Marshes (*August 15*). Slowworm: widespread, including Denbies Hillside (*August 20*).

Orchid odyssey

Sprawled on the floor of a Kent woodland, elbows scratched and knees soiled, I admire a beautiful lady. Quite the Victorian dame, she wears a white petticoat, fringed magenta, and her face is shaded by a burgundy bonnet. A lady orchid, at her finest.

Between 50 and 60 orchid species grow in Britain; the number varies with the rhythm of disputed taxonomy. Wherever the true figure lies, it is manageable: sufficient variety to get us hooked, without being overwhelming. As a first step into the plant kingdom, orchids excel.

> **"As a first step into the plant kingdom, orchids excel"**

For a start, orchids are widely distributed. You can see them from Cornwall to Orkney and the Western Isles to Sussex. They grow in beautiful places. Visit chalk downlands to enjoy pyramidal orchid, heathland mires for bog orchid, Chiltern beech hangers for violet helleborine and Caledonian pine forests for lesser twayblade.

Diversity peaks in May–July, but orchids can be seen across most months. Dorset's first early spider orchid may bloom as early as March, and Berkshire's final autumn lady's-tresses whirls through September. Orchid gatherings can be immense: 50,000 green-winged orchids transform Kent's Marden Meadows into a purple haze. Orchids vary enchantingly in size, shape and colour: be mesmerised by a bonsai musk orchid just 5cm tall or by a lissome lady orchid topping a metre.

Inspect an orchid flower spike closely for a treat. You may discern florets resembling monkeys, bees, spiders or lizards (in addition to Victorian ladies). This is pure evolutionary and ecological wonder: some orchids exaggerate features of insect pollinators to coax them into 'mating'.

Erotic and exotic in equal measure, orchids are also steeped in mystery. How did the sawfly orchid – a Mediterranean plant – discovered in Dorset during 2014 get there? (It is not as if flowers can fly!) When, if ever, will ghost orchid flower again? Several species have distinctive variants. None is more dramatically different than the 'wasp' orchid, a rare and graceful take on the bee orchid.

Indeed, rarity caps orchids' undoubted allure – often to their detriment, as collection remains a live threat. Fen orchid now survives in just a couple of areas. The tropical-looking lady's slipper has been introduced to Lancashire's lime pavements to alleviate visitor pressure on the two remaining wild plants. Go see them, and rejoice.

With its reptilian tail and odour of goat, the lizard orchid is one remarkable plant. (JL)

Fragrant flora

WHERE Kent
TARGETS common poppy, late spider orchid, lizard orchid, black-veined moth & Rambur's pied shieldbug
ACCESSIBILITY ②
CHILD-FRIENDLINESS ③

Thank heavens for long June days. Given the natural richness of Kent's chalk downland, optimise use of daylight to max out on an array of rarities. Start, however, with a reminder that the commonplace should never be sniffed at. Nuzzling the easterly car park at Plantlife's Ranscombe Farm Reserve high on the North Downs, there is a field of fire. Set ablaze by the rising sun, thousands of common poppies – one of Britain's five types of crimson poppy – nod in the breeze. A spectacle best appreciated in wide angle: the field, rather than individual flower, is the unit.

> **❝Thousands of chalk fragrant orchids turn meadows as pink as my six-year-old daughter's bedroom❞**

The opposite is true at Kent Wildlife Trust's HQ at Tyland Barn, where your quarry is Rambur's pied shieldbug. Park outside the reserve gates, and scrutinise kerbside vegetation for black horehound: lanky, with stinky nettle-like leaves and lilac flowers. Search each plant carefully to reveal youngsters of this rare black and cream insect, first discovered in Britain during 2011.

Bug bagged, take the M20 east to Wye Downs. Pretty much anywhere on the escarpment looming north of the Wye–Stowting minor road merits exploration. Your target is a rare day-flying moth – black-veined white – that flies solely here. Despite such localised distribution, this stunner is not uncommon, so you may spot several lounging in long grass.

Wye also offers abundant floral interest. Various orchids thrive: you may encounter man, bee, chalk fragrant, pyramidal and common spotted. The local star is the late spider orchid, which grows only between Wye and Folkestone. With a population as tiny as 500 plants, it is not for this guide to divulge the exact locations of this über-rarity. Contact the land managers, Natural England, if you wish to see it!

◀ Britain's 500 or so late spider orchids grow solely in Kent. (JL)

An 'instar' (young) Rambur's pied shieldbug (JL)

For a fiery start to your day, visit the poppy field at Ranscombe Farm. (JL)

Given that Park Gate Down (*May 26*) lies but a few kilometres northeast, it would be rude not to pop in. Mid-June sees thousands of chalk fragrant orchids turning the meadows as pink as my young daughter's bedroom. (Today, June 12, is her birthday, so please indulge me.) Common spotted orchids and common twayblades abound, but you will need sharp eyes to spot the musk orchids that punctuate the middle path in the third meadow. There's a chance of late spider orchid here, and the odd tardy monkey orchid may still bloom.

For the day's final plants, peruse the coastal golf course and gardens at Sandwich Bay. The summer's first lizard orchids should be twirling their way up stout stems and smelling, unattractively, of damp goat. For a finer and final floral fragrance, look for clove-scented broomrape near, ahem, the golf course toilet block. If you can't spy them, perhaps follow your nose...

WHERE TO GO Ranscombe Farm is immediately southwest of the M2, junction 2. The car park is by the A228 (♀ TQ718675 📱 tinyurl.com/Ranscombe). Tyland Barn is 1km north of M20 junction 6, signposted off the A229 (♀ TQ754593 📱 tinyurl.com/TylandBarn). At Wye National Nature Reserve (eg: ♀ TR075451 📱 tinyurl.com/WyeNNR) park carefully along Wye–Stowting road, and scramble upwards. Park Gate Down: see *26 May*. Sandwich Bay: leave Sandwich east on Sandown Road. Pause at St George's Golf Course (♀ TR349581) or continue to the bird observatory (♀ TR356575 📱 www.sbbot.org.uk) then explore the roadsides.
FLEXIBILITY Early June to early July for all target species.
MAKE IT A WEEKEND Visit East Blean Woods for heath fritillary, and Westbere Lakes for Norfolk hawker.
ALTERNATIVE LOCATIONS Lizard orchid: Devil's Dyke (*July 5*). Common poppy is widespread. Nowhere else for other targets.

Day 30: June 13

Frozen in time

WHERE County Durham
TARGETS spring gentian, Teesdale violet, mountain pansy, shrubby cinquefoil & whiskered bat
ACCESSIBILITY ①
CHILD-FRIENDLINESS ②

'If you want to see what an Ice Age field looked like,' enthuses Peter Marren in *Britain's Rare Flowers*, 'go to Upper Teesdale. Here are flowers whose heyday was 12,000 years ago, before woods filled the dales.' Hugging the River Tees from Middleton-in-Teesdale to Langton Beck is a luxuriance of upland flower meadows, each vying to be the most colourful. Above them, the moorland of Cronkley and Widdybank Fell safeguard an array of plants so rare in Britain that they have become collectivised as the 'Teesdale Assemblage'.

In the morning, explore between Bowlees and England's tallest waterfall, High Force. First, pootle round the quarry by the car park. Flat sedge and long-bracted yellow-sedge grow here, and the deep purple of wood cranesbill abounds. Orchids bewilder, with numerous hybrids between northern marsh and common spotted orchids. Posing no such problem are unadulterated common twayblade and greater butterfly orchid.

> **"Heath fragrant orchid blotches meadows pink, bird's-eye primrose contributes pale lilac, mountain pansy opulent purple"**

Then cross Wynch Bridge and follow the Tees' southern bank. Meadows of globeflower nod agreeably. Shrubby cinquefoil, restricted to northern England, sprawls on river islands, while alpine and common bistorts stand out on riverbanks. Heath fragrant orchid blotches meadows pink, while bird's-eye primrose contributes pale lilac, and mountain pansy opulent purple. There are birds too, for unimproved meadows are manna for upland waders. Lapwings perform aerial pirouettes, redshanks bleat and curlews bubble.

Fortified by a substantial lunch, dedicate the afternoon to ascending Widdybank Fell. Head south from Cow

Spring gentian is the county flower of Durham.
(Richard Becker/FLPA)

Teesdale violet flowers in just three areas of Britain.
(Bob Gibbons/FLPA)

Green car park, keeping the reservoir to your right. After about 1.25km (around ♀ NY817300), you should start to see 'exclosures', fenced areas designed to protect flowering rarities – the Teesdale Assemblage – from nibbling herbivores.

The botanical stars are spring gentian, right at the end of their flowering season regrettably, and Teesdale violet. Here too are Scottish asphodel, the delicately pink alpine meadow-rue, and common moonwort, a small fern that was once believed to have magical properties. Where the path crosses small, chortling streams (locally known as 'sykes'), check for further scarce plants: variegated horsetail, hair sedge, alpine and three-flowered rushes, and bird's-eye primrose. The list goes on.

Return carwards and treat yourself to an early dinner. Afterwards, park up in Middleton-in-Teesdale for a relaxing post-prandial stroll – just the thing to ease aching calf muscles. From the B6277 road bridge, follow Teesdale Way east, on the river's northern bank. Even before dusk gathers, whiskered bats start hunting overhead and Daubenton's bats whoosh low over the Tees. Upper Teesdale may be a botanist's nirvana, but it offers much, much more besides.

WHERE TO GO Use the B6277 to access various parts of Moor House–Upper Teesdale National Nature Reserve (🖱 tinyurl.com/UpperTeesdale 🖱 tinyurl.com/ BSBIUpperTees). Use Bowlees car park (♀ NY908282), explore the disused quarry (♀ NY908286) then walk west along the River Tees towards High Force waterfall (♀ NY880284). From Cow Green Reservoir car park (♀ NY811309), take the footpath south over Widdybank Fell. Park in Middleton-in-Teesdale, then follow the Teesdale Way east (♀ NY947251).
FLEXIBILITY June is ideal for most of the plants, but spring gentian is better in May. Whiskered bat: June–August.
MAKE IT A WEEKEND From Hankley Shaws car park (♀ NY867298), walk onto Cronkley Fell for more alpine flora. Hannah's Meadow (♀ NY933189 🖱 tinyurl.com /HannahsMeadow) is another brilliant upland hayfield. Try quiet roads around Langdon Beck for black grouse.
ALTERNATIVE LOCATIONS None for the 'Teesdale Assemblage'; that's the point!

Day 31: June 14

Bee good
to yourself

WHERE London & Hertfordshire
TARGETS bee orchid, early marsh orchid, white-legged damselfly
& hairy dragonfly
ACCESSIBILITY ④
CHILD-FRIENDLINESS ④

It is the ultimate British orchid, the perfect bloom. It is among Britain's most sumptuous flowers and one of its most remarkable. The bee orchid is neither rare nor localised, yet spotting your first of the year never fails to excite. It is an unequivocal sign of summer's arrival.

The River Lee flows serenely, surreptitiously, towards the Thames, passing underneath the vehicular bedlam of London's orbital motorway, the M25. Oddly, this juxtaposition of peaceful and hectic, natural and artificial, fails to jar. On the Lee's banks lies Rammey Marsh. This area of straggly grassland – not quite a meadow, but entirely welcome given its capital location – is smattered with the poached eggs of ox-eye daisies, their yellow core circled with white.

It is in the shelter (the Lee's lee?) of the ox-eyes, north of the union of paths by the canal, that bee orchids flourish. And what plants they are. As Richard Mabey writes in *Flora Britannica*, 'the first sight of a bee orchid is an experience few flower-lovers ever forget. There is nothing quite like the sculptured *oddity* of the blooms, perched like sunbathing, pink-winged bumblebees on the stalk. They are beautiful, bizarre and exotic.' In yesteryear, say the old orchid hands, there were thousands of them scattered around Rammey Marsh. The current population is an order of magnitude lower, but no less special for that.

For a different orchid experience, follow the Lee towpath north for 2.5km (or drive) to Pindar car

▶ Bee orchids may be common and widespread, but seeing one always gets the juices flowing. (JL)

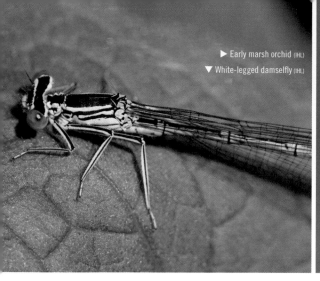

▶ Early marsh orchid (IHL)

▼ White-legged damselfly (IHL)

park. If you walk along the Small River Lee, you may hear a water vole nibbling or spot one swimming: a buoyant, warm-brown feather duster. Once at Pindar, trails lead to the North Metropolitan and Bowyers Orchid meadows. Here you should see two species of pink or magenta marsh orchid – southern and early – plus a few subtle common twayblades.

Should the afternoon be bereft of wind and offer at least a glimmer of sun, watch dragonflies at Cornmill Water Meadows east of the Lee. There are three star species to track down, each a very different take on what it means to be a dragonfly. Hairy dragonflies are blue-and-black striped, compact-bodied predators, their flight fast but also often undulating as if yanked by an invisible string. Banded demoiselles bounce jauntily along, unhurried, with black wingspots flashing. The most sedate and discreet member of the trio is the white-legged damselfly, a specialist of slow-flowing rivers. Lingering over them makes the M25 flyover seem but a distant memory.

> **66 Banded demoiselles bounce jauntily along, unhurried, with black wingspots flashing 99**

WHERE TO GO Bee orchids are at the north end of Rammey Marsh (♀ TQ372993); park on Smeaton Road, Enfield (♀ TQ371987) and walk north. For Bowyers and North Metropolitan Orchid Meadows, use Pindar car park (♀ TL367023), east of the B176 in Cheshunt. Cornmill Water Meadows is off the B194 north of Waltham Abbey (♀ TL384016).
FLEXIBILITY Bee orchid: late May to late June. Marsh orchids: June–July. White-legged damselfly and hairy dragonfly: May to late June.
MAKE IT A WEEKEND Look for heath fritillaries and more in Essex (*June 11*).
ALTERNATIVE LOCATIONS Bee orchids: widespread, particularly on poor soils and waste ground. Marsh orchids likewise, but on wetlands. White-legged damselfly: Arun Bridge (West Sussex). Dragonfly: Strumpshaw Fen (*June 15*), Dungeness (*June 16*), Wicken Fen (*July 27*).

A swallow's tale

WHERE Norfolk
TARGETS swallowtail, Norfolk hawker, scarce chaser & Chinese water deer
ACCESSIBILITY ⑤
CHILD-FRIENDLINESS ⑤

Ablur the shade of clotted cream infiltrates your vision, then vanishes. Within seconds, it loops back, tearing over your shoulder before careering to a halt at the ivory flowers of dame's violet. Wan yellow in colour, spurred and fringed a lacy black, with red eye-spots caressed by blue iridescence, this is unequivocally and emphatically a swallowtail, Broadland's lord of the butterflies.

Britain's swallowtails are a quixotic breed. The subspecies *britannicus* inhabits only East Anglian fens, where its life cycle is unhelpfully contingent on milk parsley, a localised plant that National Trust butterfly expert Matthew Oates berates for being 'rather neurotic.' Oates was speaking to nature writer Patrick Barkham who described his own encounter with a Norfolk swallowtail in *The Butterfly Isles*: 'it had the flashy familiarity of a famous person in the flesh – like a celebrity... somehow more glossy, perfect and compact in real life.'

> **❝Territorial swallowtails readily boss birds away, as well as fellow butterflies❞**

Despite its rarity and tight distribution, seeing a swallowtail is easy. Pick a sunny day with a light breeze and you should succeed at any number of sites. For a properly wild Broadland experience, yomping through towering reeds and soggy fens, try Wheatfen, How Hill or Catfield Fen. A moderate approach would be to walk Weaver's Way footpath south of Hickling Broad, checking yellow flag irises near Rush Hill scrape hide.

The most sedate site is Strumpshaw Fen: dame's violet in the nectar garden at the reserve entrance is proving irresistible to swallowtails. Sugar-rich patches such as this and the famed doctor's garden along the public footpath to the north are such prime real estate that territorial swallowtails readily boss *birds* away, as well as fellow butterflies.

◀ Swallowtail: Lord of Broadland butterflies (IHL)

Although not native to Britain, Chinese water deer is gradually spreading through East Anglia's damper habitats. (JL)

Be aware that Strumpshaw sometimes overflows with swallowtail-watchers, so visiting before mid-morning provides the calmest experience.

Strumpshaw also excels for another Broadland speciality, Norfolk hawker. Whilst this dragonfly is no longer exclusive to the county – it now breeds in Suffolk, Cambridgeshire and Kent – it remains most abundant in the Broads. At Strumpshaw, the best area is the dyke that opens the Meadow Trail, where its preferred aquatic vegetation, water-soldier, abounds. Ideally, visit early on a sunny, calm day to spot the Granny-Smith-green-eyed insects at rest, before they are fuelled by solar power and become incessantly airborne.

Spend the remainder of the day uncovering Strumpshaw's other secrets. Hobbies may scythe through the sky. Scarce chasers meander along the river bank. Marsh harriers should be quartering and Cetti's warblers scolding. A bittern should be booming, as if blowing across the mouth of a bottle. Chinese water deer bark angrily at one another. Strumpshaw is Broadland at its best.

WHERE TO GO RSPB Strumpshaw Fen (♀ TG341065 👆 tinyurl.com/RSPBStrumpshaw) is signposted from a minor road east of Brundall in the Yare valley. Wheatfen (♀ TG325057 👆 www.wheatfen.org) lies on the opposite bank of the Yare. Catfield Fen (♀ TG368214 👆 tinyurl.com/CatfieldFen), How Hill (♀ T370211 👆 http://howhilltrust.org.uk) and Hickling Broad (♀ TG428222 👆 tinyurl.com/NWTHickling) are in 'core' Broadland, to the northeast.
FLEXIBILITY Swallowtails: late May–mid-July; Norfolk hawker: early June–mid-July. Chaser: mid-May to July. Deer: resident.
MAKE IT A WEEKEND Combine with Lakenheath (*June 10*) or Breckland (*June 20*). Or look for natterjack toads in small pools on Winterton Dunes (♀ TG495205).
ALTERNATIVE LOCATIONS Swallowtails and Norfolk hawkers: Upton Fen (Norfolk). Norfolk hawkers are also in Suffolk (including at Minsmere), Cambridgeshire (Paxton Pits) and Kent (Westbere Lakes). Scarce chaser: Lakenheath (*June 10*), New Bridge (West Sussex). Deer: Woodwalton Fen (Cambridgeshire).

Prospect Cottage, Derek Jarman's ground-breaking garden at Dungeness (JL)

Shingle sensations

WHERE Kent
TARGETS Nottingham catchfly, sea pea, toadflax brocade & white-spot
ACCESSIBILITY ③
CHILD-FRIENDLINESS ④

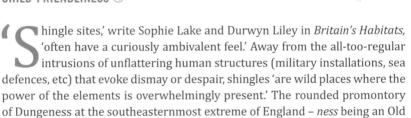

'Shingle sites,' write Sophie Lake and Durwyn Liley in *Britain's Habitats*, 'often have a curiously ambivalent feel.' Away from the all-too-regular intrusions of unflattering human structures (military installations, sea defences, etc) that evoke dismay or despair, shingles 'are wild places where the power of the elements is overwhelmingly present.' The rounded promontory of Dungeness at the southeasternmost extreme of England – *ness* being an Old Norse word for headland – is a case in point.

I recall once giggling at an estate agent's prospectus for a house on this remote peninsula, Europe's largest tract of shingle jutting into a graphite sea. An enticing abode, but the details somehow omitted mention of the property's aspect over the nuclear power station for which Dungeness is infamous. Strange, that. Or, actually, not so strange. Local residents seem not to notice the imposing monstrosity – perhaps because their eyes are transfixed by outstanding flora and fauna.

Coastal vegetated shingle is a rare habitat, and the UK's 5,700 hectares are of global importance. This is a dynamic and fragile realm, created by wave action that deposits stony sediment, then colonised by pioneering plants.

> **"This dynamic and fragile realm is created by wave action then colonised by pioneering plants"**

Appropriately then, part of today focuses on flora.

A remarkable third of all Britain's plant species – some 600 – grow here. Their number includes classic shingle fodder such as sea kale, yellow horned-poppy and sea holly. Prostrate broom and the Nationally Scarce sea pea both sprawl over the ground. Older shingle ridges mimic the coastline. Their more established flora includes sweet vernal-grass, wood sage and common sorrel, while viper's bugloss glows blue and sea campion splashes Tippex-white. On steep banks by the bird observatory, look for another star plant: Nottingham catchfly. The pinkish-white flowers, wrapped into quiffs, waft a heady scent into the calm evening air.

Although this is a guide to summer *day*-trips, try to stay overnight at Dungeness. This enables you to participate in nocturnal moth-trapping sessions – and to trawl any prized hauls from nearby 'moth-ers' the following morning.

Unfortunately, it is three weeks too early for Dungeness's stellar moth, Sussex emerald, although checking wild carrot might reveal its caterpillars. Instead, hope that the opening of the trap(s) bring June specialities such as toadflax brocade – formerly known only from 'Dunge' and environs, but now spreading across the Home Counties and beyond – dark tussock (which, at rest, extends its forelegs like a stretching cat), yellow belle, white-spot (which nectars on Nottingham catchfly) and mullein wave. See them all, and any initial ambivalence will have been vanquished by unequivocal rapture. Just keep blotting out Dungeness B...

WHERE TO GO Dungeness National Nature Reserve (🖥 www.dungeness-nnr.co.uk) is 4km southeast of Lydd. Park by the old lighthouse (📍 TR089170) and explore northwards. Dungeness bird observatory (📍 TR084174 🖥 www.dungenessbirdobs. org.uk) is 500m northwest. Warden David Walker runs moth traps most summer nights. Moth information is summarised at 🖥 tinyurl.com/AtroposDunge.

FLEXIBILITY Nottingham catchfly: May–July; sea pea: June–August. Toadflax brocade: May–June; other moths mentioned June–July.

MAKE IT A WEEKEND Adjacent RSPB Dungeness has bittern and bearded tit and gives you a shot at the recently reintroduced short-haired bumblebee.

ALTERNATIVE LOCATIONS Nottingham catchfly: Great Orme (*July 3*); sea pea: Shingle Street (Suffolk); moths: harder to predict. Other coastal vegetated shingles include Shingle Street (Suffolk) and Lepe (Hampshire).

▶ Formerly a Dungeness speciality, toadflax brocade is spreading north and west in England. (JL)

Day 34: June 17

Musky frogs

WHERE Hampshire
TARGETS musk orchid, frog orchid, common juniper & bastard toadflax
ACCESSIBILITY ③
CHILD-FRIENDLINESS ③

The world may be a big place but chalk grassland is entirely confined to a small area of northwest Europe. Much of it is in Britain, yet we and our forefathers have long mustered an ambivalent relationship to it.

At times, we have treated chalk as special. Many grasslands have an ancient feel and, indeed, prehistoric burial mounds, hillforts and old trackways are commonplace. But our use of chalk downland has been exploitative – quarrying the raw material – as well as reverent. Today, as Sophie Lake writes in *Britain's Habitats,* 'the notion of settled pastoralism evoked by chalk landscapes is often tempered by... the effects of cultural eutrophication.'

Hampshire's Noar Hill captures this quandary. It is the site of medieval chalk workings, yet the abandoned gouges are now carpeted by garlands of flowering plants. Noar's ridges and funnels, exposed banks and sheltered depressions furnish varied niches that enable many different species to thrive. Noar Hill has become a botanist's dream.

Ascending the steep trackway that parts intensely agricultural land does little to prepare you for the wonders that await. Once through the kissing gates into the reserve, however, everything changes.

Pyramidal orchids and common twayblades rise to greet you – and their respective tones (pink, yellow) immediately set the site's base colour scheme.

WHERE TO GO Leave Selborne south of the B3006, immediately turning west towards Newton Valance. Take the first left; there is limited parking at the base of two tracks on the left that lead southeast/uphill to Noar Hill reserve (♀ SU738321).
FLEXIBILITY May–August is good for plants and butterflies, but June–July is optimum for the target flora.
MAKE IT A WEEKEND Check out the River Itchen at Ovington (*May 25*), Pulborough Brooks (West Sussex) or the New Forest (Hampshire).
ALTERNATIVE LOCATIONS Musk orchid: Cleeve Common (Gloucestershire) and Park Gate Down (*May 26*). Frog orchid is widespread. Ditto bastard toadflax on southern chalk downlands. Juniper: Upper Teesdale (*June 13*), Cairn Gorm (*July 4*), Aston Rowant (Oxfordshire).

Dwarf thistle, quinancy-wort, common spotted orchid and chalk fragrant orchid infiltrate the grassland with rose. Horseshoe vetch, cowslip, lady's bedstraw and common rockrose smother the ground with gold. Other colours are less abundant, but still present – often in the guise of rarities. The sprawling stems of the irresistibly named bastard toadflax culminate in titchy white flowers, whilst chalk milkwort is decadently purple.

In the sheltered hollows (those quarries) beneath the information panels, look for little and large. The latter – the ancient bushes of common juniper – will not trouble your eyesight. The wee plants, however, demand an ant's-eye perspective. Fortunately, once you have spotted one musk orchid, and reconciled search image with eyes, you will discern hundreds, perhaps thousands. Noar Hill hosts Britain's heftiest population of this delicate plant; here the rare is gloriously common.

❝Sprawling stems of the irresistibly named bastard toadflax culminate in titchy white flowers❞

One notch bigger is frog orchid. Whereas musk orchids favour sheltered basins, frogs prefers their banks and rims. Whilst this orchid is subtly stunning, only the most gifted of imaginations could possibly construe an amphibian in its form. Ambivalence is integral to Noar's plants themselves, not just the scarce habitat of which they are part.

▶ Musk orchid is a delicate plant: this picture is at least twice life size! (JL)

Noar Hill: a brilliant chalk downland site with excellent flora. (OS)

Day 35: June 18

Largin' it

WHERE Somerset
TARGETS large blue, six-belted clearwing, pyramidal orchid & 'wasp' orchid
ACCESSIBILITY ②
CHILD-FRIENDLINESS ④

Health warning: loving nature risks engendering despair. All too frequently, we learn of a species that has gone extinct, or another that is suffering catastrophic population declines. So when conservationists have something to celebrate, we should down tools and cheer. The reintroduction of the large blue, a glorious butterfly with wings the hue of a perfect summer sky, is one such magnificent success. Today is about toasting that achievement and honouring those who made it happen.

So to Collard Hill, a secluded grassy slope in Somerset's Polden Hills. Managed by the National Trust, Collard is the epicentre of a Butterfly Conservation-led programme to return to Britain a charismatic critter that succumbed to extinction in 1979. All the effort looks to have been worth it. 'It is now merely one of Britain's rarest butterflies,' writes Patrick Barkham in *The Butterfly Isles*. The clue that enabled what Barkham calls 'this strange and miraculous reversal' was unravelling the intimate, treacherous relationship between the large blue butterfly and red ants of the genus *Myrmica*.

Ants are seduced into carrying caterpillars into their nests, only for the guest to feast on the host's own offspring. Understanding the ant's habitat requirements became integral to providing conditions in which large blues could thrive. The butterfly has now been introduced to 100 sites across southwest England, but unfettered visitor access is restricted to Collard

❝Collard Hill is the epicentre of a Butterfly Conservation-led programme to return the large blue to Britain❞

◀ At the start of the 1980s large blue was extinct in Britain. It now flies at 100 sites. (OS)

Hill. Come on a sunny morning in the month from mid-June, and you will be unlucky not to see at least one large blue nectaring on wild thyme.

Check the National Trust blog for the season's prime locations, but typically the lower slopes in the eastern glade and quarry are reliable. Other butterflies on the wing include common blue (which, unlike its rarer relative, has underwings adorned by orange blotches), marbled white (often feeding on field scabious), ringlet (a chocolate button with a distinctive bouncing flight), small heath and brown argus. Six-belted clearwing, a wasp-mimic moth, occurs, typically feeding on or around the yellow flowers of common birdsfoot trefoil.

Collard's other charm – aside from stunning views over the Somerset Levels (*June 25*) – is its orchids. Pyramidal orchids grace the reserve's southernmost reaches with their pink cones. Harder to find, but often marked with sticks, are 'wasp' orchids. Whilst not a species in their own right, these are a scarce, stunning variant of the bee orchid. 'Wasps' have a long, narrow tapering lip and elongated sepals. Cherish their difference, love Britain's diversity and celebrate conservation.

▶ The pyramidal orchid's dense clump of flowers is distinctive. (JL)

WHERE TO GO Collard Hill (♀ ST488340 📱 tinyurl.com/CollardHillNT & 📱 tinyurl.com/CollardHillWalk) is 2km south of Street. Park west of the B3151 (♀ ST485344) on Cockrod, opposite the youth hostel. Walk east to the reserve. A blog gives daily information on large blue sightings (📱 www.ntlargeblue.wordpress. com) and a useful map indicates favoured locations (📱 tinyurl.com/CollardHillMap).
FLEXIBILITY Check the blog for up-to-date information, but large blue generally flies and 'wasp' orchid flowers from mid-June to mid-July. Six-belted clearwing: June–July. Pyramidal orchid: early June to late July.
MAKE IT A WEEKEND Elsewhere in Somerset, visit Haddon Hill (📱 https://tinyurl. com/HaddonHill) for heath fritillary or Avalon Marshes (*June 26*).
ALTERNATIVE LOCATIONS Somerset Wildlife Trust has several open days for large blue at its Green Down reserve. Other large blue sites are private. Clearwing: widespread, including Cherry Hinton (*June 9*) and Devil's Dyke (*July 5*). Pyramidal orchid: widespread, mainly in England. 'Wasp' orchid: best here.

Day 36: June 19

Manxie and thrifty

WHERE Gwynedd
TARGETS thrift clearwing, chough, Manx shearwater & grey seal
ACCESSIBILITY ③
CHILD-FRIENDLINESS ⑤

The lichen-crusted dry-stone wall against which you recline has been warmed by the June sun, two days shy of the solstice. You doze, soaking up the radiance of summer on Bardsey Island, famed resting place of 20,000 saints. Meadow pipits parachute towards a cropped turf overlain by rugs of candyfloss-pink thrift. Wheatears bob, call and flirt, displaying white bums that give them their Old Norse name. Otherwise all is calm. Then you hear an echo of a caterwauling emanating abruptly and inexplicably from the depths of the ground below your seat! What on earth...?

Have you offended some Celtic spirit? Or are you daydreaming? Then you click. The banshee wailing is real, not imaginary. It is the territorial song of a male Manx shearwater, a sound so terrifying that Norse sailors believed the Scottish island of Rhum to be inhabited by trolls. 'Manxies' typically sing at night, but often by day too. Thanks to sensitive wardening, these seabirds are doing well on Bardsey. Up to 20,000 pairs may now breed (one per saint?).

Thrift clearwing, a tiny wasp-mimic moth, atop its namesake plant. ULI

"As you approach the island by boat, Manx shearwaters scythe past in an unending parabola"

20,000 pairs of Manx shearwater breed on Bardsey. (RC)

Bardsey lies 3km off the tip of the Llŷn Peninsula, making it an easy and delightful day-trip from a jetty near Aberdaron. Greater butterfly orchids greet you as you descend from the mainland car park to the departure cove. As you approach the island by boat, Manx shearwaters scythe past in an unending parabola. Guillemots and razorbills charge out to sea from the cliffside nesting colonies. Fulmars glide past, stiff-winged and aloof. A raven croaks overhead, its smoker-voice matched by a throaty, deep-jowled form.

Docking at the eastern slipway, you are greeted by a slew of mermaids. More than 100 grey seals are hauled out on the seaweed-coated rocks, and they yodel cheerily at each other. As you tread towards the lighthouse – striped red and white like an archetypal barber shop's sign – at the island's southern extremity, house martins beat the cover for aerial insects. A rabble of choughs – scarecrows in silhouette – lazes along the low cliffs, their calls searing the air with the freedom to fly.

The slope below the lighthouse has the island's densest flush of thrift, and you will need to enter the world of these pink flowers to search for Bardsey's star invertebrate. To do so involves lowering your eye level to flower height. Part the thrift heads carefully, looking for a remarkable tiny moth that mimics a wasp and is wholly dependent on this maritime bloom: thrift clearwing. You could of course 'cheat' by using a pheromone-infused vial to lure a libidinal male – but an hour on your tummy should do the trick.

WHERE TO GO Bardsey island (♀ SH120215 🖰 www.bardsey.org) lies off the Llŷn Peninsula. There is a bird observatory (🖰 www.bbfo.org.uk). The nearest town is Aberdaron. Day trips usually depart from Porth Meudwy (use the car park at ♀ SH159259 and walk downhill; see 🖰 tinyurl.com/BardseyDay).
FLEXIBILITY Seabirds are present March–August. Thrift clearwing: June–July. Chough and grey seal: resident.
MAKE IT A WEEKEND Anglesey has much to offer, including Sandwich and Arctic tern colonies at Cemlyn Bay plus red squirrel (*August 9*).
ALTERNATIVE LOCATIONS Thrift clearwing: Lizard Peninsula (*May 31*) and Anglesey. Manx shearwater: Borth (*August 17*). Chough: many west coast locations, including South Stack (Anglesey) and Stackpole (*May 27*). Grey seal: widespread.

Day 37: June 20

Field wormwood (JL)

Proliferous pink (JL)

Spanish catchfly (JL)

Pretty in pink

WHERE Suffolk
TARGETS proliferous pink, field wormwood, Spanish catchfly, powdered grass-veneer & marbled clover
ACCESSIBILITY ④
CHILD-FRIENDLINESS ④

Kneeling amidst an immense picnic rug of mustard-coloured kidney vetch and beneath a cobalt sky worthy of the South Pacific, the individual buzz and collective hum of hundreds of bees drifts over you. The sandy heathland of the Brecks, straddling the county border between Norfolk and Suffolk, is Britain's answer to the steppes – 'a world apart from the rest of East Anglia,' writes Peter Marren in *Britain's Rare Flowers*. A mid-summer day here is immensely enjoyable – but also thought-provoking. Unearthing Breckland's botanical riches may force you to question both your concept of rarity and your philosophy of conservation.

Start at Cranwich Camp, a long-deserted military base on which several Breckland botanical specialities are striving to reassert themselves. The car park itself, specifically the perimeter of an obvious rectangular concrete block, is one of just two sites nationwide for proliferous pink. Like many Breckland plants, the rosy flower is tiny, so it pays to get your eye in by searching for the tall spindly stems with a bulging calyx just shy of its tip. This nationally threatened plant was only discovered in Britain as recently as

1993, yet many thousands flourish in this most inconsequential of locations. How wonderfully disconcerting that a rarity can abound.

Powdered grass-veneer, a smart micro-moth (JL)

Then enter the meadow, searching for further scarcities to a hymenopteran soundtrack. Small lilac dabs alert you to purple milk-vetch, another nationally threatened plant. Small discrete blotches of yellow may be the star-shaped flowers of biting stonecrop.

At an obvious sandy rectangle with more bare terrain than vegetation, proceed carefully. Another major rarity, Spanish catchfly, grows commonly here. Like proliferous pink, it is titchy – indeed, markedly dainty and weedy – and scarily susceptible to obliteration by a misplaced boot.

“The Artemisia reserve's incongruous brownfield location provokes disturbingly contradictory emotions”

Then check out clumps of the vigorous, purplish-blue viper's bugloss. This is the favoured foodplant for marbled clover, an energetic, nationally rare day-flying moth. Search too for other classic Breckland moths such as powdered grass-veneer, oblique striped and straw-barred pearl, as well as the more widespread forester and six-spot burnet moth.

If you can drag yourself away, visit the tiny Artemisia reserve in Brandon, national stronghold of an incredibly rare plant. Field wormwood has declined by 77% in 40 years. A protected area barely the size of two tennis courts, Artemisia's incongruous brownfield location – an unprepossessing industrial estate – provokes disturbingly contradictory emotions. Should we celebrate the rescue of this biologically rich parcel of land? Or despair that human activity expels our rarest biodiversity to such fragile margins? Breckland enthrals – and unsettles.

WHERE TO GO Cranwich Camp is 3km west of Mundford south of the A134 (car park ♀ TL775942). Artemisia reserve (♀ TL773855) is in southwest Brandon. From the A1065 enter the industrial estate on Highbury Road, then take the first right.
FLEXIBILITY Throughout June–July for most Breckland specialities.
MAKE IT A WEEKEND Join a public nocturnal moth-trapping session run by the Suffolk Moths Group or West Stow Country Park. By day, try for yellow-legged clearwing (a wasp-mimic moth) at Barnhamcross Common (♀ TL864811). More botanising at Maidscross Hill for sand catchfly, etc. Military orchids at Rex Graham reserve, Mildenhall Woods.
ALTERNATIVE LOCATIONS Other good sites for Breckland flora and moths include Tuddenham Gallops, Icklingham Triangle, Wangford Heath and Rampart's Field.

Day 38: June 21
Small is beautiful

WHERE Powys
TARGETS small white orchid, heath fragrant orchid, wood bitter vetch & small pearl-bordered fritillary
ACCESSIBILITY ③
CHILD-FRIENDLINESS ④

S welling upwards from a clandestine valley escaping from the Cambrian Mountains is a petite but enchantingly rich grassland reserve. Vicarage Meadows was once owned by local clergy. Horses and cattle were grazed, and hay harvested – all in tandem with natural cycles. Brecknock Wildlife Trust now manages the site, continuing the traditional approach that enables a botanical bonanza of wildflowers to flourish. This gorgeous meadow merits a full day of relaxed – indeed, often supine – exploration.

> **❝This gorgeous meadow merits a full day of relaxed – indeed, often supine – exploration❞**

Take both time and picnic, and insinuate yourself amidst Vicarage Meadows' sights, sounds and smells.

The western meadow is packed with summer orchids, with several species to track down. Heath spotted orchids abound on damp ground atop acidic soil. Unlike their common spotted cousins, these are rather delicate, attractive blooms which culminate in billowing petticoats. You should compile quite some palette, from whitish through various pinks to mauve and even dusky red. The 'spotting' also varies in intensity, meaning that neighbouring plants rarely look alike.

Even daintier is heath fragrant orchid, a small but erect orchid crested by a spike with relatively few pink flowers. Even more graceful still, you may spot a few greater butterfly orchids, which holds its ivory flowers with unrivalled elegance. But it is a smaller white orchid that forms your top target in the western meadow. Or, precisely, *it is* small white orchid.

Unimaginatively named, for sure, but this is a teeny cracker of

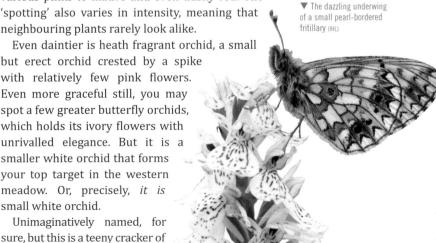

▼ The dazzling underwing of a small pearl-bordered fritillary (IHL)

Heath fragrant orchid (IHL)

Small white orchid (IHL)

a plant – when you find it. Amidst a cover of long grass, it is hard to spot, even for experienced plant-hunters. It pays to search methodically with your eyes as near to ground level as your spine grants. Once you spy its unassuming form, reward yourself with an intimate examination. Each individual flower on the orchid's densely packed spike is truly tiny: as little as 2mm in diameter yet still distinctively bell-shaped and displaying a tri-lobed lip. Bonsai perfection: small is beautiful.

Objective met, enjoy the rest of the meadow. Wetter areas glitter with the golden spikes of bog asphodel. The mauve blooms of devil's-bit scabious are glorious; some may be adorned with the fire of nectaring small pearl-bordered fritillaries. Best of all, the stunning and Nationally Scarce wood bitter vetch creeps and clusters in select spots, its purple and pink flowers provoking gasps of awe. This is a treasure of a British meadow.

WHERE TO GO Vicarage Meadows (♀ SN850526 🛈 tinyurl.com/VicarageMeadows) adjoins the hamlet of Abergwesyn, along a minor road from Beulah or Llanwrtyd Wells. Park near the gates south of the River Irfon, south of Abergwesyn. Cross the gate nearest the river. Follow the track past a cottage and through two further gates to reach the reserve.
FLEXIBILITY Small white orchid: early June to early July. Heath fragrant orchid: typically mid-June to mid-July.
MAKE IT A WEEKEND King Arthur's Cave (Herefordshire) has greater and lesser horseshoe bats.
ALTERNATIVE LOCATIONS Small white orchid: Cliburn Ashby (Cumbria). Heath fragrant orchid: widespread in Scotland, grows in the New Forest and on Stoborough Heath (*July 6*). Fritillary: Heddon Mouth (*June 24*), Fen Bog (*June 29*), Ben Lawers (*July 2*). Vetch: local and best seen here.

Day 39: June 22
Seabird cityscape

WHERE Northumberland
TARGETS Arctic & Sandwich terns, puffin & guillemot
ACCESSIBILITY ③
CHILD-FRIENDLINESS ⑤

Today is bedlam. Glorious, life-enhancing bedlam. The air seethes with wings, the rocky island crammed with feathered forms. The skies resound with cries, calls and chaos. Then there's the smell: the sulphur acridity of guano from thousands of inhabitants, nesting and pooping cheek by jowl. This is a seabird colony at full throttle.

And no ordinary seabird city at that. At almost all such colonies, human visitors are kept at a distance from avian residents. We teeter on the top of a cliff, peering down. Or we sway in the swell, craning our necks upwards from the 'comfort' of a boat. Not so on the Farne Islands, an archipelago of 20-odd volcanic islets dotted over the North Sea off the Northumberland coast.

Nearly 70,000 pairs of seabirds breed on the Farnes, and the fleets of auks on the water are bettered only by the blizzard of terns above the rocky outcrops. Visitor numbers to the only two regularly accessible islands – Staple and Inner Farne – are carefully managed, so it makes sense to advance-book your boat from Seahouses. Choose carefully to maximise your time ashore. Dress appropriately, which means robust head gear for reasons that become clear once you disembark on Inner Farne.

The Farnes' star denizens are Arctic terns. Having migrated to Antarctica and back, a mere 70,000km (and that without factoring in daily fishing trips),

Crammed cheek to jowl, guillemots raise young on the narrowest of ledges. (DT)

> **"On Britain's answer to the Galápagos, resist the temptation to touch the birdies"**

Arctic terns top the bill at the Farne Islands. (DT)

Arctic terns are understandably single-minded about raising their brood. These delicate sea swallows do not take kindly to what they perceive as intruders. As you enter a tern's patch, prepare to be dive-bombed. This is no mock-offensive; terns possess sharp bills that readily draw blood.

Once you have dealt with the shock of birdlife approaching you, it's your turn (ha ha!) to return the favour. Boardwalks wheedle through a richness of marine birds. Photographers may wonder why they bothered lugging their super-telephoto; a wide-angle is of greater service. Most birds – be they puffins, guillemots or razorbills; kittiwakes, shags or Sandwich terns – go about their business within inches of human admirers. On Britain's answer to the Galápagos, resist the temptation to touch the birdies.

It is all too easy to be overwhelmed by the Farnes. So much life, so close. If that describes your experience, simply pick one individual bird and sit down, at a respectful distance. Focus your attention on it, and grant yourself the treat of intimacy by entering its life. Watch the comings, the goings and the stayings. The bedlam retreats – and the beauty resounds.

WHERE TO GO Boats depart from Seahouses harbour for the Farne Islands (⚲ NU230370 🖥 www.nationaltrust.org.uk/farne-islands). Operators including Billy Shiel's Boats (🖥 www.farne-islands.com) and Serenity Tours (🖥 www. farneislandstours.co.uk) run trips lasting 2–6 hours.
FLEXIBILITY Boats operate May–July.
MAKE IT A WEEKEND Dive with grey seals off the Farnes (with Sovereign Diving or Farne Islands Diving Charters). Visit Coquet Island (*May 28*) or Hauxley (🖥 www.nwt. org.uk/reserves/hauxley) for roseate tern.
ALTERNATIVE LOCATIONS Sandwich tern colony: Blakeney Point (*August 3*). Arctic tern colonies: Shetland. Colonies of both terns: Cemlyn Bay (Anglesey). Puffins: Flamborough Head (East Yorkshire) and Sumburgh Head (Shetland). Guillemot: Stackpole Quay (*May 27*), Bempton (*June 3*), Bardsey (*June 19*), Great Orme (*July 3*).

Day 40: June 23

For peat's sake

WHERE Shropshire
TARGETS white-faced darter, common hawker, large heath &
common raft spider
ACCESSIBILITY ③
CHILD-FRIENDLINESS ③

There is something apposite about the discovery of a Bronze Age axe in a 3,400-year-old layer of peat at Whixall Moss. In recent decades, peat has formed a battleground between sparring horticulturalists and conservationists – but the wildlife is finally winning through.

Given widespread drainage of peat bogs for conversion to agriculture and forestry, and the extraction of peat for fuel, livestock bedding and gardening, it is remarkable that Whixall Moss survives at all. For this we thank conservationists who designated the area as a national nature reserve, then restored Britain's third-largest bog. This is important stuff; Britain is responsible for a chunky proportion of the world's remaining raised peat bogs. But what's all the fuss about?

At first sight, the Moss looks unassuming, unspectacular, even ordinary. Between you and the horizon stretches an organic medley of greens and browns. But let's dwell on that thought. The horizon is distant, the sky everywhere, and you are alone; Whixall is huge, Whixall is wild, Whixall is wilderness.

Walking the waymarked trails helps you unearth the Moss's heterogeneity. There are dry bits and wet bits, bogs and pools, sandy tracks and deep ditches. All across this wilderness, nature thrives. Curlews bubble in territory-defining flight, and teal pipe from a concealed pond. Skylarks yodel above a patchwork

"Always in a hurry, the large heath bounces relentlessly across the heathland"

To see a large heath perched like this, visit very early in the morning. (OS)

A young common raft spider, literally walking on water. (JL)

quilt of sphagnum bog-mosses, carnivorous sundews and the bobbing white thistledown-heads of common cotton-grass.

Impressive though this wildlife is, Whixall's star turns are invertebrate. White-faced darter is a bog-pool specialist, best seen between posts A and B, and at a larger boardwalk-flanked pool deeper into the mire. Whixall's second special dragonfly is among Britain's largest: common hawkers are powerful but wary, rarely granting an audience. For sure, you will get better looks at four-spotted chaser, the Moss's most obvious and fearless dragon, which will have a pop at any intruder to its air-space.

In poolside vegetation, particularly cross-leaved heath, slump to your knees to look for bog bush-crickets, which are developing from nymph to adult. This stripe-necked orthopteran is a speciality of damp terrain. Near post 7, check black pools for the eerily motionless form of a common raft spider. This supreme predator hunts by stealth, so don't expect to see it move much. The opposite is true of Whixall's final sexy invertebrate. Whilst common in Scotland, large heath is a localised butterfly this far south. Always in a hurry, it bounces relentlessly across the heathland, with only the occasional pit-stop. Or should that be 'peat-stop'?

WHERE TO GO Whixall Moss (📱 tinyurl.com/WhixallMoss) is 6km southwest of Whitchurch. Park on the east side at Moss Cottages/Manor House (♀ SJ501364). Walk west onto the Moss and follow trails. A good pool for white-faced darter is between posts A and B (♀ SJ495366), with common raft spiders 400m southwest near post 7 (♀ SJ493362).
FLEXIBILITY White-faced darter: mid-May to mid-July. Large heath and common hawker: mid-June to end July. Common raft spider: May–September.
MAKE IT A WEEKEND Prees Heath (Shropshire) has silver-studded blue (*July 14*).
ALTERNATIVE LOCATIONS White-faced darter and common hawker: Abernethy Forest (*June 4*). Large heath: Fen Bog (*June 29*), Ben Lawers (*July 2*) and Meathop Moss (Cumbria). Common raft spider: widespread on peaty pools, including at Arne (Dorset).

Get your eye in with dark green fritillary before attempting to identify Heddon's rarer butterflies. (OS)

Heddon on earth

WHERE Devon
TARGETS high brown fritillary, dark green fritillary &
silver-washed fritillary
ACCESSIBILITY ③
CHILD-FRIENDLINESS ④

I s Heddon Valley Devon's Heaven? In a single mile, from a temptingly placed pub northwards to a savagely rocky cove (Heddon's Mouth), the Exmoor footpath infiltrates a succession of contrasting landscapes. Bracken-rich slopes, sheltered wooded valleys and flower-rich meadows; steepling cliffs, rocky shores and heathery moorland. Heddon has it all. Even better, this is the top site in Britain to watch fritillaries, burning butterflies that occur here in variety and numbers.

Parking at Hunter's Inn (you'll be back, don't worry), take the footpath that snakes north along the wooded eastern slope of the valley. Keep left and gradually descend to join the South West Coast Path. Cross the bridge, and turn right to continue north, staying west of the riverbank. The fritillaries – of which there are four species – favour the stretch between bridge and beach, so check all flowering vegetation, particularly bramble, thistle and violets growing shyly beneath bracken.

> **66 An incessant and precipitous decline means that fewer than 50 high brown fritillary colonies remain 99**

But which fritillaries? At the petite end of the size spectrum, the small pearl-bordered

▶ High brown fritillary is one of Britain's two Critically Endangered butterflies. (IHL)

fritillary flies here. Its stature is clearly discernible, even in fluttering flight, so there is no chance of confusing it with the larger trio of fritillaries. You will, however, need sharp eyes and stationary butterflies to differentiate between dark green, silver-washed and high brown fritillaries.

These three species are similarly large, with fast swooping flights combining rapid wingbeats and powerful glides. Identifying a fritillary as it roars around would be a bold call, so wait until it alights. Even then, the species's markings differ only subtly – and the key is to look at the closed underwing.

The most common species is the dark green fritillary; the underside of its wing has a greenish cast and features a dozen or more large silvery-white spots. The silver-washed fritillary also possesses a greyish-green underwing, but this is decorated by diffuse silver streaks. The rarest of the trio – the insect that butterfly-enthusiasts travel hundreds of miles to see here – is the high brown fritillary. Look for russet blotches adorning its underwing.

The high brown fritillary is one of only two British butterflies considered Critically Endangered at a national level (the other being large blue; see *June 18*). Once widely distributed across England and Wales, an incessant and precipitous decline since the 1950s (and particularly since the 1990s) means that fewer than 50 high brown fritillary colonies remain countrywide. For Michael Easterbrook, author of *Butterflies of Britain and Ireland,* 'only a concerted effort by conservationists and landowners is likely to avert its extinction.' Even in Heaven, this glorious butterfly's future is far from secure.

WHERE TO GO Heddon Valley (♥ SS655482 ☎ www.nationaltrust.org.uk/heddon-valley) is 6km west of Lynton; follow minor roads north from the A39. Use the car park by Hunter's Inn, then walk north, eventually following the path along the west side of the River Heddon.

FLEXIBILITY High brown fritillary: mid-June to mid-July. Early in its season, high brown fritillary overlaps with dark green; later on it overlaps with silver-washed.

MAKE IT A WEEKEND Spend another day wandering the footpaths either side of Heddon's Mouth; brilliant walking amidst stunning scenery.

ALTERNATIVE LOCATIONS High brown fritillary: Arnside Knott and Whitbarrow Scar (Cumbria), Alun Valley (Glamorgan), Marsland Valley, Aish Tor and Hembury Woods (Devon) and Allt Dolanog (Powys). Other fritillaries are fairly widespread.

Day 42: June 25
Festival of fauna

WHERE Somerset
TARGETS great white egret, bittern, argent and sable,
& Iberian water frog
ACCESSIBILITY ⑤
CHILD-FRIENDLINESS ④

Late June at Glastonbury is all about the music. Unless you're into wildlife, in which case it is all about herons. The conical Glastonbury Tor protrudes above an extensive area of carefully managed wetlands known collectively as Avalon Marshes.

Avalon's adjoining wetland reserves, notably Shapwick Heath and Ham Wall, have become Britain's most exciting location to look for members of the heron family. When I was a juvenile birdwatcher in the 1980s, the only species I ever expected to see was grey heron. During a day at Avalon nowadays you should see at least four species.

> **In Avalon Marshes's festival of wildlife, there is competition for headliner**

This change – nay, revolution – is a sign of our climatic times. Ever-milder weather means Britain is being stutteringly colonised by species from continental Europe. Foresighted conservationists from Natural England, RSPB and elsewhere have developed habitat ahead of their arrival – Avalon's wetlands among them.

Lanky and snow-white, little egret is the poster boy for this upheaval. This was a national rarity as recently as the 1980s yet in a single day on the Somerset Levels you could now easily rack up 50 individuals. Several notches larger is great white egret. With its snake of a neck and stilts for legs, the great white towers above its relative. Nobody knows quite how many frequent the Levels, but it is at least 20 – with breeding already proven.

At a global scale, the most significant heron is the bittern, a bird as tawny as its reedbed habitat. In 2014, an amazing 41 males were counted 'booming', the territorial call equated to blowing softly across an open beer bottle. Good places for both species include Ham Wall (notably Waltons and Loxtons) and Meare Heath.

If your luck is in, you may even coincide with a rarity. Little bittern, a jaunty cream and black heron, has a toehold as a British breeder. Up to four males 'bark' their libidinal

▶ Formerly a rarity in Britain, great white egret is now a welcome fixture on the Avalon Marshes. (JL)

Avalon Marshes is the only known site in Britain for Iberian water frog. (RC)

desires here most summers. Night herons hint at oversummering, and even purple herons and glossy ibises are occasionally spotted. The smart money is on all becoming established breeders in the Avalon within our lifetimes.

All these sizeable birds need lots to eat, and amphibians are the meal of choice. Ham Wall waterways are crammed with what was thought to be edible frog but is now reckoned to be Iberian water frog, the first time this non-native species has been determined to occur in Britain. Finally, look for argent and sable, a rare black-and-white day-flying moth, with a national stronghold at Shapwick. In Avalon Marshes' festival of fauna, there is competition for a headliner.

▶ Argent and sable is a rare and attractive moth with a stronghold in Somerset. (IHL)

WHERE TO GO Avalon Marshes (🐾 www.avalonmarshes.org) stretches from Glastonbury west to the M5 near Burnham-on-Sea. Avalon comprises several reserves. The best are Shapwick Heath (🐾 tinyurl.com/ShapwickH) and RSPB Ham Wall (🐾 tinyurl.com/RSPBHamWall): use adjacent car parks (📍 ST449397) at Ashcott Corner, either side of the Ashcott–Meare road. The official visitor centre is southwest of Westhay (📍 ST424412).
FLEXIBILITY Bittern and great white egret: year-round. Iberian water frog: April–August. Argent and sable: May–July.
MAKE IT A WEEKEND The brand new wetland at Steart Marshes (📍 ST252442 🐾 www.steart.wwt.org.uk) has water vole and Somerset's first breeding avocets. Or go badger-watching at Denbury Farm (🐾 tinyurl.com/DenburyBadger).
ALTERNATIVE LOCATIONS Minsmere (*May 22*) for bittern and frequent great white egret. Iberian water frog: nowhere else... yet! Argent and sable: Glen Loy (*June 4*).

Southern hawker is a large, inquisitive and striking dragonfly. OLJ

Winged jewels

On a hot July day in 1997, an excited colleague approached my desk. He bore news of Britain's first-ever twitchable lesser emperor at a nearby lake. I confessed to lacking the faintest inkling of this was. My friend was aghast. 'It's a dragonfly, and dragonflies are brilliant! You are missing out!' he exclaimed... and dragged me out the door.

The lesser emperor proved to be a breathtaking aeronaut, scudding along at 25 miles per hour. This and other species I saw were as bejewelled as the brightest birds. That first imperial encounter hooked me. I've never looked back.

High-octane predators, dragonflies have unrivalled powers of flight and sight, dexterity and determination. Their names evoke flight styles: hawkers and skimmers, chasers and darters. Red and blue damselflies flutter meekly, demoiselles yo-yo extravagantly, and emerald damselflies helicopter gracefully.

Their world may be fast, but watching dragonflies slows you down. Loll by a waterbody in the sun then gawp as you bask. Dragons are exhilarating in motion, but entrancing at rest. All repay close perusal. Gasp at a darter's compound eyes. Wonder at the fragility of transparent veined wings. Examine spiny legs that catch prey and pincer-like jaws that crush it.

Watch damselfly pairs float aloft, locked in mating wheels, or male chasers obsessively guard egg-laying partners. Play peekaboo with a dew-encased damselfly at dawn. Find a dragonfly nymph crawling free of water for the first and only time, then watch it 'hatch' into the winged wonder of an adult.

Throughout Britain, wherever there is water — lake or pond, canal or stream, ditch or bog — there be dragons. Their winged world hums from April to October. The number of species — 40-odd — is perfect. Too few to bamboozle; enough to excite. Most are easily identifiable; some pose tantalising conundrums.

"Dragonfly names evoke flight styles: hawkers and skimmers, chasers and darters"

Excitingly, Britain's dragonfly list is lengthening as species spread from continental Europe. Unknown here 20 years ago, small red-eyed damselfly is now common across much of England. Willow emerald damselfly looks to be following suit. If finding rarities is your thing, dragonflies offer rich rewards. Even I have discovered three 'megas', as well as my very own lesser emperors. I suspect I owe my friend a pint...

Gorge yourself

WHERE Somerset
TARGETS Cheddar pink, slender bedstraw, peregrine, greater horseshoe bat & water vole
ACCESSIBILITY ②
CHILD-FRIENDLINESS ②

Visit England's largest canyon to stride spectacular clifftops looking for rare plants and powerful raptors, and to chance your arm with a nocturnal stroll targeting shy mammals. It required the end of the last Ice Age to create Cheddar Gorge. Scoured out by torrential meltwater, the limestone plateau now towers 130m above the road twisting through the gorge's nether regions. Walking the clifftop is the best way to view Cheddar's panoramas and pinnacles – and isn't bad for wildlife either.

Soaring and hovering below you should be peregrines and kestrels that breed on sheer cliff-faces between the rocky dentition of weathered crags. A breeze wafts one upwards; who is the watcher and who is the watched?

Aside from scenery, Cheddar Gorge is renowned for botany. Cheddar pink, a tufted perennial herb, grows on goat-grazed turf and inaccessible cliff-ledges here but nowhere else in Britain. A worthy county flower. Similarly scarce is slender bedstraw, whilst little robin (a geranium) is nationally rare. Most amazing of all are the whitebeams, trees related to pears. In 2009, botanists discovered – 'hidden' amongst a long-known quintet of species – three species entirely new to science here, suggesting Cheddar has become a centrifuge for whitebeam evolution.

> **Cheddar pink grows here but nowhere else in Britain. A worthy county flower**

Cheddar pink grows on rocky ledges and cliff-edge turf.
(IMAGEBROKER, MARKO KoNIG, Imageb/
Imagebroker/FLPA)

Water voles inhabit the River Yeo in Cheddar Gorge. (JL)

After circumnavigating the gorge, take an extension eastwards along Black Rock trail. Common redstarts smoulder in the woodland. Limestone fern sprouts from dry-stone walls, including opposite the limekiln at post 1. Grassland opposite post 2 heaves with wild thyme, common milkwort and common rockrose. In scrubby terrain, a dark green fritillary may hurtle past, a common buzzard may mew overhead or an adder may bask beneath sunny walls or rocks.

After the hike, catch your breath beside the river below the National Trust shop. Water voles occur here, and the RSPB may have viewing facilities set up. Aim to greet nightfall outside Gough's Cave. Greater horseshoe bats roost inside the amazing karst-limestone cavern, emerging at dusk to swarm at its mouth before heading deep into the night to feed.

Then, if the night is still and dry, return to Black Rock. Work the trail backwards from posts 8 to 6. Bat-detector in hand, you may capture the echolocatory warbling of both greater and lesser horseshoe bats. Keep alert to terrestrial activity; you may bump into pygmy shrew or a badger from a sett east of post 6. If your optimism is surging, have a crack at hazel dormouse. The coppiced woodland between posts 8 and 7, rich in hazel and honeysuckle, habours a decent population. An alert ear might just discern the rustling of leaves that betrays one of these shy mammals clambering through the canopy. You gotta be in it to win it, right?

WHERE TO GO Access Cheddar Gorge (🌐 www.cheddargorge.co.uk) from the B3135. Park in Cheddar. Gorge walk (🌐 tinyurl.com/NTCheddarwalk) starts from the 274 Steps. For Black Rock and other Somerset Wildlife Trust reserves (🌐 tinyurl.com/ SWTCheddar) park in the layby (📍 ST482546).
FLEXIBILITY Plants: June–July; mammals: June–September; peregrine: March– September.
MAKE IT A WEEKEND Explore Somerset Wildlife Trust's other reserves: Long Wood for silver-washed fritillary and herb Paris; Velvet Bottom for common lizard, meadow saffron, alpine pennycress and spring sandwort; both reserves for badger. Further south, The Perch (📍 ST480532) harbours slender bedstraw and Cheddar pink. Or Avalon Marshes (*June 25*).
ALTERNATIVE LOCATIONS Plants: none. Bat: Stackpole (*May 27*). Peregrine: widespread, including Chichester (*August 4*), Norwich (*August 22*). Vole: Arundel (*August 4*), Rainham (*August 15*), London Wetland Centre (*August 19*).

A black-necked grebe family (IHL)

Where there's muck...

WHERE West Yorkshire
TARGETS bittern, marsh harrier, avocet & black-necked grebe
ACCESSIBILITY ⑤
CHILD-FRIENDLINESS ③

I n a world where human impact on wildlife is typically associated with at least gloom and all too frequently doom – witness the ever-lengthening Red Lists of species suffering precipitous declines – we should make extra effort to celebrate success wherever we encounter it. Good-news stories rarely reach the media, but that does not mean that they *are* rare. Conservation-minded organisations, from Natural England to Plantlife, and Buglife to the Yorkshire Wildlife Trust, are moving metaphorical mountains to preserve our natural delights.

> **This is not a 'good-news story'; it is an 'astonishing-news story'**

Some – notably the RSPB – have become experts at creating something out of nothing, and nowhere is that something more special to me, personally, than at Swillington Ings. As a teenager, I regularly birdwatched at this former opencast coalmine with a view over slag heaps and spoil tips as black as night, scanning a flooded pit the depth of ten houses. Scenic it was not. Never did I imagine the revolution that the RSPB would bring about at 'Swilly'.

From muck, the charity has created not just brass, but bronze, silver and gold. Fossil-fuel wasteland has been transmogrified into a reserve of reedbed and invertebrate-rich waterbodies covering nearly 600 times the extent of

An avocet: all limbs and appendages (BHL)

Leeds United's nearby football ground at Elland Road. And how the birds have responded, with nationally rare species racing one another to colonise this extraordinary site.

In ten active years of birding in West Yorkshire, I only once saw black-necked grebes, and never had a sniff of bittern, marsh harrier, avocet or bearded tit. All five species now breed at Swillington – and the colony of grebes has become Britain's largest. This is not a 'good-news story'; it is an 'astonishing-news story'.

Mid-summer is prime time here. The black-necked grebes, enchanting waterbirds decorated in black, chestnut and gold, are feeding young – and allow amazingly close views. Bitterns flap around, seeking out aquatic provisions for their growing offspring. A drake Garganey peers out from a reedy margin, a white mask curving back from its eye. The black-headed gull colony is in full throttle, and the odd Mediterranean gull may secrete itself in their midst. Not one bird bats an eyelid at the constant passage of joggers, cyclists and other non-wildlife-watching visitors.

As I write, legal difficulties mean that the reserve – which will eventually become known as RSPB St Aidan's – is not yet formally open. Nevertheless, there is access to all key wildlife areas through a network of public footpaths. So go – and celebrate conservation success!

WHERE TO GO Swillington Ings/RSPB St Aidan's (⌨ tinyurl.com/RSPBStAidans) lies east of Oulton. Site information is currently provided by Swillington Ings Bird Group (⌨ https://sibg1.wordpress.com/sites/). Park opposite Bayford's Oil Depot at the bottom of Fleet Lane (♀ SE381284) for southern parts. Footpaths ply across St Aidan's, reached from Astley Lane with parking best at ♀ SE389288.
FLEXIBILITY Throughout spring and summer for the target species.
MAKE IT A WEEKEND Options include York for tansy beetle (*June 3*), Bempton Cliffs for seabirds (ditto), Fen Bog for large heath and wood tiger (*June 29*) or Wykeham Forest (*July 28*) for honey-buzzard and goshawk.
ALTERNATIVE LOCATIONS Black-necked grebe: Woolston Eyes (Cheshire). Marsh harrier, avocet and bittern: Leighton Moss (Lancashire), Minsmere (Suffolk), Titchwell (Norfolk).

A meadow rich in ox-eye daisies (JL)

The perfect meadow

WHERE Wiltshire
TARGETS hay-rich flower meadows with burnt orchid, great burnet & adder's-tongue fern
ACCESSIBILITY ③
CHILD-FRIENDLINESS ④

I s there a sadder loss from the English landscape than the near-wholesale disappearance of traditional flower-rich hay meadows? George Peterken, author of the eulogy *Meadows,* laments that 'in less than my lifetime, most meadows have been ploughed, drained, converted to sown grassland, fertilised to biological impoverishment or destroyed by development.'

> **❝Clattinger is a time capsule, unique in England's agricultural domain❞**

How utterly demoralising – how downright irresponsible – that we are now obliged to make a concerted visit to a far-flung meadow should we wish to laze amidst its spectrum of colours, forms and fragrances. But how special are those surviving traditional meadows. Today is about celebrating what is probably England's best-preserved fragment of such floral grassland: Wiltshire's Clattinger Farm.

Described by HRH Prince Charles as 'a magical series of wildflower meadows,' Clattinger owes its botany to the antipathy of its previous owners towards agricultural chemicals. As such, Clattinger is a time capsule, unique in England's agricultural domain. An agriculturally 'unimproved' grassland that, botanically, cannot be improved upon.

Treat yourself to dwelling day-long amidst eleven meadows spreading over 60 hectares. Explore each thoroughly while treading carefully to avoid trampling. Rejoice at the tonal paroxysm: the pinks and yellows and lilacs and burgundies. Identify – and treasure – the species that instigate this floral riot (more of which later). Recline cautiously and linger decadently, listening to the assiduity of bees and the repetitions of the orthopteran orchestra, and granting yourself the right to drift into (agri)cultural nostalgia for yesteryear.

So what of the species that make Clattinger spectacular? Great burnet, common knapweed, ragged robin and ox-eye daisy form the backdrop. Adder's-tongue ferns protrude cheekily. But orchids steal the show. Common spotted and southern marsh orchids vie for predominance, which may explain the high proportion of confusing-looking hybrids. Heath spotted, pyramidal and early marsh orchids are fewer; the former contributes further to confusing gene-mixing.

The stately great burnet (Bob Gibbons/FLPA)

The odd green-winged orchid may linger from May's excesses. Bee orchids – and their 'wasp' orchid variant – stipple the greenery. Clattinger's star orchid is also its smallest. Burnt orchid is almost exclusively a plant of chalk downland. Little surprise that Clattinger is partly responsible for the 'almost'. Roped-off areas mark, and protect, a relict population of this delectable claret and ivory flower.

In 2013, Clattinger became one of Britain's 60 'Coronation Meadows'. Collectively, these are what George Peterken terms 'the residue' of meadows, which 'survives because enough people value their wild fauna and flora, their historical associations and the gentle pleasure of tranquil places.' Visit Clattinger, and value it.

The well-named adder's-tongue fern (IHL)

WHERE TO GO Clattinger Farm (🖱 tinyurl.com/ClattingerFarm) lies 8km southwest of Cirencester. Access from the Oaksey–Somerford Keynes minor road; park at Lower Moor Farm (📍 SU007939). Cross the stile and follow paths south.

FLEXIBILITY Clattinger is good any time April–August, but plantlife varies by month. June–July is best for target species.

MAKE IT A WEEKEND Morgan's Hill, a fellow Wiltshire Wildlife Trust reserve (🖱 tinyurl.com/MorgansHill), is home to marsh fritillary, marsh helleborine and frog orchid.

ALTERNATIVE LOCATIONS For other Coronation Meadows, see 🖱 www. coronationmeadows.org.uk. The Wildlife Trusts have selected 40 top meadows (🖱 tinyurl.com/WTMeadows). Burnt orchid grows on chalk downlands including Mount Caburn (*May 17*) and Ladle Hill (*July 16*). Burnet: locally common in central and northern England. Fern: Freeman's Pasture (Lancashire), Hunsdon Mead (Hertfordshire), Oxford Meadows (Oxfordshire).

God's own

WHERE North Yorkshire
TARGETS large heath, wood tiger, green tiger-beetle, round-leaved sundew & keeled skimmer
ACCESSIBILITY ③
CHILD-FRIENDLINESS ③

Choo choo! Chugga chugga chugga chugga... A touristic steam train may provide an unexpected soundtrack but it underlines the North Yorkshire Moors's special 'feel'. Today's trip takes in one of the finest sites in 'God's own country': the raised mire of Fen Bog.

Arriving at the car park, the crescent-shaped reserve sweeps your eye towards the horizon. To your left, flowering heather is a favoured domain of nectar-sipping small pearl-bordered fritillaries. A larger orange butterfly should be dark green fritillary, but this high-octane insect rarely pauses for more than seconds. Sit and watch its smaller cousin instead.

Patches of sandy earth are the hunting ground of another energetic invertebrate. All of Britain's five types of tiger-beetle are fearsome predators, lightning quick with all-seeing eyes and unforgiving jaws. The species that occurs at Fen Bog – green tiger-beetle – is the sexiest-looking of the quintet. Its eye-catching metallic green armour is offset by seductively violet eyes.

> **❝ Tiptoe cautiously and discern the riotous joy of plants typifying saturated uplands ❞**

As you head mire-wards, keep alert for a couple of scarce moths, both in the long grass and typically within 50m of the car park. Wood tiger is a stunner; all sooty, white and umber. Small argent and sable is contrastingly delicate as it mooches on a snowdrift of heath bedstraw.

Green tiger-beetle: bulging eyes and predatory prowess (JL)

A freshly emerged keeled skimmer, wings too soft to fly (JL)

Down on the bog itself, tiptoe cautiously to the edge of the wet stuff and discern the riotous joy of plants typifying saturated uplands. Dotting a bed of purple and green sphagnum mosses are round-leaved sundews – glistening, crimson and carnivorous stars. Cross-leaved heath forms the border between wet and dry heath. Amidst the purple moor-grass, the gold sheen of tormentil and the white flags of common cotton-grass, notice the pink speckles of heath spotted orchid.

Before you depart, if the weather offers sun but little breeze, search for three final speciality insects. Bog bush-cricket skulks in the sage of bog myrtle. Get close and you may hear its stridulations which recall an insanely rapid ticking watch. Large heath is a scarce butterfly that typically hurtles past without regard for its observer. There are very few sites in England where you can see this species, so make time to try.

Keeled skimmer is more compliant, the dragonfly's body as gently curved as its name infers. Along your return uphill, a flicker of movement may divulge a common lizard, a flash of white may reveal a whinchat, and the lucky walker may encounter a curled adder. In God's own, expect the lot!

WHERE TO GO Fen Bog (♀ SE858983 ⚲ tinyurl.FenBog) is along the A169, equidistant between Pickering and Whitby. The entrance track is west of the road, 3km north of Hole of Horcum information point and just north of RAF Fylingdales.
FLEXIBILITY Large heath: mid-June to late July. Wood tiger: late May to July. Others May–August.
MAKE IT A WEEKEND Visit Bempton Cliffs for breeding seabirds (*June 3*), look for red grouse on the North Yorkshire Moors, or try Wykeham Forest (*July 28*) for honey-buzzard and goshawk.
ALTERNATIVE LOCATIONS Large heath: Meathop Moss (Cumbria), Whixall Moss (*June 23*). Wood tiger, round-leaved sundew: widespread but local. Beetle: Dungeness (*June 16*), Brownsea (*July 13*). Skimmer: Stoborough Heath (*July 6*), Thursley Common (*July 15*), Pensychnant (*July 19*).

The carnivorous round-leaved sundew feasts on insects. (JL)

Day 47: June 30

The purple empire

WHERE Northamptonshire
TARGETS purple emperor & white admiral
ACCESSIBILITY ⑤
CHILD-FRIENDLINESS ⑤

You never forget your first encounter with a purple emperor. Nor is a single encounter sufficient. Watching 'His Imperial Majesty' is so addictive that fans even devote a website to sharing experiences (🖐 *www.thepurpleempire.com*). And with good reason: Britain's joint largest butterfly is unequivocally its most powerful, soaring over high treetops then exploding groundwards. Honouring the purple empire is an unmissable day in your summer of British wildlife.

Purple emperors are an exquisite morass of contradictions: disdainful of human company yet undisturbed by it; regally garbed yet partial to faecal feasts. The empire's heart is southern England, from Wiltshire to the Weald – yet the finest place to see the butterfly is its northernmost outpost: Fermyn Woods in Northamptonshire.

> **"Male purple emperors glide above the canopy, sufficiently pumped up to chase small birds "**

▼ His Imperial Majesty, the male purple emperor (IHL)

Like Glapthorn (*May 15*), Fermyn lies within the ancient hunting forest of Rockingham. The woods' abundance of sallow – trees on which empresses lay eggs – means you could easily see 50 emperors in a day. Many observations will be at point-blank range: emperors are not merely common here, but showy too. No other site matches Fermyn.

This makes Fermyn popular with butterfly-watchers. On weekends, a hundred binocular-toting folk may throng the track leading south-southeast from the gliding club. Should you wish a more peaceful audience, several strategies are available.

Weekdays are quieter than weekends; ditto early mornings than lunchtimes.

Photographing a purple emperor feasting on dog faeces. (JL)

Stake out fresh dog poo – to which emperors are partial – or, if you can bear it, bring some yourself (or, only slightly less unpleasant, the outstandingly named 'Shito', an African fish paste). Finally, prepare to walk: the best paths are in Lady Wood, 2km from the car park.

In the early morning, look for males gliding above the canopy, sizeable black triangles sufficiently pumped up to chase small birds crossing their flight path. Emperors are larger than the only confusion species – white admiral – which also occurs here and is a winged treasure in its own right. As the male emperors warm up, they descend in search of sustenance. Once an emperor has inserted its proboscis into a dog turd or other mineral-rich substrate, it relaxes and tolerates close approach. This is its empire, after all.

Typically, the males feed with wings aloft, their undersides a sumptuous chestnut, striped and spotted white. But it is the male emperor's upperwings that elicit gasps from his worshippers. Patrick Barkham recalls his first such experience in *The Butterfly Isles*: 'The Emperor opened his wings. Glorious purple erupted from them. I felt bludgeoned, like a dazed cartoon character seeing stars.' Little wonder that Barkham subtitled his book *A summer in search of our emperors and admirals*. Like me – and like you, I wager – Barkham is addicted.

WHERE TO GO Fermyn Woods (📱 tinyurl.com/fermynw) is off the A6116 east of Brigstock (Northamptonshire). Park by the visitor centre (📍 SP955850) then walk east or use the informal roadside car park by the airstrip (📍 SP964859). Leading south from the airstrip, the Forest Horse Riding Trail is very good for emperors, as is the northwest segment of Lady Wood (📍 SP973845).

FLEXIBILITY Emperors usually fly late June to mid July. Ideally, visit as soon as you hear they have emerged. Admiral: mid-June to mid-August.

MAKE IT A WEEKEND Spend a second day in Fermyn, looking for further special woodland butterflies, either late black hairstreak or early purple and white-letter hairstreaks.

ALTERNATIVE LOCATIONS The best sites are collated on 📱 www.thepurpleempire.com/Locations/map.html. To these, add Knepp Wildland Project (Sussex; *July 11*). Admiral: Brownsea (*July 13*), Ryton Wood (Warwickshire), Dene Park (Kent).

The giant of British orthoptera, the great green bush-cricket (RC)

July

Ptarmigan – bee-wolf – dark red helleborine – lizard orchid
black-throated diver – great yellow bumblebee
Balearic shearwater – Scottish primrose – sand lizard
nightjar – brilliant emerald – minke whale – blue shark – adder
Jersey tiger – worm pipefish – great green bush-cricket

A dune tiger-beetle pauses between scurries across the sand. (DL)

Easy, tiger!

WHERE Norfolk
TARGETS dune tiger-beetle, bee-wolf & dune chafer
ACCESSIBILITY ③
CHILD-FRIENDLINESS ⑤

I t's barely breakfast-time, but that hasn't deterred the sun from intensifying. Fluffy balls of cotton wool drift across a sky of perfect blue. A wonderful English summer's day is in the offing. Ideal for a family day at the beach – particularly one packed with wildlife literally below your feet. So flip-flop your way to Thornham's dunes for several hours of kite-flying, paddling and seeking out mini-beasts on the beach.

Walking west from an isolated flint-clad barn, you gaze over saltmarsh to the right. Here oystercatchers probe the gloop and a whimbrel lazes past, calling with its distinctive seven-note whistle. Skylark song is constant: the air is flecked with these

❝Today's target is a top-drawer predator with powerful jaws as long as its head❞

avian choristers. The path is nuzzled by pink mallow, stems burning with soldier beetles, and cosseted by bronzed butterflies. There are large skippers and gatekeepers, small tortoiseshells and the odd painted lady.

Reaching the beach, set up camp between the high-tide line and the first marram-grass tussocks. Offshore, Sandwich and little terns fraternise, the former self-confident, the latter edgy. With the family primed on the order of play – mini-beast hunting before beach cricket – you walk slowly between the lilac spikes of sea holly and search the pebbly sand for movement. When you locate a subtly sheltered trough between new and old dunes, intensify your efforts and sharpen your search image.

Today's principal target is a top-drawer predator: one with powerful jaws as long as its head. The dune tiger-beetle is as fearsome and fleet-

WHERE TO GO Park at end of Staithe Lane, Thornham, near the flint barn
(♀ TF727442). Follow the coastal footpath west until you flank Broadwater
lagoon at Holme Dunes, then follow a little path north through dunes to the beach.
Scour the area either side of the dead tree, particularly on stony, sheltered areas.
FLEXIBILITY April–September for dune tiger-beetle, but hot days June–August best
for all targets.
MAKE IT A WEEKEND Look for creeping lady's-tresses in the northwest of Holkham
Pines (♀ TF890447): from the cross-tracks at the Joe Jordan hide, walk north to the
forest edge and search diligently.
ALTERNATIVE LOCATIONS Titchwell beach (Norfolk) and Sandwich Bay (Kent) for
dune tiger-beetle. Other species are widespread along sandy coasts.

footed as its feline namesake. It's also excitingly rare, occurring locally on
dune systems in East Anglia, Kent, Wales and beside the Bristol Channel.
You should spot several 'tigers' scurrying across the sand, occasionally
taking to the air for a few metres, as if the substrate scalds their feet too
much for them to remain still. All are big-eyed and striped violet-black and
cream. Stunners.

The longer you search, the more you find. On what seemed barren sands,
there is abundant invertebrate life – much of it well adapted for a sandy
existence. Dune chafers, iridescent green and auburn beetles, mooch
along absent-mindedly, climbing fronds of marram grass if the urge takes
them. Graylings, expertly camouflaged butterflies, flick up and away
at your tread. Dune robber-flies pierce victims with their proboscis
then suck the life out of them. Red-waisted spider-hunting wasps catch
and paralyse arachnids such as sand bear-spider, before dragging them to
their burrow.

Best of all is the spectacular bee-wolf, a wasp that preys on bees, hunting
persistently at tiny bee-holes excavated in the sand. Bears, wolves and tigers
on the same beach! Who needs cricket?

The walk out to Thornham's dunes is flanked by flower- and butterfly-rich terrain.

Against all odds

WHERE Perth & Kinross
TARGETS mountain ringlet, black mountain moth & arctic-alpine plants
ACCESSIBILITY ①
CHILD-FRIENDLINESS ①

The morning starts cooler and cloudier than hoped. Those kind souls at the Met Office forecast sun for midday, with mercury ascending to the upper teens. Just as well, for today's principal target at Ben Lawers will stay resolutely hidden unless the air is warmed to 15°C. Even Britain's hardiest butterfly, the mountain ringlet, is a softie at heart. But more of that later... you hope.

For now, treat grey skies as a blessing in disguise. They offer you a clear conscience to focus on the arctic-alpine flora for which this Perthshire mountain is renowned. Ben Lawers holds 17 nationally rare plants, and is also the country's most important site for lichens, with 500 species.

The most straightforward approach is to park at the mountain visitor centre then ascend Edramucky Burn nature trail. A more adventurous alternative involves yomping upslope from the reservoir and shambling wherever your botanical instincts decree. Either way, there are various plant communities to explore so do whatever serves you best.

Cushion grassland is dominated by dwarf herbs; moss campion and cyphel abound, but search hard for rarities such as alpine gentian. In high-altitude flushes, an array of sedges and rushes include russet sedge. You may find it easier to spot yellow saxifrage sprawling over damp rocks, or bog asphodel, alpine bistort and the (carnivorous!) common butterwort.

Tracking down mountain ringlet takes time, patience and fine weather. (os)

Alpine saxifrage is a star plant high up on Ben Lawers. (Bob Gibbons/FLPA)

The scattered, ungrazed mountain ledges (particularly on the southwest crags) hold dwarf montane willows such as downy and dark-leaved. In isolated crevices on lime-rich rocks, diligent perusal may reveal alpine woodsia, alpine saxifrage, mountain bladder-fern and the sweet-smelling lemon-scented fern. Tall-herb vegetation includes wood cranesbill and roseroot.

But... hang on! The sun is breaking through! It's time to search for mountain ringlet. Every moment is precious, and you must be alert to the slightest movement.

Your heart leaps as a dark-brown butterfly flops past... but this is a ringlet (much larger than and, despite its name, not closely related to our montane quarry). Small pearl-bordered and dark green fritillaries both glow orange. Small heaths rise up, and a golden-ringed dragonfly powers past, oozing malevolence. Then a suitably small winged insect flutters a few paces over the herbs... not our target, but a good sign: a black mountain moth.

Then, finally, a small, very dark butterfly hurtles past, low over a south-facing slope dominated by spiky mat-grass. It flirts with a yellow tormentil, then rushes on. Surely...?

> **"Amazingly, joyously, a mountain ringlet nectars on heath bedstraw, flashing its fiery wingspots"**

Then another, only this one plunges into a thick clump of mat-grass. You speed across, and there – amazingly, joyously – a mountain ringlet nectars on heath bedstraw, flashing its fiery wingspots. Success, against all odds.

WHERE TO GO From the A827 Killin–Fearnan road, turn north towards Bridge of Balgie. After 2km, use the Ben Lawers visitor centre car park (📍 NN608379 🖰 tinyurl.com/BenLawersNNR). Follow the nature trail north towards Ben Lawers. Alternatively, park by the reservoir and explore eastwards. For an online guide to Ben Lawers' key plants, see 🖰 tinyurl.com/BenLawersFlora.
FLEXIBILITY Mountain ringlets may fly any time late June to late July here. Moth and flora: June–July.
MAKE IT A WEEKEND Try for other montane Scottish specialities up Cairn Gorm (*4 July*).
ALTERNATIVE LOCATIONS Mountain ringlet: Honister Pass and Langdale Pikes (Cumbria), Creag Meagaidh (Highland). Various arctic-alpine plants: Cairn Gorm and Snowdonia (*May 30*). Moth and flora: Cairn Gorm (*July 4*).

The Welsh *tepui*

WHERE Conwy
TARGETS grayling, silver-studded blue, dark red helleborine, spiked speedwell & Kashmir goat
ACCESSIBILITY ②
CHILD-FRIENDLINESS ③

Venezuela's isolated *tepuis* tower above its lowlands. Isolated from one another and from the land far below, each table-top mountain is its own lost world. The limestone plateau of Great Orme Head – protruding seaward, thrusting apart Conwy and Llandudno bays, and straining towards the sky – is north Wales's very own *tepui*. And just like any truly lost world, it harbours creatures that occur nowhere else.

Great Orme's unique biodiversity comprises two dwarf subspecies of butterfly, and a plant. From the summit car park, walk east to descend the zigzag path to Invalid's Walk, then loop northwest. As you wander you should come across local variants of both grayling and silver-studded blue.

Graylings are masters of disguise, landing on the ground with wings closed to merge with bare, stone-stippled earth. Great Orme's version (subspecies *thyone*) looks the same as those elsewhere in Britain, but is much smaller – barely the size of a ringlet – and emerges a month earlier. The subspecies evolved from butterflies that were isolated during the last ice age, when Great Orme became an island.

> **“Graylings are masters of disguise, landing on the ground and merging with bare, stone-stippled earth”**

Orme's silver-studded blues are of the subspecies *caernensis*, which is smaller than normal with bluer-coloured females. Commoner butterflies include small heath, wall and brown argus. Make an effort to check any day-flying moths that flee from your tread, particularly while picking your way through common rockrose-rich scrub dotting the grassland. Orme is one of just three sites in Britain for silky wave, and the rockrose is the caterpillar's foodplant.

Talking of plants, the peninsula's famous endemic is trickier to find than the butterfly duo. Indeed, because only a dozen or so wild

▶ Dark red helleborine is one of Great Orme's stellar plants. (IHL)

Kashmir goats browse the Orme's ledges and grasslands. (RC)

cotoneaster (aka Great Orme berry) plants persist here, exact locations tend to be hushed up. Your best bet is to check the crevices of the steep slope below the mini-golf 'attraction'. Bizarre but true.

Less rare, but still a national scarcity, is dark red helleborine. You may find a few of these delightful crimson orchids at the back of ungrazed limestone ledges, particularly above head height, backed by the limestone cliff. On the stunted grassland of the plateau, look for wild thyme, salad burnet, harebell and – in a few areas – the rare spiked speedwell and hoary rockrose.

Larger fare include a decent population of feral or Kashmir goats – the origin of cashmere fabric, replete with impressive arched horns – which have been naturalised here for a century. Birdwise, choughs call their name, and the odd peregrine harries breeding seabirds such as kittiwake and guillemot. Just don't leave this Welsh *tepui* until you have seen its butterflies.

WHERE TO GO For Great Orme, leave the A55 northwest on the A470. Drive through Llandudno until you reach the tool house. Follow Marine Drive anti-clockwise to the summit car park (♀ SH756844). Footpaths traverse the area: explore widely to maximise your chances.
FLEXIBILITY Late June to end July for all targets.
MAKE IT A WEEKEND The dunes west of Point of Ayr lighthouse (Flintshire) are good for natterjack toad, shore wainscot and Portland spurge.
ALTERNATIVE LOCATIONS Dark red helleborine: Bishop Middleham (*July 17*). Spiked speedwell: Breckland (Suffolk). None for the other targets.

Day 51: July 4

The living mountain

WHERE Highland
TARGETS ptarmigan, dotterel, Scotch burnet & trailing azalea
ACCESSIBILITY ②
CHILD-FRIENDLINESS ②

We have much for which to thank the elements. Born of fire, yet formed by ice, the volcanic plug of the Cairngorm Mountains is one such recipient of our gratitude – and our wonder. Mountaineer-poet Nan Shepherd celebrated this mesmerising range in *The Living Mountain*, a eulogy that so captivated writer Robert Macfarlane that he told the story of this woman and her wild place through a 2014 BBC documentary.

Wildlife-watchers adore Cairn Gorm as much as mountaineers, for the rolling granite plateau and its ascent harbour many remarkable living entities. Seeing them is no mean feat, however, and your first decision to make is how to journey upwards. Ideally you should hike, so as to freely explore corries and plateau with their habitat jigsaw of montane heath, mountain ledge and montane scrub. But for those with wee legs or low on stamina, climb aboard the funicular, then book on a guided walk.

> **Black mountain moth adapts to the rasping wind by crawling rather than flying**

If you DIY, venture into Coire an t-Sneachda to see rugs of globeflower and roseroot. On the walls of the northern corries, alpine and highland saxifrages grow obstinately. On the plateau itself, whether with guide or without, look for pink blotches that betray trailing azalea, for dwarf juniper and for the five-petalled cloudberry or the black-fruited crowberry.

▶ A ptarmigan proclaims its territory. (OS)

The latter is the foodplant for caterpillars of the black mountain moth, a dapper insect that adapts to the rasping wind that scours all life at this altitude by usually crawling rather than flying. Separate the crowberry's stems and you may reveal an egg-laying female. The same plant is favoured by northern dart, a supremely camouflaged moth. Spotting patches of a

130

Montane beauty: a dotterel (os)

third plant, the cudweed-like mountain everlasting, is your cue to search for another moth. The crimson-and-sooty Scotch burnet basks in sunshine, but skulks in other weathers (which, up here, means most of the time).

You have a better chance of spotting Cairn Gorm's birdlife, but even feathered residents may demand a cryptograph to decipher them. Ptarmigan – a montane grouse – blends in effortlessly with tussocky, rocky vegetation. A male dotterel – the British bird most troubled by climate change – sits tight on its nest, undetected until you approach within a few metres. It may feign a broken wing to distract your attention from its eggs or chicks. Snow buntings tinkle to attract your attention, but even then can be difficult to spot on scree slopes. The same visual challenge applies to mammals: there are mountain hares around, but they hunker down in hollows until there is no option but to zigzag away. *The Living Mountain*, indeed.

WHERE TO GO Cairn Gorm (🐚 http://visitcairngorms.com) is 15km east of Aviemore, signposted along the B970 then a minor road. Park in the ski centre car park (♀ NH990061). Walk up or take the funicular. The latter confines you to the ski centre unless you take a guide (🐚 www.cairngormmountain.org/guided-walks).
FLEXIBILITY Dotterel: May to early July. Ptarmigan: year round. Moths: June–July. Burnet and azalea: June–July.
MAKE IT A WEEKEND Phew! Where to start? Abernethy Forest (*June 5*) would work, plus twinflower in Curr Wood near Dulnain Bridge and creeping lady's-tresses at Loch Mallachie car park. Or watch pine martens with Speyside Wildlife near Loch an Eilean.
ALTERNATIVE LOCATIONS None are as accessible as Cairn Gorm, although you could try Stob Coire Raineach (Argyll & Bute) for trailing azalea and Pendle Hill (Lancashire) for passage dotterel.

Lizard orchids twirl into the distance. (OS)

The Devil's goat

WHERE Cambridgeshire
TARGETS lizard orchid, pasqueflower, chalkhill blue & Daubenton's bat
ACCESSIBILITY ③
CHILD-FRIENDLINESS ③

This is surely the strangest-looking orchid growing in Britain. It is also the foulest smelling. The winner of this pair of accolades is the lizard orchid, and one of the finest places to admire it (or to acquaint yourself with its odour) abuts one of the country's most famous sporting venues.

Devil's Dyke, a 12km-long, 10-metre-high ridge, serves as the boundary of Newmarket's July racecourse. The Dyke's original purpose was different, of course: this Anglo-Saxon earthwork was designed to control movement along Roman roads. Creating a cracking site for wildlife was never part of the plan – but this unintended consequence is very welcome.

> **❝ Lizard orchid is like no other flower: extravagant, hooded and long-tailed; lilac, ivory and green ❞**

The Dyke's linear form makes a there-and-back walk the only viable approach. Vary a two-way wander by walking along the apex path in one direction, then return along the foot of whichever slope is sunny to optimise chances of butterflies. Starting from the south, you have to walk northwest about 1km to encounter the first lizard orchids.

This is a dramatic plant. Thrusting upwards with robust stems, these are resolute, self-confident orchids. The flower is like no other in Britain: extravagant, hooded and long-tailed; lilac, ivory and green. If you squint, you *might* be able to construe its form as that of a long-tailed reptile. A vivid imagination would certainly help.

Daubenton's bat (JL)

However contested the visuals may be, no doubt attaches to this plant's odour. Even through nasal passages congested by hay fever, lizard orchids indubitably smell of... goat, a creature sometimes linked with the Devil. Freaky, huh?

Neighbouring the lizards are the wispy seedheads of what, during the spring, were glorious pasqueflowers. Whilst they are clearly no longer decadently purple, I am mesmerised by the dreamy floral skeletons which seem to float and merge and transcend. In these plants named after Easter, it is as if the Devil has extracted the pasqueflowers' souls from his Dyke, but left us their bodies.

Chalkhill blue (OS)

From plants to winged insects. July is *the* month of the chalkhill blue, a powdery butterfly that flies here in numbers. Track down patches of the yellow c ommon birdsfoot trefoil at the foot of the Dyke, and you may encounter six-belted clearwing, a yellow-and-black striped moth that flies by day.

End the excursion by indulging in a classic touristic activity with a twist, in the Varsity town of Cambridge. All summer long, punts coast serenely along the River Cam. On selected evenings, some dusk sorties are dedicated to bat-watching. What more luxurious way to watch Daubenton's bats swoop low over the water, snaffling lackadaisical insects?

WHERE TO GO Devil's Dyke is 2km southwest of Newmarket. Park by the A1303/A1304 roundabout (♀ TL617613) and follow the footpath northwest as far as the A14. In central Cambridge, bat-watching punting trips are offered by Scudamore's in conjunction with the local Wildlife Trust (🐭 www.scudamores.com/bat-safari-punting).

FLEXIBILITY Lizard orchid: mid-June to mid-July. Chalkhill blue: late June to August. Pasqueflower blooms mid-April to early June. Bat: best May–September.

MAKE IT A WEEKEND Cherry Hinton chalkpits (Cambridgeshire) for moon carrot, orchids, peregrine and six-belted clearwing (*June 9*).

ALTERNATIVE LOCATIONS Lizard orchid: Sandwich Bay (*June 13*). Chalkhill blue: Aston Rowant (Oxfordshire), Warham Camp (*August 3*), Sharpenhoe Clappers (Bedfordshire) and Denbies Hillside (*August 20*). Pasqueflower: Therfield Heath (Hertfordshire), Barnack Holes and Hills (*May 19*). Daubenton's bat: widespread.

Boggy bonanza

WHERE Dorset
TARGETS bog bush-cricket, bog orchid, brown beak-sedge,
keeled skimmer & Lulworth skipper
ACCESSIBILITY ②
CHILD-FRIENDLINESS ③

Kneeling delicately as if in prayer, adjust your weight to avoid compressing the fragile mire vegetation. Deftly part the stems of bog myrtle to unveil your quarry. From under its stormtrooper helmet, the bog bush-cricket regards you with bulging eyes: this is an expert starer. Its preposterously long antennae twitch madly, gleaning information about you. This scarce orthopteran favours sodden habitats on moors and – as here at Stoborough Heath – wet heathland. It is a distinctive looking creature – and a good find.

Still prostrate, scrutinise miniature islands protruding above the dribbling water of this peaty seepage. Startlingly crimson carnivorous plants – round-leaved sundews – are common. So too is the spiky bog asphodel with golden stars for flowers. With enormous luck, you might spot a tiny green spike, luminous against russet sphagnum moss. Barely longer than two knuckles of your little finger, this is Britain's titchiest orchid: bog orchid.

A burning flash nearby gives away a small red damselfly. This slight insect floats to a horizontal perch and freezes. Another dragonfly, a keeled skimmer, zips past. Sky-blue in colour, this is a male. On the mire surface, another skimmer has just emerged from its larval form. It airs shiny wings, waiting for them to harden sufficiently to enable flight.

Stoborough keeps on giving. On small black pools, common raft spiders loiter; inattentive little fish beware... Britain's largest grasshopper, large marsh grasshopper, kicks legs against wings to produce a characteristic ticking. In the large central bog, bright green splashes of vegetation gleam

The dramatic-looking bog bush-cricket (JL)

Stoborough Heath has a good population of the rare brown beak-sedge. (JL)

amongst the 50 shades of brown. These are white beak-sedges and the rare (if visually uninspiring) brown beak-sedge.

A strip of cross-leaved heath forms the frontier between bog and dry heath. On the pink flowers of bell heather, silver-studded blues flash their wings; these are attractive and delicate butterflies. Where the heather stands deep and is interspersed with gorse, Dartford warblers jeer and a heath grasshopper sulks. Purple splatters signal sprigs of Dorset heath, which grows almost nowhere else in Britain. The desiccated corpses of heath fragrant orchid stand sadly, a reminder of floral delights earlier in summer.

After lunch, take in another Purbeck delight. Above Ulwell, Ballard Down rises steeply and unmissably northwards. There's no need for a map here. Linger in the colourful roadside meadow. Packed with greater knapweed, devil's-bit scabious, fleabane

66 Purple splatters signal sprigs of Dorset heath, which grows almost nowhere else in Britain 99

and common ragwort, this hums with butterflies. Marbled whites blizzard through. Meadow brown and small heath flit diffidently. A dark green fritillary refuels on pink thyme, then blazes off.

Finish the day by clambering up the escarpment until you spy a tiny, boggle-eyed, golden-toned butterfly on a grassy tussock. The entire British range of Lulworth skipper is confined to southeast Dorset. What a county!

◀ In Britain, Lulworth skipper occurs only in a small area of Dorset. (JL)

WHERE TO GO Stoborough Heath is east of Stoborough, northeast of the A351. Park carefully by gate marking the southern tip of an old tramline (♀ SY936845). Bog bush-crickets and dragonflies are around ♀ SY937853; the main mire is at ♀ SY935851. For Ballard Down, head northwest from Swanage towards Ulwell. Park in the southern layby east of Ulwell road (♀ SZ021808). Pass through the gate, then explore northeastwards through meadow and up the escarpment.
FLEXIBILITY Late June to late July for most species.
MAKE IT A WEEKEND Where to start? Purbeck is phenomenally wildlife-rich. Explore dry heath on Hartland Moor for dotted bee-fly and Purbeck mason-wasp; RSPB Arne for reptiles and sika deer; Brownsea Island (*July 13*) or Kimmeridge Bay (*July 23*).
ALTERNATIVE LOCATIONS New Forest (Hampshire) for most species.

Highland fling

WHERE Highland
TARGETS azure hawker, northern emerald, black-throated diver
& creeping lady's-tresses
ACCESSIBILITY ③
CHILD-FRIENDLINESS ②

The road northwest from Inverness is a rollercoaster. Rugged moorland smoulders bronze, and red deer stand like statues by the tarmac. As Benn Eighe rises austerely to your left, the hidden valley before you opens into Loch Maree. This is Scotland's Highlands at their finest.

Clouds are scudding across the sky, precluding any chance of dragonfly activity for a few hours yet. Pass the time by checking the islands in the Loch's northwest, scanning for a special waterbird. You may hear black-throated divers before you see them; a mournful, echoing wail. Attired like a City lawyer, pin-striped with black, grey and white, this stunning creature breeds solely on remote Scottish lochs. This bird alone is worth the trip.

But the diver is merely the entrée. The sky is brightening, which calls for dragon-hunting. With sun a sporadic resource in Wester Ross, it pays not to waste a moment of suitable weather should you wish to see three of Scotland's speciality insects. Azure hawker is bold and blue, northern emerald dapper and dark green, and white-faced darter sleek and (mostly) black. The supporting cast is mighty fine too: common hawker (voracious and energetic), golden-ringed dragonfly (a cruise-missile of an insect) and the Highland form of common darter (enigmatic and confiding).

Creeping lady's-tresses has a refined whirl of flowers. (IHL)

There are three principal sites to try along the western shore of Loch Maree – and you may need to visit them all to 'clean up'. With breaks in the weather at a premium, it pays to concentrate on the very best locations.

At Slattadale Forest, use the lochside car park, walk 200m north, cross the bridge, bear left

> **With sun sporadic in Wester Ross, it pays not to waste a moment**

When the sun finally emerges, so too should dragonflies such as this northern emerald. (IHL)

and follow the track for 150m to a clearing. At Bridge of Grudie, explore pools on both sides of the road, particularly in spots sheltered by trees. Large heath, a butterfly fond of northern bogs, flies here too. At Benn Eighe visitor centre, try the boggy wooded clearing by the car park, the path ascending the hillside from the car park and the 'village trail' which leads east.

To celebrate seeing all three target dragonflies, or as consolation for not seeing any, explore Benn Eighe's Caledonian pine forests for a very Scottish orchid. Creeping lady's-tresses should be starting to flower, and their delicate, hirsute ivory flowers are a miniature treat. The mossy floor may be damp to the touch, but there is something gloriously self-indulgent about letting your weight press into it as you eyeball the flowers. After your energy-intensive Highland fling, it is tempting to close your eyes, if only for a minute...

WHERE TO GO Access to Loch Maree is off the A832. From north to south, the best sites are: Slattadale Forest (car park at ♀ NG886723), Bridge of Grudie (roadside parking ♀ NG965678) and Benn Eighe (🛈 tinyurl.com/BennEigheNNR; visitor centre car park ♀ NH019630). Coille na Glas-Leitir car park (♀ NH001650) is worth a stop, ditto good-looking boggy pools by the A832.
FLEXIBILITY Dragonflies: early June to end July. Black-throated diver: May–August. Creeping lady's-tresses: July to mid-August.
MAKE IT A WEEKEND Scan for golden eagles from Kinlochewe viewpoint. Pine marten may be seen at dusk along the A832; Loch Ruthven has breeding Slavonian grebes (south of Inverness ♀ NH638281). White-faced darters are at Monadh Mor (west of Inverness ♀ NH579525).
ALTERNATIVE LOCATIONS Dragonflies: Coire Loch (♀ NH289284). Creeping lady's-tresses: Abernethy Forest (*June 5*), Holkham (Norfolk). Black-throated diver: Loch Shiel (Highland).

Bumbling through the machair

WHERE Argyll & Bute
TARGETS corncrake, great yellow bumblebee, moss carder bee, machair & basking shark
ACCESSIBILITY ④
CHILD-FRIENDLINESS ④

It's unclear how, but you appear to have woken up in the Seychelles. Either that or the Caribbean. Or the South Pacific. Whatever, the paradisiacal combination of powder-blue sky, sapphire sea and white sand cannot possibly be British... can it? Welcome to the west coast of Coll, an island Utopia just 20km long in Scotland's Inner Hebrides.

The sand's colour derives from finely crushed shells of long-dead crustacea. Where these greet peat-based meadows, one of Europe's most remarkable landscapes develops: the machair. To experience its wonders, the RSPB reserve on Coll, centered around Totronold, is the place to be.

By this stage in summer, the floral intensity borders on overload. Saturated yellows and pinks predominate with contributory plants including red fescue, lady's bedstraw, bloody cranesbill, common birdsfoot trefoil and red clover. Look closer to spot orchids dotting the meadow with magic. The Hebridean form of common spotted orchid is here. So too are frog orchid and early marsh-orchid of the scarlet subspecies *coccinea*. The odd lesser butterfly orchid – ivory-coloured and refined – stands aloof from the brighter-toned masses.

❝By this stage in summer, the floral intensity borders on overwhelming❞

Great yellow bumblebee, a striking and rare insect (RP-J)

Linger in the machair, for there is nowhere else like it in Britain. Linger too, for three very particular bumblebees nectaring on the blooms. Great yellow bumblebee is aptly named, being chunky and golden-yellow. During the 20th century, it vanished from 98% of its range, and is now a real rarity. Red-shanked carder bee has a similarly sorry tale: it is now more common on Coll than anywhere else (and its nearest home otherwise is southern England). The final member of the trio is moss carder bee, another declining species – and one that is superficially similar to great yellow bumblebee.

A typical view of a corncrake, peering out from vegetation. (IHL)

Before forsaking the machair, spend time with its breeding waders. Lapwing, snipe and redshank abound, and their collective voices resound from boggy hollow, fencepost and air. Then make your way to hay fields ('in-bye land') by the warden's cottage. If you haven't heard a corncrake thus far, you will surely do so now.

Upwards of 60 pairs of this skulking land-rail breed on the RSPB reserve, and the male's mechanical rasp persists throughout the summer. So insistent are corncrakes on proclaiming their territory that each male may repeat its comb-like call a million times in a single breeding season. Might the rasp, one wonders, be due to a perpetually sore throat?

Finally, return to the coast and scan offshore. On kelp-rich rocks, an otter gnaws at a crab. Beyond the waves, straggly lines of guillemots, razorbills and puffins commute between fishing grounds and breeding cliffs. Further still, in deeper water, the double triangle of basking shark fins sears the water surface. Another day in paradise.

WHERE TO GO Caledonian MacBrayne ferries (🖱 www.calmac.co.uk) sail daily from Oban to Coll in the Inner Hebrides (🖱 www.visitcoll.co.uk), taking three hours. Thursday's timetable enables a full day on Coll. Hope to see dolphins, minke whale, seabirds, white-tailed eagle and basking shark en route. Alternatively, fly from Oban with Hebridean Air (🖱 www.hebrideanair.co.uk). On the island, local custom is to hitch; alternatively hire a bicycle from Arinagour village or walk.
FLEXIBILITY Machair and corncrake: May to end July. Bees and basking shark: June–September.
MAKE IT A WEEKEND Stay on Coll. There's plenty to do. Or take a basking shark trip from Oban (*August 10*) with Basking Shark Scotland (see ad, page 240).
ALTERNATIVE LOCATIONS Uists and Tiree for machair, bees and corncrake. Shark: Coll (*July 8*), Lyme Bay (*July 9*), Lundy (*August 6*), Mull (*August 10*).

Clear water means great views of white-beaked dolphins. (JD)

Leaping clear

WHERE Dorset
TARGETS white-beaked & common bottlenose dolphins, Balearic
shearwater & basking shark
ACCESSIBILITY ④
CHILD-FRIENDLINESS ④

It's funny how one thing can lead to another. For biologist Tom Brereton – research director of the charity MARINElife – surveying offshore for the most globally threatened bird to occur in Britain was his entrée to discovering Europe's most southerly population of a striking marine mammal. Today's outing is an expeditionary excursion into Lyme Bay that seeks both species, Balearic shearwater and white-beaked dolphin, plus Britain's largest fish.

❝As recently as 2007 Tom Brereton discovered white-beaked dolphins in Lyme Bay❞

Balearic shearwater, a close relative of the Manx shearwater, is in serious trouble. Globally, it is classified as Critically Endangered, the highest category of threat for any living species. In some cases, this means a 50% chance – the flip of a coin – of the species becoming extinct within ten years. Just 2,000 pairs are thought to persist, all breeding in a tiny area of the Mediterranean, and this titchy remaining population is rapidly declining.

In recent years, global warming has pushed northwards the fish shoals on which Balearic shearwaters feed. Many birds now routinely summer off southwest England's coasts; Lyme Bay is a good area to find them. To do so, join an organised trip aboard a mid-sized motorboat (or gather a group of like-minded souls and charter) to explore the sheltered waters.

Typical seabirds passing the boat include fulmars, gannets and kittiwakes. You may spot a group of European storm-petrels, fluttering above the boat's foamy wake. Manx shearwaters lounge on the sheeny swell before pattering along and coasting away on stiff, elongated wings. Keep your eyes peeled for a chocolate-and-oatcake-coloured version of the Manxie. This will be a Balearic; feathered gold-dust.

◄ Balearic shearwater is the avian star of Lyme Bay. (RC)

All the time watch for an arched dorsal fin breaking the sea surface. It was as recently as 2007 that Brereton discovered a pod of white-beaked dolphins in Lyme Bay. Whilst this cold-water cetacean is known from the North Sea (particularly from Yorkshire northwards; see *July 17* and *August 8*), sightings along the English Channel were previously rare.

Upwards of 100 individuals have now been observed, enticed to the cold, relatively deep shelf waters of Lyme Bay by its abundant cod and whiting. With harbour porpoise and common bottlenose dolphin also feeding here, you could potentially enjoy a three-cetacean day.

At three metres in length, white-beaks set the pulses racing, particularly if they act as police outriders for your boat by bow-riding. But they are dwarfed by the day's final target. Britain's biggest fish is the basking shark, a beatific plankton-slurper that wends its leisurely way around Britain's western and southwestern coasts each summer. How good would seeing that be?

WHERE TO GO There are three ways to explore Lyme Bay. Wildlife-travel company Naturetrek (🐚 www.naturetrek.co.uk/tour.aspx?id=164) offers day-long trips each summer; dates vary and are demand-driven. Alternatively volunteer for a survey with marine conservation charity MARINElife (🐚 www.marine-life.org.uk). Finally, charter: try Chris Caines (📞 07976 766169).

FLEXIBILITY Dolphins: year-round. Basking sharks and Balearic shearwaters: June–September. Calm seas essential.

MAKE IT A WEEKEND Cliff tiger-beetle can be seen at Eype and scaly cricket at Branscombe (*June 8*). Purbeck excursions include *July 6*, *13* and *23*.

ALTERNATIVE LOCATIONS White-beaked dolphin: Northumberland (*July 17*), Stonehaven (Aberdeenshire) and Shetland. Basking shark: Coll (*July 8*), Isle of Man (*July 21*) and Penzance (*August 7*). Balearic shearwater: headlands in southwest England, including Portland Bill (Dorset), Berry Head (Devon) and Porthgwarra (Cornwall). Common bottlenose dolphin: Moray Firth (*May 20*), Cardigan Bay (*July 25*).

A male emperor moth recuperates after chasing the scent of a female. (JL)

Moth-ers of invention

'At what point in my evolution as a naturalist,' I demanded of a fellow wildlife-watcher, 'do I resort to moth-trapping to get my kicks?' The answer, I hoped, was never. Nothing seemed duller than moths. Small, drab and nondescript, they were surely the ultimate 'little brown jobs'.

In response my friend displayed a poplar hawkmoth that he had enticed into his garden the previous night. My jaw dropped. What a beast! What a beauty! Large, angular, strikingly patterned, sweetly furry and endearingly placid, this was lepidopteran royalty. I was transfixed.

Starting 'moth-ing' was undeniably daunting. Identification uncertainties are compounded by Britain's sheer number of species: 800-plus large moths ('macros') and 1,600 small moths ('micros'). So I trod the path of least resistance – day-flying moths – effectively treating them as surrogate butterflies. This proved immensely rewarding. The summer's highlight was black-veined moth, a sumptuous scarcity restricted to very few Kent downs.

> **As a family, we giggled at moths' magical monikers**

I caught the bug. Investing in a Robinson-style moth trap the following spring, I illuminated my tiny suburban garden, retired to bed and woke early to check the night's catch, the anticipation almost overwhelming. By the time we moved house mid-summer, the whole family was confirmed moth-ers.

We were astonished to record 200 different species visiting our London terrace. How many more were hiding in and around our small patch of lawn and flowers? We gasped at the nightly totals: 2,500 moths in one memorable catch (even if 90% were a single species, horse-chestnut leaf-miner). If you can't make it out to watch wildlife, let it come to you!

As a family, we giggled at moths' magical monikers. There are wainscots and waves, flames and footmen, beauties and bloodveins – and who could forget shears and snout? Above all, we were mesmerised by a wide cast of hawkmoths, notably small elephant (as pink as candy) and lime (Art Deco green and grey): all made saucers of my daughter's eyes.

It transpires that H is for hawkmoth, not just for hawk. Moths became our very own Project Wild Thing: smitten, my daughter refused to move house unless 'Daddy's moths can come with us.' Let moth-ing hook you too.

Primrose pilgrimage

WHERE Orkney
TARGETS Scottish primrose, orca, great skua & corncrake
ACCESSIBILITY ①
CHILD-FRIENDLINESS ③

The small, weathered sculpture looks seaward, forlornly. Not one reader of this book has seen the species of bird it represents, yet few would fail to recognise it. It is a great auk, the last British example of which was shot, here at Fowl Craig on the Orcadian island of Papa Westray, in 1813. Your visit today is a pilgrimage, and – after a long trip north – reaching the statue prompts reflection.

Why do we drive to extinction the creatures with which we share this planet? Why do we annihilate the natural resources on which we depend? Why do we not learn from actions past? Why?

> **❝July sees the second coming of a very special flower, Scottish primrose❞**

Extracting yourself from contemplation, you follow the statue's gaze to celebrate the continued existence of the great auk's brethren. Guillemots and razorbills breed here at the RSPB's North Hill reserve, and their chicks are readying themselves for a death-defying, life-affirming leap from cliff into foaming sea. Puffins are here too, albeit in reduced numbers – a legacy of plummeting sand eel stocks.

Inland, Arctic terns judder overhead, shrieking at any human venturing too close to their nests. Or at any bird: Arctic and great skuas loiter ominously at the edge of the tern colony. As the skuas take to the air and drift out to sea, take the opportunity to scan to the horizon. Orcas and Risso's dolphins regularly circumnavigate Orkney; seeing either will make your heart sing.

Waders do well on North Hill's maritime heath. Oystercatchers, piebald exhibitionists with a carrot for a bill and a kumquat for an eye, pipe in agitation. Lapwings tumble from the sky or trot along the rough grassland, leading you away from

▶ The great skua or bonxie is a dramatic, powerful seabird. (OS)

Visit Orkney for the second flowering of the stunning Scottish primrose (Peter Wilson/FLPA)

their chicks. A curlew lopes nonchalantly, pausing to probe the humid soil with its preposterously long, arched bill.

The odd corncrake is here too, although it may not announce its presence until nightfall. That corncrakes breed here at all is testament to local crofters' convivial approach to land management that, in turn, reflects constructive engagement by the RSPB.

July is excellent for wildflowers on Orkney, with abundant species including thrift, common birdsfoot trefoil, kidney vetch and sea campion. This month also sees the second coming of a very special flower, Scottish primrose. Found only in scattered localities in Caithness, Sutherland and Orkney, this is a real rarity. It is also heart-stoppingly beautiful, with tiny but exquisite flowers of an intense purple. Scottish primrose thrives best where traditional crofting and grazing methods are used. Perhaps, your pilgrimage seems to be telling you, we are finally learning from actions past?

WHERE TO GO Fowl Craig (♀ HY507544) is on the east coast of RSPB North Hill (🖱 tinyurl.com/RSPBNorthHill) on Papa Westray, Orkney. From Kirkwall (mainland Orkney) there are daily flights to Papa Westray (🖱 www.loganair.co.uk) and daily ferries to Westray, connecting via minibus with the passenger boat to Papa Westray (🖱 www.orkneyferries.co.uk).
FLEXIBILITY Scottish primrose: May–June and again July–August. Seabirds and corncrake: late April to end July. Orca resident, but peak June–October.
MAKE IT A WEEKEND Visit the RSPB Noup Cliffs seabird colony on neighbouring Westray.
ALTERNATIVE LOCATIONS Scottish primrose: Hill of White Hamars on South Walls (Orkney), Strathy Point (Highland), Holborn Head and Dunnet Head (Caithness). Skua: Shetland (*June 6*), passage along coasts. Orca: Shetland. Corncrake: Coll (*July 8*), North Uist (Western Isles).

Broad-leaved helleborine is the most sun-loving of Britain's helleborines. (IHL)

Beech bum

WHERE Surrey & Sussex
TARGETS narrow-lipped helleborine, broad-leaved helleborine,
silver-washed fritillary & purple emperor
ACCESSIBILITY ⑤
CHILD-FRIENDLINESS ③

Britain's beech hangars are aristocratic woodlands. Their trees stand proud; tall and robust. The luxuriant canopy exercises control over the sun's desire to reach the floor. The leaves harness solar energy for their own needs before condescending to sieve the surplus groundwards. This makes for ethereal early mornings, with fragmented rays filtering through silhouetted trunks, and for a sparse understorey free of vegetative riffraff.

A sparse understorey – but a special one. Here at Sheepleas on Surrey's North Downs, a scarce and mysterious plant ekes out an existence: narrow-lipped helleborine. Helleborines are orchids, but not as you know them. Between ten and 13 species of helleborine grow in Britain – the uncertainty stems from controversy on what constitutes a 'species' – and most are undemonstrative, understated plants. Not for vivid helleborines the pinks of marsh orchids, the ostentation of bee orchids or the reptilian idiosyncracy of lizard orchids. Helleborines are leggy, willowy and aloof. Aristocratic orchids, if you will.

> **Helleborines are leggy, willowy and aloof. Aristocratic orchids, if you will**

Stroll one minute northeast from the car park to enter this particularly shady, notably enchanted woodland. Commanding beeches rear skyward.

At their feet, in cool muted light, a score of narrow-lipped helleborines are marked (for you) or protected (from nibbling herbivores) by wire cages. Their sparse florets repay proximate inspection, with tinges of pink, purple, yellow and ivory discernable amidst the green.

Stroll northwards for a few minutes, until the trees cease and open scrub dominates. Here grows the most ostentatious and sun-loving helleborine. The stunning pink or purple flowerheads of broad-leaved helleborine can teeter more than a metre above ground. Here too are butterflies, mostly commoners such as ringlet and meadow brown, but also the extravagant silver-washed fritillary. Sizeable and stately, with burnt-gold wings embroidered black with interwoven silver diamonds. An aristocratic butterfly, if you will.

Aristocratic, but not royalty. For that, head south into West Sussex to Knepp. This major 'rewilding' site, which seeks to 'drive the forces of habitat regeneration,' contains abundant sallows, the plant on which female purple emperors lays eggs. For this reason, Knepp has become a fabulous location to watch our grandest, most incontrovertibly majestic butterfly. It is predicted to eventually eclipse Northamptonshire's Fermyn Woods (*June 30*) as Britain's finest location.

You can pay to join an organised safari, led by emperor-obsessives such as Matthew Oates of the National Trust. Alternatively, you may explore six kilometres of trails alone, including climbing up to viewing platforms in the canopy. A butterfly's-eye view of royalty? Count me in!

▶ A large blaze of orange signals the arrival of a silver-washed fritillary. (OS)

WHERE TO GO Sheepleas (🖱 tinyurl.com/sheepleas) lies in Surrey's North Downs, 1.5km southeast of West Horsley. Use Shere Road car park (♀ TQ084514) and walk northeast. For Knepp (♀ TQ150205 🖱 tinyurl.com/KneppEmperor) leave the A24 at Dial Post, 4km south of the A272 crossroads. Turn first right into Swallows Lane then first left, signposted New Barn Farm. Use the car park.

FLEXIBILITY Narrow-lipped helleborine flowers any time in July. Purple emperor: late June to late July. Broad-leaved helleborine: mid-July to end August. Fritillary: late June to mid-August.

MAKE IT A WEEKEND Thursley Common (*July 15*) has dragonflies and silver-studded blue.

ALTERNATIVE LOCATIONS Narrow-lipped helleborine: Warburg Nature Reserve (*July 30*). Broad-leaved helleborine: widespread: try Dryhill (Kent). Silver-washed fritillary: widespread, for example Heddon Valley (*June 24*). Purple emperor: the best sites are collated on 🖱 www.thepurpleempire.com/Locations/map.html and include Fermyn Woods (*June 30*).

Down on the dunes

WHERE Merseyside
TARGETS red squirrel, sand lizard, natterjack toad, northern dune tiger-beetle & dune helleborine
ACCESSIBILITY ④
CHILD-FRIENDLINESS ⑤

'Footprints in the mud: two sets of prints, walking northwards. A man and a woman, companionably close, moving together, shore-parallel, at around four miles per hour: journeying, not foraging.' So starts Robert Macfarlane's exploration of Formby's prehistoric footprints in *The Old Ways*, his ode to a landscape of human footfall. Walking Formby's silts at low tide, following the trails of humans and beasts of yester-millennium, is a must. So too is enjoying the present-day wildlife of Merseyside's fabulous Sefton Coast.

A rippled beach, backed by heaving, shape-shifting sand dunes. Inland, a protective arm of salty pinewoods shielding the coast. A sanctuary for Britain's scarcest wild critters, within minutes of Liverpool's urban intensity.

Start with the star. Formby's red squirrels have had their ups and downs, but the pinewood population is currently recovering. Animals are most easily seen on National Trust land (there are also National Nature Reserves, local nature reserves and Wildlife Trust sites, which stretch north to Ainsdale).

Dune helleborine (IHL)

A male sand lizard (JL)

A calling male natterjack toad (JL)

> **"A sanctuary for Britain's scarcest wild critters, within minutes of Liverpool's urban intensity"**

As you explore the pinewoods, search the ground in sunny glades for a rare orchid found solely in Britain. The world population of dune helleborine may number as few as 10,000, more than half of which occur here. This green and pink plant flourishes in higher, drier dune slacks, often below creeping willow, and under pines. Another good spot is the woodland edge north of Ainsdale's West End Lodge.

Should you spot a similar but all-green orchid, you have probably found green-flowered helleborine. With your eye in, continue flower-seeking. The slacks should glow with colour; special blooms include seaside centaury, yellow bartsia, bog pimpernel and round-leaved wintergreen. On sandy grasslands, heath dog violet abounds alongside the first flush of Britain's largest colony of field gentian.

Wherever nectar is offered, the percussion of bees accompanies you. So too does the flitting of butterflies, notably dark green fritillary and grayling. Wandering north through the dunes towards Ainsdale, a flicker of reptile catches your eye. Common lizards are common, but a thousand sand lizards are scattered across the site. Persistent checking of ridges and gullies may pay off. Or you may be rewarded with another rarity, northern dune tiger-beetle, sprinting across the sand as if it were hot coals.

Finally, wherever you encounter shallow pools in dune slacks – particularly towards Ainsdale but also east of Formby's Lifeboat Road car park – peer downwards. These are the domain of the 'Birkdale nightingale', a local nickname for natterjack toad. The amphibian chorus will be over, but you may encounter adults loitering or spy tadpoles wriggling. You may even spot a great crested newt, another rarity. So much wildlife! Just don't forget to follow the tread of Mesolithic man...

WHERE TO GO The Sefton Coast comprises several adjacent reserves. Formby Hills (♀ SD274082 🛈 www.nationaltrust.org.uk/formby/) is on Victoria Road, Formby. For Formby Point, use Lifeboat Road car park (♀ SD274065). Freshfield Dune Heath (♀ SD298091 🛈 tinyurl.com/FreshfieldDH) is off Brewey Lane, Formby. Use Ainsdale-on-Sea beach car park (♀ SD297126) for Ainsdale Dunes National Nature Reserve (🛈 tinyurl.com/AinsdaleDunes ♀ SD304113; off Coastal Road, Ainsdale) and Ainsdale Hills local nature reserve.
FLEXIBILITY Dune helleborine: late June to early August. Natterjack toad and sand lizard: April–August. Tiger-beetle: May–September.
MAKE IT A WEEKEND Martin Mere (Lancashire) is always worth a visit.
ALTERNATIVE LOCATIONS Sand lizard: Hankley (*July 15*). Red squirrel: widespread, including Brownsea (*July 13*). Natterjack toad: Walney (*June 7*), Sandscale Haws (Cumbria). Dune helleborine: Newborough Warren (Anglesey). Tiger-beetle: local on coastal dunes in Lancashire and Cumbria.

Day 60: July 13
Small is beautiful

WHERE Dorset
TARGETS red squirrel, Sandwich tern, yellow-legged gull & common lizard
ACCESSIBILITY ⑤
CHILD-FRIENDLINESS ⑤

Small islands always get the juices going. They are tiny worlds – their *own* tiny worlds – and that distinctness, that otherness, stokes a wildlife-watcher's adrenalin. What lives there? What might appear there? Then there's the journey. The water dividing mainland from island demands non-standard transport: wheels are redundant. The extra travel effort heightens anticipation and thus delays gratification.

And, boy, is Brownsea worth it! For British wildlife-watchers, this Dorset island is unique as no sea crossing is involved. Snugly secluded in Poole Harbour and ringed by land, Brownsea's surrounding water is tidal rather than coastal, which exerts a profound influence on the wildlife of an island best known for galvanising Robert Baden-Powell into establishing the Scout and Guide movements.

> **"As the ferry docks, a confetti of terns provides the greeting line"**

At distance, Brownsea looks gentle and wooded. As the ferry docks, a confetti of terns provides the greeting line. There are Sandwich terns (large, angular and confident) and common terns (smaller, slimmer and subordinate). To watch terns fly is to appreciate why they are known as 'sea swallows'; they *are* aerial elegance and dexterity.

Brownsea encourages you to familiarise yourself with another dimension to tern life: happy families. Use the concealment offered by hides overlooking the shallow brackish lagoon – Macdonald to see Sandwich tern and Low for common tern – to play voyeur. The terns have made their home on the pebble islets closest to each hide; on Brownsea, there are no mammalian predators to fear. Their chicks should be approaching fledging; the air is dense with calls and wings.

Among ample nesting gulls, fresh, biscuit-coloured juvenile black-headed gulls catch the eye. Brownsea is also famed for holding Britain's only nesting pair of yellow-legged gulls – a variation on the archetypal 'seagull'. Scan for the dapper Mediterranean gull, which started breeding here in 2015.

▶ An adult Sandwich tern returning to its nest with prey. (IHL)

Common lizards bask in sheltered spots (JL)

The lagoon attracts wading birds, particularly when Poole Harbour's muddy feeding grounds are inundated. Ginger at rest, black-tailed godwits flash black and white in flight. Greenshanks stride with silvery purpose. An avocet shimmies along the muddy catwalk, whilst little egrets dart and spoonbills doze.

Save time to explore the other habitats that cram Brownsea. Some 200 red squirrels inhabit its alder carr, free from interference from the non-native grey, particularly visiting feeders at Villa. In wetlands, look for sika deer, water vole and dragonflies such as emperor.

Bizarrely, the Mediterranean land snail *Papillifera papillaris* anoints stonework and statues, having hitched a ride 200 years ago; it occurs at only one other British site. Common lizards bask atop logs; white admirals amble past. Common spotted orchids flower along the track, southern marsh orchid in the meadow. Green tiger-beetles scurry beneath the heather. Brownsea Island may be small, but this ark is beautiful.

WHERE TO GO Brownsea Island (♀ SZ022878 🖱 tinyurl.com/NTBrownsea) lies in Poole Harbour. It is served by a half-hourly boat service from Sandbanks and Poole Quay (🖱 www.brownseaislandferries.com 🖱 www.greensladepleasureboats.co.uk). Part of the island is a Dorset Wildlife Trust reserve (🖱 tinyurl.com/DWTBrownsea); the remainder is National Trust.
FLEXIBILITY Most species mentioned should be seen any time April–August.
MAKE IT A WEEKEND Combine with a day out elsewhere on Purbeck (*July 6* and *23*).
ALTERNATIVE LOCATIONS Red squirrel: RSPB Abernethy (*June 4*), Ainsdale (Merseyside) and Anglesey. Yellow-legged gull: Rainham Marshes (*August 15*). Nesting terns: Coquet Island (*May 28*) or Farne Islands (*June 22*).
Lizard: widespread including Thursley (*July 15*), Wicken Fen (*July 27*), Wykeham Forest (*July 28*).

Day 61: July 14

Bolt from the blue

WHERE Shropshire & Staffordshire
TARGETS silver-studded blue, hobby, woodcock & nightjar
ACCESSIBILITY ④
CHILD-FRIENDLINESS ②

A common for centuries, an airfield during World War II, arable farmland for 60 decades and a heathland restoration project presently: Prees Heath has had multiple identities. The airfield control tower still looms large on the northern skyline, but the only current winged users of this Butterfly Conservation reserve are birds, butterflies and their ilk. Today, Prees is the silver-studded blue's last haunt in the Midlands.

Britain's population of this delicate heathland butterfly has halved since 1980, making Prees Heath worth saving. Following decades of cultivation, bell heather seedlings were sown and thousands of plants bedded to regrow the site's heathland. Silver-studded blue has certainly benefited, with a peak count of 7,000. Look for it feeding on bell heather and the paler pink ling.

> **Britain's population of silver-studded blue has halved since 1980, making Prees Heath worth saving**

If the day is warm, scan upwards for hobbies. These falcons are all angles, all speed: agility in avian form, with Prees dragonflies at their mercy. To watch one plummet from upon high, only to pull out inches above heather or waterbody, a dragonfly clasped between its talons, is a quintessential – and, joyously, increasingly common – summer wildlife experience.

To help restore Prees, conservationists spread heather cuttings from Cannock Chase over the soil surface. The Chase, Central England's largest remaining lowland heathland, forms this evening's destination. Park at the Katyn memorial and descend to Sherbrook Valley, where birch trees cede to heathland.

Should you spot a sizeable isolated birch, look for the emergence holes of Welsh clearwing. Locally distributed in Wales, this moth was thought extinct in England until an alert lepidopterist discovered 5mm-wide exit holes at Cannock. The Chase's population may now be Britain's largest.

◀ Prees Heath is now the only place in the English Midlands where you can see silver-studded blue. (IHL)

Heathland at Prees Heath (IHL)

Unfortunately, you are unlikely to see the moth itself: mid-July is towards the end of its flight season, and its daytime activity ceases by midday.

By now, the light is failing, the sky smudging. Take your seat for Cannock's showtime. With a broad purview over the heathland, fine-tune your vision and prick up your ears. First up will probably be a woodcock, a bizarre woodland-dwelling wader that performs a 'roding' display flight above the treetops.

A mechanical churring draws your attention to a nightjar beating low over the heather before clapping its wings together in territorial defiance. The Chase is probably Central England's most important site for this nocturnal insectivore. If you are really lucky, you may spot a long-eared owl quartering the slopes. With such avian riches to conserve, little wonder Staffordshire Wildlife Trust is learning lessons from Prees Heath to restore 50 football pitches' worth of heathland to connect Cannock Chase's otherwise isolated patches. Conservation in the Midlands has turned full circle.

▶ Hobbies sear overhead, hunting inattentive dragonflies. (JL)

WHERE TO GO Prees Heath (📍 SJ557363 🖱 tinyurl.com/PreesBC and 🖱 www.preesheathcommonreserve.co.uk) is sandwiched between the A41 and A46, 3km south of Whitchurch (Shropshire). Access from the A49, opposite the road to Steel Heath. Cannock Chase (🖱 www.cannock-chase.co.uk 🖱 visitcannockchase.co.uk) covers a large area of Staffordshire, lying between the A34, A460, A51 and A513. Park at Katyn memorial by Springslade Café (📍 SJ978165) on Camp Road east of the A34. Walk east along the Heart of England Way.
FLEXIBILITY Silver-studded blue: mid-June to end July. Woodcock: resident. Hobby and nightjar: mid-May to mid-August. Nightjar: Mid-May to Mid-August.
MAKE IT A WEEKEND Visit Woolston Eyes (Cheshire) for black-necked grebes (permit required).
ALTERNATIVE LOCATIONS Nightjar: Wykeham Forest (*July 28*), Clumber Park (Nottinghamshire), Salthouse Heath (Norfolk). Silver-studded blue: Great Orme (Conwy), Stoborough Heath (Dorset). Hobby, woodcock: widespread.

Black darter, a stunning heathland dragonfly (IHL)

Heavenly heathland

WHERE Surrey
TARGETS brilliant emerald, downy emerald, black darter, true lover's knot & sand lizard
ACCESSIBILITY ⑤
CHILD-FRIENDLINESS ④

Pulling into the Moat car park on Thursley Common prompts a nervous glance upwards. Britain's take on 'summer' – sporadic sun and warmth, if we're lucky – foists uncertainty upon wannabe wildlife-watchers. Success today is contingent on the weather deities blessing you with light winds and bright spells. Hence peering skywards... and hoping.

The 'Moat' is a medium-sized, dark lake with a shoreline fringed with pines and silver birches. Look here for small, dark dragonflies patrolling the shoreline, a metre or so up, pausing for a count of five before continuing their beat. If you clock vividly green eyes, you are watching a downy emerald. This vigorous species emerges in late May so is nearing the end of its flight season.

'Downies' just about overlap here with a rarer cousin. Brilliant emerald shimmers metallic green and flies both higher and further from shore. This dragonfly has an oddly disjunct distribution in Britain, occurring solely in northwest Scotland and southeast England. Seeing one would be special.

As you walk around the Moat, keep your eye on damselflies fluttering feebly in lakeside vegetation. If any of them glow scarlet rather than blue or black, chances are that it is small red damselfly, a retiring speciality of boggy parcels in southern and western heathlands. Talking of which, you now have a dilemma. Do you first explore Thursley's dry heathland, or tread the boardwalk into its mire?

In the former, the target dragonfly is black darter, the male sumptuous, sleek and shiny. The key butterfly is silver-studded blue, a flimsy waif. Day-flying moths include true lover's knot, a stunning mosaic of chestnut, black and white. Pink crab spiders skulk between bell heather blooms. You may hear a rattling Dartford warbler, and should – assuming your step is light and your shadow short – spot common lizards scuttling between vegetated clumps.

Heather 'done', follow the boardwalk across a mire rich in common cotton-grass and round-leaved sundews, the latter a haemoglobin-red carnivorous plant. Here fly dragonflies in abundance. Imperious and bright blue, emperors make the air their own. Not even an instinctively pugnacious four-spotted chaser is sufficiently brave (or foolhardy) to challenge them. Keeled skimmers certainly know their place, preferring the bog's squidgy edges and keeping their heads down.

One Thursley inhabitant too tricky to see here is sand lizard. So relocate to nearby Hankley Common, where our rarest native reptile frequents a trackside bank. Seeing it involves treading lightly, and scanning ahead of you for lounging lizards atop sun-trap tree stumps or clearings in the vegetation. Another reason for the weather gods to play ball.

True lover's knot (JJ)

❝Day-flying moths include true lover's knot, a stunning mosaic of chestnut, black and white❞

Bright eyes

WHERE Hampshire
TARGETS burnt orchid, chalk milkwort, marsh fragrant orchid &
marsh helleborine
ACCESSIBILITY ②
CHILD-FRIENDLINESS ③

S hould you be of a certain age, you may find yourself humming Art Garfunkel's *Bright Eyes* as you ascend the escarpment south of Sydmonton. To your left climbs Watership Down, setting for Richard Adams' allegorical novel of the same name, featuring rabbits named Fiver, Hazel, Bigwig and more. This brush with your childhood may prompt weepy reverie so let things play out before venturing back further in time.

Park at the summit of the hill, then follow the Wayfarer's Walk westwards to the Iron Age hillfort crowning Ladle Hill. The circular earthworks would have enjoyed a commanding vista, the better to repel invaders. Nowadays, the view is simply a reward for friendly visitors.

The fort's earthworks have been spared excavation, enabling a rich chalk downland flora to develop. You should soon spy wild thyme, salad burnet,

Burnt orchid is unusual in having two flowering seasons. (IHL)

fairy flax and hairy violet. Chalk milkwort spatters the ground purple, with magenta blotches drawing your eye to pyramidal and chalk fragrant orchids. Hairy rockcress strains upwards towards knee-height, and clustered bellflower does likewise on the slopes.

Ladle Hill's botanical highlight grows in the southwest section of the fort. This is the rare, late-flowering form of burnt orchid. Unusually among orchids, this burgundy-tipped delight has two distinct flowering seasons in the British summer. Colonies bloom either in May and June or in July and August. If you missed the spring showing (*May 17*), be sure to indulge in this second coming.

Once you have wended your way back to the car, drive 20 minutes southeast to a gem of a reserve skirting Old Basing. Lauded by

"Lauded by botanists as 'Hampshire's richest half-acre', Mapledurwell Fen is outstanding for its size "

Close-up of a marsh helleborine: a striking beauty (JL)

botanists as 'Hampshire's richest half-acre,' Mapledurwell Fen is outstanding for its size. Tread carefully over the sodden ground and cherish the density and diversity of orchids.

Southern marsh orchids predominate and come in a bewildering variety of forms. There are even plants that resemble Pugsley's (aka narrow-leaved) marsh orchid, a species that Kew botanist Richard Bateman has revealed through DNA analysis to occur only in northwest Scotland! Confusion is exacerbated by hybrids between southern marsh and common spotted orchids.

If all this risks bamboozling you, stick instead to locating two distinctive orchids, neither of which even contemplate hybridisation. The long, slender and curved spurs of marsh fragrant orchid set it apart from Mapledurwell's other orchids, whilst the pockets of exquisite marsh helleborines – rose, ivory and mustard-yellow – may well bring tears to your eyes. Weeping twice in a day? What would Bigwig say?

WHERE TO GO For Ladle Hill (⚲ SU478568), leave the A34 east towards Kingsclere. Traverse Sydmonton then turn south at the first crossroads. Climb Watership Down then park on the roadside (⚲ SU493566). Follow Wayfarer's Walk west 1.5km to the hillfort. For Mapledurwell Fen (⚲ SU678523 🖱 tinyurl.com/Mapledurwell), park on Greywell Road, 100m south from the A30, immediately southeast of Old Basing.
FLEXIBILITY Burnt orchid: July. Mapledurwell orchids: mid-June to end July. Fragrant orchid: Beeston Common (Norfolk). Milkworth: Denbies Hillside (*August 20*).
MAKE IT A WEEKEND Spend some time in the New Forest (*July 24*).
ALTERNATIVE LOCATIONS Burnt orchid: Mount Caburn (*May 17*), Clattinger Meadows (*June 28*). Marsh helleborine: Sandwich Bay (Kent), Wells-next-the-Sea (Norfolk).

Not so dinky minke

WHERE Northumberland & County Durham
TARGETS minke whale, white-beaked dolphin, dark red helleborine & northern brown argus
ACCESSIBILITY ④
CHILD-FRIENDLINESS ⑤

After waiting what feels like an eon, you spot it. A roll, speedy but lengthy, of a leaden back, crested by a dorsal fin swept sharply backwards. This is no dinky dolphin. This is a *whale*. This is a *minke* whale! This is *your* minke whale. And you *never* forget your first whale.

Whale-watching has rocketed as a global ecotourism activity. But there remains a preconception that you must travel to far-flung destinations to see gargantuan leviathans: Iceland, California, South Africa. Not so. We have whales around Blighty – and today is about seeking them out.

> **❝White arrowheads – gannets – spear the water, plunging in pursuit of a shoal of fish❞**

For decades wisdom had it that British whale-watching was confined to the Inner Hebrides. How things change. We now know that minkes visit the North Sea each summer, particularly between Seahouses (Northumberland) and Whitby (North Yorkshire). Today, join a pelagic excursion off Tyneside to search for cetaceans.

At first all you spot from the converted lifeboat are seabirds. But what seabirds – and in what numbers! Three species of auk dawdle on the sea.

A typical view of a minke whale, rolling above the sea surface. (MK/NEWT)

The white 'beak' on white-beaked dolphins is surprisingly easy to see. (MK/NEWT)

Puffins with their ridiculous-looking bills, sleek guillemots and chunky razorbills. Kittiwakes, neat seafaring gulls, bounce past casually. Fulmars and the odd Manx shearwater sail by arthritically. This duo are 'tubenoses', proper oceanic wanderers with bills adapted to sift salt from marine water.

Then you spot a flurry of wings, a frenzied cloud of activity, a mass of feather crowding a small volume of airspace. White arrowheads – gannets, our largest breeding seabird – spear the water, plunging in pursuit of a dense shoal of fish. And that's when the call comes. *Minke!*

When the excitement abates – minkes have a tendency to simply vanish – the skipper directs the boat to a pre-determined spot. A group of fins spike the surface, much smaller than the minke but hardly petite. A platinum go-faster stripe between dorsal fin and head reveals the mammal's identity: white-beaked dolphin.

Back on dry land an hour later, replaying your mental video of each cetacean encounter, head south into Durham. Your next quarries occur, well, in a quarry. Teetering up from the magnesian limestone of Bishop Middleham Quarry is half the British population of dark red helleborine. More than 2,000 seductively crimson orchids luxuriate here. Lying amidst them is an indulgence – and also a fine way of seeing your other target, a dapper chocolate butterfly called northern brown argus. Starting with a minke whale and ending with a dinky insect: a day impossible to forget!

WHERE TO GO In Northumberland, the charity MARINElife and Northern Experience Wildlife Tours collaborate to offer pelagic trips of various durations (🖥 www. newtltd.co.uk; see ad, page 242), departing from North Shields, Beadnell and Seahouses. In Durham, Bishop Middleham Quarry (📍 NZ331326 🖥 tinyurl.com/ BishopMiddlehamQuarry) is 0.75km north of Bishop Middleham. Park in the roadside laybys and walk east into the quarry.
FLEXIBILITY Pelagic trips: June–September. Dark red helleborine: July–August. Northern brown argus: mid-June to late July.
MAKE IT A WEEKEND Dive with grey seals around the Farne Islands (*June 22*). Look for 'Tyne' helleborine, which smart money suggests is a species distinct from dune helleborine, at Williamston (Northumberland).
ALTERNATIVE LOCATIONS Minke whale: Whitby (*August 8*). Dark red helleborine and northern brown argus: Gait Barrows or Arnside Knott (Cumbria). Dolphin: Lyme Bay (*July 9*), Whitby (*August 8*).

Badgerland

WHERE Dorset
TARGETS badger & fox
ACCESSIBILITY ⑤
CHILD-FRIENDLINESS ⑤

There can be few more controversial animals in Britain. Persecuted for centuries and stigmatised (culled!) for its unwitting role in perpetuating cattle malady, the badger has many foes. But Brock also has abundant friends; folk who cherish this hefty, monochrome mammal for its doughtiness and cultural resonance.

The badger is familiar to us all – yet those who have seen one alive are surprisingly few. In general, our badger-encounters are with cylindrical, motionless lumps on the roadside, victims of our motorised lifestyle. Accordingly, your summer of British wildlife would be incomplete without bringing to life these mysterious mint-humbugs.

Badgers occur widely across Britain, so you could bump into one in many of this book's itineraries that last until twilight. But there are three main ways to watch badgers *intentionally*. You could follow countryside clues – spotting badger walkways or tell-tale bare earth riddled with holes like a Gorgonzola cheese – to discover your 'own' sett, near home. Second, seek landowner permission to visit a known sett, closeting yourself into the crook of a trunk in pursuit of concealment and comfort.

Thirdly, pay to view from an established watchpoint over a sett. Landowners across Britain have cottoned on to the income-generating potential of enabling people to view badgers. Dorset's Old Henley Farm is one such location. Here two spacious hides, each comfortably housing a dozen observers and filled with relaxed seating and carpeted floors, offer luxury badger-watching.

Take your seat well before the gloaming deepens. As natural illumination dissipates, so floodlights flick on. Anticipation mounts. A smidgeon of movement! But just a rabbit. It starts and flees. A fox strolls through, indifferent to the pairs of eyes staring at it from behind glass. Foxes may be common and widespread, but seeing one is never less than a delight.

Whilst waiting to see a badger from the hide, you may spot a fox. (JL)

Britain's most controversial mammal, the badger (JL)

> **"Having determined the coast to be clear, the badger emerges, incontrovertible and much-appreciated"**

Then – a tremor of white, the merest hint of badger. Minutes pass; nothing. Then a strange whickering noise, answered by an abrupt grunt. Adrenalin screams through your body. And is released when a black lump of coal expands into a snout sniffing the air. Having determined the coast to be clear, the badger emerges, incontrovertible and much appreciated.

Then another. And another. Within minutes a handful of these grizzled, hunchbacked Old English sheepdogs are snorting up peanuts generously scattered around the viewing area. One badger grooms another. A third animal squats to mark the clan's territory. A fourth and fifth, this spring's cubs perhaps, snuffle in tandem.

After 20 communal minutes, individuals part – each trundling off into the darkness, intent on a night of gainful foraging. Controversial they may be, but badgers are also stunning, engaging, mesmerising creatures. Never pass up an opportunity to spend a summer evening in their company.

WHERE TO GO Old Henley Farm (⚲ ST696043 📱 www.badgerwatchdorset.co.uk) is one of several locations countrywide that offer organised badger-watching opportunities. The farm lies off the B3143, 1km south of Buckland Newton in north Dorset. Booking essential.
FLEXIBILITY Any time February–September works for badger-watching. Fox: resident.
MAKE IT A WEEKEND Try Durlston and Kimmeridge (*July 23*) for moths and marine life.
ALTERNATIVE LOCATIONS The Badger Trust (📱 tinyurl.com/WTWBadgers) has compiled a list of commercial and charitable badger-viewing operations. Venues include College Barn Farm (Oxfordshire), Aigas (Highland), Falls of Clyde (Lanarkshire), Ipswich (*August 16*), Rutland Water (*August 12*) and Wakehurst Place (Sussex). Fox: widespread.

Allure of the rare

WHERE Conwy
TARGETS Ashworth's rustic, Weaver's wave, true lover's knot & chough
ACCESSIBILITY ④
CHILD-FRIENDLINESS ③

What is it about rarity that gets our juices flowing? Rarity captivates, enthralls and obsesses. Charlie Elder, who dedicated a year of his life to searching out Britain's rarest animals, argued in *Few and Far Between* that scarcities have 'an undeniable allure' embodying 'a tragedy of loss that pricks at our conscience.' Being elusive, uncommon or unprecedented can make even the most drab of creatures beautiful, desirable and illicit.

Dedicate today to seeing two of the country's most elusive and least common – and thus most illustrious – moths. Within Britain, Ashworth's rustic and Weaver's wave occur solely in a small area of montane Wales. Pretty much the only chance to see them is to participate in the 'Ashworth's rustic weekend' at Pensychnant in Conwy, held annually in mid-July.

To be frank, Weaver's wave is not a looker. Petite and narrow-winged, it is a drab creamy-grey ruffled with brown bars. The slaty Ashworth's rustic is more striking, being adorned with ripples, kidneys and diphthongs, but even so it is an acquired taste compared to heart-throb insects such as elephant hawkmoth.

The rustic favours rocky ground on south-facing slopes and the wave adores (and often adorns, even by day) lichen-encrusted rocks. Synchnant Pass, just above Pensychnant Nature Conservation Centre, is rich in both

Chough regularly fly through Pensychnant Pass. (IHL)

Pensychnant is the best place in Britain to see Ashworth's rustic. (TB)

66 Within Britain, Ashworth's rustic and Weaver's wave occur solely in a small area of montane Wales 99

micro-habitats. More widely the area contains mountains and moorland, oak woodland and pastures.

There are laidback and full-on approaches to making the trip your own. You could join the hardy moth-ers on Saturday evening, setting light-traps in suitably sheltered spots and staying up all night checking them. What you will lose in sleep, you will gain in adrenalin; each 'trap-round' could produce the winged treasure. Or you could let others do the work, and piggyback on their stoic determination by visiting the Centre the following morning, when the night's catch will be on show.

Even if you don't connect with either of the two targets, providing the night has not been a total wash-out (an outcome eminently feasible in a Welsh 'summer'), there should be a handful of new and exciting moths for you. July belle is nailed-on, with crescent dart, confused and northern spinach to be expected. Commoner fare should include spectacular species such as garden tiger and true lover's knot, plus the patterned mosaic that is triple-spotted clay.

Whether you trap by night or gape at moths by day, spend a few hours exploring the wider Pensychnant reserve. Choughs should swoop, crumple-winged around the crags, whilst a few common redstarts and pied flycatchers may hang on in the oak woodland. Alternatively explore Gwern Engan, a sphagnum-bog lake, for dragonflies such as four-spotted chaser, keeled skimmer and black darter. None may be rare, but none is to be sniffed at either.

WHERE TO GO Pensychnant is 3km west of Conwy. Leave the A55 at junction 18, passing through Conwy on the A547. Follow the minor road west to Synchnant Pass. Park at Pensychnant Nature Conservation Centre (♀ SH752770 📖 www.pensychnant.co.uk). Gwern Engan is 400m east of the Centre; park at ♀ SH755767.

FLEXIBILITY Target moths fly June–August (peak July). Check events page of website for the specified weekend. Chough is resident.

MAKE IT A WEEKEND Pay a visit to Great Orme for dark red helleborine, feral goat and grayling (*3 July*). Or Anglesey for red squirrel and dune helleborine (*August 9*).

ALTERNATIVE LOCATIONS Ashworth's rustic: none. Weaver's wave: Lake Vrywny (*May 24*). True lover's knot: widespread on heathland, including Ashdown Forest (*July 15*). Chough: widespread in western Britain including Stackpole (*May 27*), Lizard Peninsula (*May 31*) and Bardsey (*June 19*).

True blue

WHERE Cornwall
TARGETS blue shark, porbeagle shark & short-beaked common dolphin
ACCESSIBILITY ②
CHILD-FRIENDLINESS ③

ach summer, tabloid newspapers work up a frenzy about man-eating sharks patrolling British coasts. As with many silly-season stories, the copy is nearer fiction than fact. For sure, there are sharks in British waters – but they certainly aren't great whites salivating at the prospect of a human buffet.

Even seasoned wildlife-watchers may be taken aback that a score of shark species inhabit our waters – and particularly that it takes relatively little effort to see some. Granted, Britain's total includes benign-looking creatures such as catsharks and dogfish, but we also have species fitting the archetypal search image of... Shark!

So head to Cornwall's north coast to join a dedicated shark-watching trip out of Bude, Newquay or Padstow. Genuflect to the weather gods, for strong winds and heavy seas will kybosh the outing. Assuming clement conditions,

Don't fret: the blue shark is more scared of you than you are of it. (IMAGEBROKER, MICHAEL WEBERBERGER/Imagebroker/FLPA)

you will board a small vessel that furrows several nautical miles across the leaden sea, littering a foamy wake.

At a suitable set of co-ordinates – kept secret from those whose preference is to catch sharks – the skipper cuts the engine and starts 'chumming'. If your understanding of 'chum' is as a synonym for 'friend', prepare for a shock. For those seeking marine wildlife, 'chum' is a floating slick of fishy innards. Protein-packed bait for predators – but unremittingly stinky and frequently vomit-inducing for their human admirers.

Seabirds will be the first to arrive. Gulls for sure, perhaps with the sublime kittiwake among them. Delicate European storm-petrels flutter over the swell. Perhaps a Manx shearwater or two admit to curiosity. Then bigger fare. Much bigger.

A harbour porpoise heaves briefly, too shy to linger. Perhaps a family pod of short-beaked common dolphins, their flanks segmented with stripes. But with no bow to ride (a motionless boat is no fun), they do not deviate from their plotted course. Then... Shark!

> **66** Its owner slips under the boat, a two-metre-long torpedo. Blue shark! Or is it porbeagle?! **99**

A triangular dorsal fin tentatively pierces the sea surface, testing the tranquility of the atmosphere above. Its owner slips under the boat, a two-metre-long torpedo. Blue shark! Or is it porbeagle?! The views from the boat into the water, from one element into the other are good, but frustrating. The adventurer in you craves more.

And so you take more. Already clad in wetsuit, you don mask and snorkel as the cage is prepared. Britain's Cornwall may not be South Africa's Cape, but we also do cage-diving for sharks. You slip into the water, gasping at the chill. Visibility is ten metres, no more. Then the murk is parted, as the torpedo returns. The blue shark, saucer-eyed and long-snouted, gawps your way, then departs. It is no more man-eater than you.

WHERE TO GO Shark-watching trips, both fixed departures and charters, typically operate out of Bude, Newquay and Padstow. Travel with a member of the Cornwall Cage Diving Operators' Association, who follow a code of conduct that minimises disturbance to sharks. Companies include Atlantic Diver (🖱 www.atlanticdiver.co.uk) and Newquay Sea Safaris and Fishing
(🖱 www.newquayseasafarisandfishing.co.uk).
FLEXIBILITY June–September. Calm weather essential.
MAKE IT A WEEKEND Track down rare plants on the Lizard Peninsula (*May 31*) or look for basking sharks off Penzance (*August 7*).
ALTERNATIVE LOCATIONS Boat trips off the Isles of Scilly sometimes encounter the sharks. Dolphin: off Penzance (*August 7* and *18*), Coll (*August 10*), Skye (*August 14*).

A rough diamond

WHERE Essex
TARGETS round-leaved wintergreen, green-flowered helleborine,
common spotted orchid & brown-banded carder bee
ACCESSIBILITY ②
CHILD-FRIENDLINESS ②

Every so often, when travelling the country in search of wildlife experiences, I trip over a natural jewel in a wholly unexpected location. Hidden away in Thamesside Essex, barely visible from surrounding roads and unknown to the majority of residents, is one such site. Step forward Grays Chalk Quarry, a diamond in the land of geezer.

Having ascended a short chalky bank to enter the reserve, you see the land dropping away into an industrial-looking lake. An emperor dragonfly patrols the ridge, untroubled by your presence. You

> **" Step forward Grays Chalk Quarry, a diamond in the land of geezer "**

stroll east, gently uphill, a mini-meadow with salsify, grasshoppers and bees at each flank. Gatekeepers and meadow browns abound; both sun-loving butterflies thrive here.

Round-leaved wintergreen is scarce nationally, but abundant here at Grays. (JL)

A stand of teasel, lanky and spiky, draws the eye. If doing so floats your boat, check its flowerheads for a Nationally Scarce flea beetle formally known as *Longitarsus fowleri*. On the bare path below your feet, a ruby-tailed wasp scurries around – another hint at Grays' invertebrate wealth.

After a few minutes, light woodland takes you under its wing. Common spotted orchids quickly catch your attention. Tall, sturdy; pink, spotted and lined purple. Common yet classy. There are chalk fragrant orchids too, uncompromisingly candy-pink and long-spurred.

Intriguing long-stalked white flowers grow parallel to the track, carpeting the base of a steep incline. A curving, pink, tongue-like style protrudes from each saucer-shaped flower. These are round-leaved wintergreen, a national scarcity and a Grays' speciality. Typically associated with fens and dune slacks, a few wintergreen populations exist in old quarries flushed with chalky water. Grays fits the bill – and is one of very few sites in southern England. Across the quarry, there are thousands and, hearteningly, they seem to be increasing year-on-year.

A few minutes further on, clump down the steep steps plummeting to a triangular suntrap. The meadow's accumulation of flowering plants attracts numerous butterflies, hoverflies and bumblebees. Check the latter for two Red Data Book species that adore such Essex brownfield sites: shrill and brown-

Brown-banded carder bee has a distinctive auburn hoop on its abdomen. (JL)

banded carder bees. Along the clearing's southern edge, just snatched by the woodland, stand desiccated carcasses of bird's-nest orchids – a reminder of spring's richness.

Exit the clearing northwards and make your way along muddy paths towards the lake. As you veer east, check the wooded fringes for two final orchids: broad-leaved and green-flowered helleborines. Both are very rare in Essex, and the latter – shy, drooping, serene – is considered Nationally Scarce. Even unassuming plants make Grays Chalk Quarry sparkle.

WHERE TO GO From the A13, turn south on the A1012 towards Grays then right at the second roundabout on to Devonshire Road. Park near the junction with Drake Road (♀ TQ607792), cross Devonshire Road and climb the steps to enter Grays Chalk Quarry, part of Essex Wildlife Trust's Chafford Gorges reserve (♣ tinyurl.com/ChaffordG). Paths cross the site. Helleborines are at ♀ TQ608790, 200m north of the meadow.

FLEXIBILITY Helleborines: July–August. Common spotted orchid & round-leaved wintergreen: June–July. Brown-banded carder bee: June–September.

MAKE IT A WEEKEND Rainham Marshes (*August 15*) should provide encounters with water vole, small red-eyed damselfly and marsh frog.

ALTERNATIVE LOCATIONS Round-leaved wintergreen: Upton Fen (Norfolk), Sandscale Haws (Cumbria). Helleborines: Warburg Nature Reserve (*July 30*). Carder bee: Benfleet Downs (*July 26*) and Rainham Marshes. Orchid widespread.

Day 69: July 22

The heath at
Pooh Corner

WHERE Sussex
TARGETS adder, golden-ringed dragonfly, black darter, woodlark & nightjar
ACCESSIBILITY ③
CHILD-FRIENDLINESS ③

Literary pilgrimages make for popular tourism. Wordsworth's Lake District and the Brontë sisters' Yorkshire throng with cultured types seeking to appreciate the visual inspiration for famed works. So too does Ashdown Forest in the Sussex Weald, setting for A A Milne's tales of Winnie-the-Pooh. Should the urge take you (or your children), you may follow trails around the Forest that connect the real-world locations of 'Eeyore's sad and gloomy place', 'Roo's sandy pit' and '100 Aker Wood'.

Quite aside from cultural heritage, the heathlands of Ashdown Forest offer some of the finest wildlife-watching in southern England. The nature reserve at Old Lodge is worth a full day (and evening, more of which later) exploration. A stonechat serves as car-park attendant, clacking from atop a gorse bush. Wandering onto a heath

◀ Adders never fail to excite. (JL)

clad in rich purple (bell heather) and pink (ling), a woodlark flies up at your approach, short-tailed and rectangular-winged, calling with a liquid warble. This prompts a Dartford warbler to jeer from the gorse.

Amongst the scratchy vegetation, small, pale blue butterflies flicker in the sunlight. Silver-studded blue is a classic heathland butterfly, named for the reflective scales adorning its underwing. As you brush past a copse of silver birch, a young common redstart flashes russet whilst another calls from the leafy cover above.

Heading downslope you chance upon an adder coiled at the toe of a sandy bank. High summer is a tricky time to see Britain's sole viper, so the encounter is worth cherishing. Likewise the arrival on your personal scene of a dragonfly-cum-Apache helicopter. Golden-ringed dragonfly, banded black and yellow with limes for eyes, looks ferocious. And so it is... for smaller insects. As a hunting machine, this dragon takes some beating.

> **The heathlands of Ashdown Forest offer some of the finest wildlife-watching in southern England**

A less domineering dragonfly – Britain's smallest, no less – but one similarly delighting in acid heathland, is black darter. Mature males can be wholly sooty, whilst females are largely endive-yellow. Around Keeches Brook, look for brilliant emerald, recently discovered in the Ashdown Forest and a rarity away from its Scottish stronghold. Finally, in denser, damper vegetation, look for small red damselfly, a waif that keeps its own counsel.

As both heat and hubris leave the day, take up position with a vista over the intersection of heathland and pinewood. As the sky thickens, creatures of the night emerge. No, not bears (nor donkeys), but nightjars – strange insectivorous birds with long wings and gaping mouths. Listen for the male's mechanical churring, and watch its rakish form twisting across A A Milne's nighttime sky.

WHERE TO GO In Ashdown Forest, Old Lodge Nature Reserve (https:// sussexwildlifetrust.org.uk/visit/old-lodge) lies west of the B2026 between Hartfield and Maresfield. Use the car park at ♥ TQ468308 and follow trails, exploring as many micro-habitats as possible, including trickling streams and mires for dragonflies.
FLEXIBILITY Woodlark: resident. Nightjar: mid-May to mid-August. Adder: late February to September. Dragonflies: July–August.
MAKE IT A WEEKEND Thursley Common (*July 15*) offers a dragonfly-fest.
ALTERNATIVE LOCATIONS Dragonflies: Thursley Common. Adder: Minsmere (*May 22*), Wykeham Forest (*July 28*). Woodlark: Minsmere. Nightjar: Salthouse Heath (Norfolk), Cannock Chase (*July 14*), Cropton Forest (*July 28*).

Jersey tiger has only recently colonised parts of southern England. (JL)

Marvellous moths

WHERE Dorset
TARGETS Jersey tiger, silver y, worm pipefish & tompot blenny
ACCESSIBILITY ③
CHILD-FRIENDLINESS ⑤

O nce a week during the school summer holidays, at the foot of a coastal castle with an imperious aspect over the English Channel, you have the opportunity to experience night – by day. Whereas day-flying butterflies appear universally loved – witness the fad for releasing captive-bred painted ladies during weddings – their nocturnal cousins, moths, are oft received with ignorance, indifference or a nervy shudder.

> **"This is easy wildlife-watching; someone else grafts, enabling you to sit and gape"**

But attitudes are changing. Moths are emerging from obscurity into the light of popularity. Moth-trapping is widening its appeal, as the series of events at Durlston Country Park demonstrates. Durlston is renowned for its array of breeding moths – collectively attracted and nourished by the site's flowery landscape of cliffs, meadows, scrub and woodland – and its position draws in migrant moths.

In sheltered locations around the country park, insomniac lepidopterists routinely entice moths down to box-like traps with eyeball-searing lights. Arrivals are identified, counted and released unharmed the following evening. On weekend mornings, park staff invites the public to help 'open' traps and examine their winged contents.

This is easy wildlife-watching; someone else grafts, enabling you to sit and gape. The park moth-list tops 650 species; a single trap may contain 300 individuals of

70 species! As each egg-box is lifted out of the trap, anticipation mounts: this is Christmas, in July.

The stunning, punky tompot blenny (A&GS)

A classic July crowd-pleaser is Jersey tiger, a recent colonist, with triangular, tiger-striped black-and-cream forewings cloaking a blazing hindwing. The trap might contain crescent dart, Kent black arches and the sensuously scalloped annulet, all localised breeders of rocky cliffs. Migrants will assuredly include silver y, an energetic immigrant from continental Europe, but rarer possibilities are endless.

Upon the session's close, a good call would be to amble along Durlston cliffs and across limestone meadows, searching for day-flying moths such as the spectacular six-spot burnet, butterflies such as Lulworth skipper or other insects such as grey bush-cricket. A brilliant alternative would be to wend westwards along Purbeck's Jurassic Coast, don wetsuit and snorkel in Kimmeridge Bay.

Soft shale cliffs lend shelter to Britain's finest snorkelling location – tropical diversity spliced into Dorset. A self-guided marine trail explains what to look for amidst swirling kelp, above rocky reefs and on sandy beds. A rainbow of wrasse – corkwing and ballan – flicker amongst sponge-encrusted rocks. A worm pipefish wriggles past, slender and pliable.

Molluscs and crustaceans abound: blue-rayed limpets flicker neon, and velvet swimming crabs float in currents. Petite fish peek out from a seaweed tarpaulin: the punk-horned tompot blenny, gobies and clingfish. Even the marine plants mesmerise as they sway: golden Japanese seaweed and the stunning tamarisk seaweed. Marine magic to complement marvellous moths.

▶ Silver y is one of our commonest immigrant moths. (JL)

WHERE TO GO Follow signs south from Swanage for Durlston Country Park (♀ SZ033774 🖱 www.durlston.co.uk). Experienced 'moth-ers' may request Park officials' permission to run their own traps. For Kimmeridge Bay (♀ SY909789 🖱 tinyurl/com/KimmeridgeDWT) leave the A351 at Corfe Castle, heading via Church Knowle to Kimmeridge. Dorset Wildlife Trust runs the Fine Foundation Marine Centre, which rents masks and snorkels.

FLEXIBILITY Durlston moth-ing is good April–October. Public events usually run each Saturday during the school holidays, but check website for details. Marine life: resident.

MAKE IT A WEEKEND Try any Dorset day suggested in this book. If you do Kimmeridge Bay today, explore the rest of Durlston on day two – and vice versa.

ALTERNATIVE LOCATIONS Local branches of Butterfly Conservation, some RSPB reserves and county Wildlife Trusts offer moth mornings or evenings. Marine life: Wembury (*July 29*).

Whale of a time

You never forget your first whale. Be it a tantalising glimpse of a minke whale, the jaw-droppingly long roll of a fin whale's back, or the breathtaking power of an orca (aka killer whale), the sight will be indelibly inscribed on your retina. And once you've seen your first whale, you will want to see another... and another. Watching whales and dolphins – collectively termed cetaceans – can be addictive.

The habit is not as bad for your pocket as you might think. A flawed assumption is that cetaceans inhabit only far-flung places. Fortunately, there's no need to travel to tropical or polar regions to wonder at whales or delight at dolphins. Britain has ample species that can be seen in widely dispersed locations – a clear advantage of living on an island!

July and August are the best months to watch cetaceans in Britain. To see them, look out to sea from land, often from headlands known for their seabird passage.

An encounter with a pod of orcas (aka killer whales) cannot possibly fail to enthral. (OS)

Alternatively, join boat trips offered by specialist operators that seek encounters close to shore; several are celebrated in this book.

So what to look for where? Minke whales are Hebridean stars, but occur increasingly in the North Sea from Grampian to Yorkshire. Humpbacks are also becoming more frequent. Harbour porpoises favour shallow waters and are easy to see from land: the Penzance area is a hotspot. Common bottlenose dolphins occur widely, with stellar locations including Cardigan Bay and the Moray Firth. White-beaked dolphins are best off Northumberland, Risso's dolphin off west coast headlands. Orca is a a Shetland and Orkney speciality. Whichever is the first species you see, and wherever you first see it, it will be lodged forever in your memory bank.

> **❝Once you've seen your first whale, you will want to see another... and another❞**

Sounds of summer

WHERE Hampshire
TARGETS large marsh grasshopper, woodland grasshopper, bog bush-cricket, scarce blue-tailed damselfly & southern damselfly
ACCESSIBILITY ④
CHILD-FRIENDLINESS ③

They furnish the orchestra accompanying your summer strolls; the incessant yet unseen percussion of whirrs, churrs and clicks. They spring ahead of your footfall, reaching heights equivalent to you leaping a column of ten double-decker buses. And then they disappear, perfectly camouflaged in the dense shroud of vegetation. You hear them everywhere yet glimpse them only momentarily. Today's visit to the New Forest will change that. Welcome to the world of grasshoppers and crickets.

> **❝Gawp should you spot a mating pair; the female is twice the male's size!❞**

Park at Wootton Bridge car park and head west, exploring the triangle bounded by two minor roads and the northern perimeter of Wootton Coppice Inclosure. The Inclosure itself blends coniferous and broadleaved woodland with sunny, grassy glades; perfect for butterflies such as silver-washed fritillary and that archetypal high-summer insect, gatekeeper. Hoverflies buzz wherever there is nectar – the larger ones suspended mid-air, observing you, curious and courageous.

It is Wootton's sylvan borders, and the subsequent transition from dry heath through wet heath to bog, that is the orthopteran Mecca. The New Forest holds Britain's greatest diversity of crickets and grasshoppers, and is the best place to track down notably scarce species. It helps to be familiar with the

A mating pair of southern damselflies, a nationally threatened species. (JL)

Large marsh grasshopper inhabits the wettest areas of heathlands. (RC)

'stridulations' produced by each species (those with smartphones should download the excellent Field Studies Council app *iRecord grasshoppers*), but otherwise descend to hands and knees each time you spy movement.

First, acquaint yourself with common species such as meadow, field and lesser marsh grasshoppers. This helps prepare search images for rarer fare. In scrubby woodland, the speciality is woodland grasshopper. Where the ground moistens, bog bush-cricket and long-winged conehead reside – and both enthrall at close range. The star, with adults freshly emerged, is large marsh grasshopper. This cracker adores the wettest areas dominated by purple moor-grass and sphagnum mosses. Prepare to gawp should you spot a mating pair; the female is twice the size of the fluorescent yellow-green male!

As you search, various dragonflies catch your eye. Energetic, pugnacious four-spotted chasers. Keeled skimmer: delicate and curved, the males powder-blue. A marauding golden-ringed dragonfly, huge and predatory.

To see scarcer species, relocate a short distance north to Ober Water. Park on the A35 at Markway Bridge and walk downstream. Here you should discover weedy small red damselflies hidden amongst sedges. Southern damselfly – nationally threatened – takes patience to locate. On boggy seepages north of the copse 600 metres downstream, look for the undemonstrative scarce blue-tailed damselfly. Just as you find one, a scissoring emanates from adjacent bog myrtle. A bog bush cricket, reminding you of the primary reason for exploring the New Forest today.

WHERE TO GO Both sites are in the New Forest National Park (www.newforestnpa. gov.uk). For Wootton Coppice Inclosure, turn east off the A35 – 1.5km north of B3058 junction. After 2km turn south and park (SZ250998). Walk west. For Ober Water, take the A35 4km north. Park at Markway Bridge (SU250038) and walk east along the stream.

FLEXIBILITY Late July to September for orthopterans. Mid-June to early August for dragonflies.

MAKE IT A WEEKEND Elsewhere in the New Forest, try Acres Down for honey-buzzard, Ogden's for dragonflies or Stoney Cross for bog orchid.

ALTERNATIVE LOCATIONS Various New Forest sites are good for orthopterans; so too is Purbeck (Dorset). Scarce blue-tailed damselfly: Dowrog Common (*July 25*). Southern damselfly: Corfe Common (Dorset).

You try and be bored while watching common bottlenose dolphins! (JD)

Welsh dragons

WHERE Pembrokeshire & Ceredigion
TARGETS small red damselfly, scarce blue-tailed damselfly, common hawker & common bottlenose dolphin
ACCESSIBILITY ③
CHILD-FRIENDLINESS ④

The Welsh Dragon: vigorously scarlet, its clawed foot raised and spear of a tongue threatening. A national motif signifying courage, vitality and pride. And Welsh dragonflies, varied in colour, size and form, dwell in high-quality wetland habitats near the western tip of Pembrokeshire.

Start today with a morning visit to Dowrog Common. A sizeable expanse of dry and wet heathland, it is Dowrog's boggy pools that particularly excite. Spotting black darter or keeled skimmer suggests that you are in the right place. Both these dragonflies are winged prizes in themselves, and an early arrival enables you to see them before they have warmed up and taken off.

> **66 To be close enough to a dolphin to hear it breathe is a remarkable feeling 99**

The same is true for two larger dragons, every bit as fiercesome as the reptile of lore. Golden-ringed dragonflies are gigantic, ostentatiously black and yellow, and take no prisoners. Common hawkers are a notch down the size ladder, unequivocally wary and persistently airborne.

The stars are smaller still, tiny in fact: literally damsels rather than dragons. The small red damselfly is a specialist of boggy heathland. As flaming in colour as the Welsh Dragon, but far more retiring, it clings to tall sedges and grasses.

Equally diminutive, but more at home on the bog surface itself, is scarce blue-tailed damselfly. Loathe to fly more than a metre or two, this black needle is marked with sky-blue towards the tip of its abdomen.

Dowrog hosts rare plants too. Before you depart, look for bog pondweed, pale dog-violet and both wavy and marsh St John's worts. On the swampy fringes of Dowrog Pool, reedmace and water horsetail predominate, but marsh cinquefoil and bogbean thrive as well.

From freshwater to seawater. Head north to New Quay and join a dolphin-spotting boat trip. Cardigan Bay is renowned for harbouring a sizeable population (some say 250 or so) of common bottlenose dolphins.

Small and shy, small red damselflies try to remain unnoticed. (u)

They can be seen from shore, so landlubbers need not miss out entirely. But the cetaceans are best experienced via offshore excursions.

Trips vary in duration from one to eight hours, so pick one that best matches your itinerary. Boats typically follow a fixed circuit within the bay that is mindful of both dolphin feeding grounds and the respect wildlife-watchers must show them. As a bow-riding bottlenose breaks the sea surface, it exhales noisily. To be close enough to a dolphin to hear it breathe is a remarkable feeling. The dolphin – unlike the Welsh Dragon of yore – is unequivocally present, irrefutably real.

WHERE TO GO In Pembrokeshire, Dowrog Common (◉ SM772274 ⚲ tinyurl. com/Dowrog) is off the A487, 3km northeast of St David's. Park on the roadside and follow paths southwest. Boat trips into Cardigan Bay (⚲ www. cbmwc.org) depart from New Quay in Ceredigion. Operators include A Bay to Remember (⚲ www.baytoremember.co.uk) and Dolphin Survey Boat Trips (⚲ www. dolphinsurveyboattrips.co.uk).

FLEXIBILITY Dolphin boat trips run April–September, with the best chance of sightings June–September. Dragonflies: June–August.

MAKE IT A WEEKEND Stackpole Quay is good for otter, dragonflies and chough (*May 27*). Or take a longer boat trip and explore Cardigan Bay for basking shark, ocean sunfish and harbour porpoise.

ALTERNATIVE LOCATIONS Dragonflies: New Forest (*July 24*). Dolphin: Chanonry Point (*May 20*) and Durlston (*July 23*).

Day 73: **July 26**

The colours of summer

WHERE Essex
TARGETS great green bush-cricket, white-letter hairstreak, scarce emerald damselfly, marbled white & brown-banded carder bee
ACCESSIBILITY ③
CHILD-FRIENDLINESS ③

A murky start has blossomed into a postcard-perfect summer's day. Token attempts at clouds saunter across an afternoon sky that speaks of the Mediterranean more than your Thamesside location. The sensation ('sunsation'?) is heightened by the solar power charging your limbs as you round the steep escarpment that squints south towards England's famous river. The grassy slopes of Benfleet Downs hum with the stridulations of summer's orthopteran orchestra: the constant, consistent sewing-machine buzz of Roesel's bush-cricket and the pulsating wheeze of stripe-winged grasshopper.

Roesel's is a stripe-necked beast of an insect, but today's first target is bigger still. Indeed, the great green bush-cricket is by far Britain's largest example of either cricket or grasshopper. This insect is precisely what it says on the tin: huge and intensely verdant. Spotting one munching in juncus along

A male scarce emerald damselfly (JL)

White-letter hairstreak (JL)

" Benfleet Downs hum with the stridulations of summer's orthopteran orchestra "

Great green bush cricket (JL)

▶ Marbled white is an embroidered beauty. (IHL)

ditches perpendicular to Benfleet Creek may startle even the expectant. Better to listen for this bush-cricket's penetrating, rattling 'song' that carries an impressive distance, then track it down with hands cupped over your ears to serve as parabola.

Late afternoon is when this bush-cricket gets going. It is also the optimum time for Britain's most overlooked butterfly to cease spinning in territorial combat above elms, and descend to brambles for supper. White-letter hairstreaks are small, unobtrusive dark triangles that settle with their wings firmly closed, but tilted towards the sun. Find a sheltered ride with a sunny patch of bramble or dog-rose, and you should spot one... or more.

Easier to encounter are two common butterflies of open grasslands that undulate east towards Hadleigh Castle. Marbled white may not seduce you through rarity, but it is certainly eye-candy. Juddering low over the ground, this chequered butterfly, says Patrick Barkham in *The Butterfly Isles*, recalls 'a spectacular European species you might chase in an Alpine meadow... it would be feted for its beauty if only it were rarer.'

Here too is Essex skipper, a tiny flame of a butterfly with bulging eyes that is one of worryingly few British species extending its range. Whenever you spy one nectaring on a flower, it serves as a cue to check any nearby bumblebees. Benfleet is excellent for brown-banded carder bee, a localised and declining insect distinctively hooped in ginger.

For this summer's day's final colours, return to creek-side ditches. Readying themselves for evening repose by clinging to the juncus should be scarce emerald damselflies. As well named as the bush-crickets with which today started, these insects await the obscurity that promises to envelop our summer visit.

WHERE TO GO Benfleet Downs forms the western sector of Hadleigh Castle Country Park (🖥 http://hadleighcountrypark.co.uk). Park on St Mary's Road in Benfleet (♀ TQ785859); walk southeast onto the Downs. Follow rides, looking for sucker elms (eg: ♀ TQ783857) for the hairstreak; walk meadows for marbled white and carder bee; and descend to the creek south of the railway line (♀ TQ790855) for the bush-cricket and damselfly.

FLEXIBILITY Mid-June to late July (hairstreak) or to August (others).

MAKE IT A WEEKEND Try Wat Tyler Country Park (🖥 www.wattylercountrypark.org.uk) for a shot at the exceedingly rare blue-eyed hawker, or RSPB Rainham Marshes for water vole and more (*August 15*).

ALTERNATIVE LOCATIONS White-letter hairstreak: Stockbridge Down (Hampshire), Alners Gorse (Dorset), Hardwick Dene (County Durham) and Homefield Wood (Buckinghamshire). Wat Tyler Country Park for other species.

Vision

WHERE Cambridgeshire
TARGETS southern hawker, broad-bodied chaser, drinker, milk parsley
& marsh pea
ACCESSIBILITY ⑤
CHILD-FRIENDLINESS ⑤

As you pause on a bench, processing solar energy, a southern hawker hovers at face-level, its sheer wings working overtime. The dragonfly eyeballs you. And with what eyes! Its ocular spheres are compound structures, each comprising tens of thousands of discrete seeing devices. Three-quarters of the dragonfly brain is devoted to processing the visual data received. Dragonflies have superlative vision.

So too does the National Trust. This august conservation body, frequently accused of looking backwards through its relentless preservation of heritage buildings, is definitively looking forward in its Fenland operations. The Trust's 'Wicken Fen Vision' seeks to 'rewild' 50 square kilometres of Cambridgeshire, creating a 'space to breathe, to think and to explore.'

The geographical start of the vision, Wicken Fen, is not only the Trust's very first nature reserve, but is home to Britain's first Dragonfly Centre. Open at weekends and more frequently during school holidays, the centre is run jointly with the British Dragonfly Society. This makes Wicken the perfect location to relax while getting to grips with the behaviour and splendour of these winged wonders.

Close-up of a southern hawker (JL)

Southern hawker is the most curious and unabashed of Wicken's dragonflies, routinely buzzing humans. Of similar size, but turquoise in colour and more indifferent in attitude, is the emperor. Each 'emp' beats up and down its stretch of waterbody. Common darters have started to emerge from their watery life as nymphs; look for adults basking on wooden structures such as boardwalks and benches (if the numerous common lizards give them a look-in). Smaller, and with searingly scarlet males, are ruddy darters. These are more diffident creatures, preferring vegetated seclusion.

Drinker, a disarmingly cute moth (JL)

Broad-bodied chaser: common but striking (JL)

The list continues. Four-spotted chasers attack any aerial invader, whatever its size. Broad-bodied chasers have sweaty black 'armpits' and a swollen abdomen. Male banded demoiselles flash their wingspots from prominent perches, seeking to seduce passing females. A trio of damselflies – azure, common blue and variable – flutter millimetres above the watery lodes, greener females clamped to blue males in procreational purpose.

> 66 **Southern hawker is the most curious and unabashed of Wicken's dragonflies, routinely buzzing humans** 99

As you reach the Butterfly Trail, your attentions turn to different winged insects. Commas, gatekeepers and meadow browns mingle with green-veined whites and peacocks. There are non-butterflies too, with singular moths such as drinker (what a shape!) among a site list topping 1,200 species. This is not a day for chasing invertebrate rarities, but Wicken Fen does its botanical equivalent effortlessly. As you wander, keep an eye out for milk parsley and marsh pea, both Nationally Scarce plants characterising quality fenland and thus integral to the National Trust's inspiring 100-year vision.

WHERE TO GO Wicken Fen (♀ TL563705 🖰 www.nationaltrust.org.uk/wicken-fen) is off Lode Lane, southwest of Wicken village. Boardwalks and trails of various lengths dissect the fens. The Dragonfly Centre is open weekends May–September, and more frequently during summer holidays.

FLEXIBILITY Dragonflies: various species on the wing May–October. Milk parsley: July–August. Marsh pea: May–July. Drinker: mid-June to mid-August.

MAKE IT A WEEKEND Ouse Washes (Cambridgeshire) should produce garganey. Or try Cherry Hinton for moon carrot and six-belted clearwing (*June 9*).

ALTERNATIVE LOCATIONS Dragonflies and drinker: widespread. Milk parsley: Norfolk Broads. Marsh pea: Upton Fen (Norfolk), Suffolk Broads.

Tell 'em about the honey, mummy

WHERE North Yorkshire
TARGETS honey-buzzard, nightjar, tree pipit, common lizard & adder
ACCESSIBILITY ⑤
CHILD-FRIENDLINESS ②

There is something therapeutic about sky-watching. There is a calmness above, a remoteness from the hurly-burly of human life below. Pillows of cloud drift belligerently across the pale blue. Observing them slows us down, pausing our ant-like hyperactivity. The langour is not even boring; from your perch high in North Yorkshire's forests, the vista in successive minutes is never precisely the same. And then there are the birds.

For it is birds, specifically birds of prey, that you have come to see at Wykeham Forest. Park yourself at Highwood Brow viewpoint, and ensure you face the widest horizon possible. Then scan above the tree-tops, near and far. You are looking for long-winged shapes that signify raptors. And one special raptor in particular: honey-buzzard.

> **Whereas most raptors its size devour mammalian prey, the honey-buzzard feasts on titchy hymenopterans**

Just a score of honey-buzzard pairs breed across Britain each year. Exact numbers are hard to determine, for these are secretive birds that spend much of their time inside the woodland canopy, tracking down then scoffing the contents of wasp nests. Yes, that's right. Whereas most raptors its size devour mammalian prey, the honey-buzzard feasts on titchy hymenopterans and their products. Fortunately for those intent on seeing one, birds regularly soar above the forest canopy, both in display and to move between feeding sites, so keep scanning for their flat-winged, long-winged and long-tailed form.

◄ Honey-buzzard is one of Britain's rarest breeding raptors. (David Tipling/FLPA)

A displaying male nightjar, flashing white spots in its wings and tail. (DT)

You may chance upon other raptors whilst sky-watching. A goshawk – a hulking great thing – would make for a red-letter day, but you are more likely to see its smaller relative, sparrowhawk, and common buzzard. To widen your wildlife experience, keep an eye on the ground as well as the sky.

Common lizards are frequent here, and adders frequently coil in sunny, sheltered spots. Keep ears pricked too for the calls of airborne birds: a crossbill may fly over, a siskin may drop to head height, or a tree pipit may parachute from the sky.

If activity has quieted, take a drive into the North York Moors proper. Three species of heather – bell heather, cross-leaved heath and ling – will be flowering, washing purple tones across the moorland. Along the roadside, red grouse should be enjoying their last month of freedom before the hunting season opens (*August 11*).

Return to the forests for dusk, this time near Egton in Cropton Forest. Locate a suitable clearing where trees have been managed out and heathland vegetation is hinting at a return. This is nightjar terrain. As darkness takes the upper hand in its rote battle with daylight, so male nightjars start churring from isolated pines. Revert to your meditative sky-watching, and you should see a long-winged silhouette angle past, mouth agape, hungry for airborne insects.

WHERE TO GO For Wykeham Forest, leave the A170 at Wykeham, heading north to Highwood Brown viewpoint after 3km. Turn west, continue 600m to the car park (♥ SE936887), then walk 300m north to the raptor viewpoint. In nearby Dalby Forest, the viewpoint overlooking Deep Dale is worth a visit (♥ SE916909). Many forest clearings could hold nightjars, but a good site is in Cropton Forest, 2km northeast of Rosedale Abbey on Hancow Road, where Russell Wood meets Hartoft Moor (♥ SE740963). For red grouse, any road crossing open moorland could be good.
FLEXIBILITY Birds: mid-May to August. Reptiles: March–September.
MAKE IT A WEEKEND Visit Fen Bog (*June 29*) for small pearl-bordered fritillary and large heath.
ALTERNATIVE LOCATIONS Honey-buzzard: Acres Down (Hampshire) and Clumber Park (Nottinghamshire). Other species widespread.

Velvet swimming crab gets its name from the velvety covering to its carapace. (JL)

Rockpool ramble

WHERE Devon
TARGETS cirl bunting, snakelocks anemone, velvet swimming crab
& Cornish sucker
ACCESSIBILITY ④
CHILD-FRIENDLINESS ⑤

The view south across the unpolished sapphire sea is headlined by the Great Mewstone. A rocky island the shape of a squashed triangle lies half a kilometre offshore from Wembury Point. It mesmerises your eye... until your ear overrides it, and you swivel inland.

A rattling song like an incomplete, inconsequential yellowhammer ('a little bit o' bread...') emanates from a scrubby bush. Putting binoculars to eyes, you discern a cirl bunting. Relative of the yellowhammer, this stripe-headed seedeater used to be one of Britain's rarest birds. The bunting remains scarce, but a partnership between the RSPB and local farmers (across south Devon) plus the National Trust (here at Wembury) has reversed its fortunes: here agricultural need and conservation benefit marry.

> **❝Rockpooling is a real-life treasure hunt – but it is also seriously good wildlife-watching❞**

Observing cirl buntings is a delightful way to pass the time, but tides are unforgiving masters. The waters are discernibly retreating, so head east to the Wembury Marine Centre and take a time machine back to your childhood. For who did not enjoy rockpooling as a youngster? And who would not enjoy it now, if offered the opportunity?

Cornish sucker: highlight of any rockpool ramble (D P Wilson/FLPA)

Rockpooling is a real-life treasure hunt – but it is also seriously good wildlife-watching. At low tides, the saltwater forsakes nooks, crannies and ledges, rendering accessible creatures that would otherwise be both out of your reach and your element. Even better, no two shores are ever the same – and the tide's ebb and flow means that two days are never the same on a single shore.

As with most wildlife-watching, there's a technique to rockpooling. Understanding *when* to look is key: the lowest tide possible is ideal, as this exposes stretches of the foreshore normally under water. As for *where* to look, explore as many micro-habitats as possible. Search in muddy sediment under boulders, on rock-sides, beneath overhangs, in pools and surge gullies, amidst seaweed, on the sand and in the sand. Search in shady areas and sunny spots, in areas with ample water and spots with none.

So what can you hope to see? In pools, common, orange and turquoise cushion starfish, for sure; perhaps spint starfish too. Both beadlet and strawberry anemones, but perhaps also snakelocks anemone. Hermit crabs, collectively humping around various models of shell. In gullies, the tiny ridged shells of Arctic and spotted cowries. Hiding beneath boulders, broad-clawed porcelain and velvet swimming crabs. Kelp beds teem with crabs and starfish, worms and sea squirts. Top of the wants list are Cornish sucker (aka clingfish), a fish covered in slime to keep it damp when the tide drops, and topknot, a titchy flatfish. Wembury's wave-cut platform keeps on giving; your inner child joyously receives.

WHERE TO GO Go for a rockpool ramble on Wembury Beach (♀ SX519484 🐭 www.nationaltrust.org.uk/wembury), south of Wembury village. Use the National Trust car park, visit the Wembury Marine Centre (🐭 www.wemburymarinecentre.org). The South West Coast Path hems the cliff top (head west for Wembury Point), and footpaths lead inland (Churchwood Valley is good for cirl bunting).

FLEXIBILITY All-year for rockpooling and cirl bunting. The lowest tides (a few days after the new moon) unveil the greatest expanse of rocky reefs and residual pools.

MAKE IT A WEEKEND The sand dunes of Braunton Burrows (north Devon) provide high-quality plant-searching.

ALTERNATIVE LOCATIONS Cirl bunting: several sites across south Devon (🐭 tinyurl. com/RSPBCirlBunting). Rockpooling: West Runton (Norfolk), Kimmeridge Bay (*July 23*), Cresswell (Northumberland) and many more (🐭 www.wildlifetrusts.org/rockpools).

Helleborine's angels

WHERE Oxfordshire
TARGETS narrow-lipped, violet & broad-leaved helleborines,
striped lychnis & yellow birdsnest
ACCESSIBILITY ④
CHILD-FRIENDLINESS ④

A wrinkled, pliable chipolata, splodged with Day-glo yellow and green, squirms its way up spindly herb. Up and up the caterpillar spirals until it decrees that lunch is served. The 'cat' is the larval form of a rare, localised moth – striped lychnis – on the yellow-flowered skyscrapers of its food plant, dark mullein.

This insect occurs at very few chalk-based locations in southern England. Rarity and nocturnal habits make it tricky to see winged adults, but at Warburg's visitor-centre garden, you may admire the striking caterpillar at your leisure.

This is a privileged opening to a principally botanical day at one of the Home Counties' finest reserves. Cocooned in a sheltered valley, Warburg Nature Reserve combines sunny, scrubby slopes with the wooded cool of beech hangars. From the Wildlife Trust centre, follow the footpath north then contour west along a chalky slope. Carline thistle grows commonly here; a mini-sun of a plant confined to such habitat. Gatekeepers flit daintily past, silver-washed fritillary is frequent and day-flying moths such as mint moth recharge on solar rays.

Just before a gate, broad-leaved helleborines – tall orchids drooping purplish florets – protrude from scrub downslope. Returning to the path, traverse a wood and descend the bridlepath into the valley bottom then climb steeply into a calm cathedral of towering beeches.

Where the track flatlines, small wire cages dot the open ground on either side. Inside these protective structures grow Warburg's rarest orchid, narrow-lipped helleborine. The recent steep decline of this delicate species gives conservationists sleepless nights. For years, writes Simon Harrap in *Orchids of Britain and*

▶ The caterpillar of a striped lychnis moth wriggles up its foodplant, dark mullein. (JL)

> **Warburg Nature Reserve combines sunny, scrubby slopes with the wooded cool of beech hangars**

Yellow birdsnest, a bizarre parasitic plant (IHL)

Ireland, 'a case of mistaken identity allayed fears... but it is now clear that this surprisingly attractive helleborine is in need of friends.'

Further cages hold violet helleborines, a more obvious, dramatic beauty. Small dark basal leaves cede to a purplish stem that rises upwards towards an impressive spike of pale green flowers with rosy lips. With three species of helleborine under your belt, descend to a flint track and wend your way eastwards back to the car park.

For today's botanical denouement, drive south beyond Bix where a fourth helleborine awaits. A roadside beechwood holds green-flowered helleborines, self-effacing orchids that typically clench their flowers tightly closed. Look too for the eerie yellow birdsnest, a nationally threatened, orchid-like plant. Lacking chlorophyll, the nodding yellow spikes are parasitic, using a fungus to purloin nutrients from living trees. The yellow birdsnest may be a plant, but not as you know it.

WHERE TO GO Warburg Nature Reserve (♀ SU717879 🖱 tinyurl.com/WarburgReserve) is 6km northwest of Henley-on-Thames. Leave the A4130 at Bix and head north, signposted Bix Bottom. Broad-leaved helleborines are at ♀ SU17838815; narrow-lipped at ♀ SU71678779. Green-flowered helleborines and yellow birdsnest are in Lambridge Wood, south of Bix. Pull in on the left, 150m past the junction (♀ SU73198431).
FLEXIBILITY Narrow-lipped helleborines here are best mid-July. Violet and broad-leaved helleborines are best early August. Striped lychnis caterpillars are prominent July–August. Birds nest: June–August.
MAKE IT A WEEKEND Aston Rowant (Oxfordshire; 🖱 tinyurl.com/AstonRowant1) is a chalk downland with frog and chalk fragrant orchids, plus marbled white.
ALTERNATIVE LOCATIONS Narrow-lipped and broad-leaved helleborines: Sheepleas (*July 11*). Violet helleborine: Great Merrible Wood (*August 12*). Yellow birdsnest: Anglesey (*August 9*). Lychnis: best here.

Drum and Bass

WHERE East Lothian
TARGETS gannet, fulmar, shag & northern brown argus
ACCESSIBILITY ③
CHILD-FRIENDLINESS ⑤

A gleaming white harpoon with a gold-suffused nape and wing-tips dipped in ink plunges from on high. The whoosh of feather through air intensifies as the seabird accelerates. Milliseconds before stabbing the water with its dagger of a bill, the gannet draws in its wings. The plummeting form continues its trajectory underwater, emerging seconds later with a wriggling silver fish clenched in its bill. You exhale. Wow!

Britain's largest seabird is a spectacular creature – and Bass Rock hosts the world's heftiest breeding colony. As your boat rides the swell towards this 100-metre-high, 300-million-year-old volcanic plug protruding into the Firth of Forth, hundreds – nay, thousands – of gannets swarm around you. Each bird is hungrily awaiting underwater movement from a shoal of small fry. When prey is spotted, the water froths with feather.

> **66** The plummeting form continues its trajectory underwater, emerging with a wriggling silver fish **99**

Gannets return to Bass Rock in January, remaining until October. At the peak of the breeding season, 150,000 may be present – one-tenth of the

Immerse yourself in Bass Rock's gannet colony. (DT)

▶ Fulmars sail past on stiff wings.
(Simon Litten/FLPA)

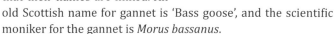

world's population. So close and long-standing is the relationship between this pairing of seabird and site that their names are linked. An old Scottish name for gannet is 'Bass goose', and the scientific moniker for the gannet is *Morus bassanus*.

Landing on Bass Rock may bring tears to your eyes, for reasons of wonder... and odour. Gannets are *everywhere*, filling the air and smothering the ground; who needs an albatross colony? Just take care not to trip over them. And gannet guano (poo) is everywhere too; treading in it is inevitable.

Other British seabirds benefit from the island's predator-free environment. The east coast's biggest colony of puffins will largely be out at sea now, and there will be fewer guillemots and razorbills than during high summer. But fulmars still sail around the higher ledges, with shags decorating the lower rocks and kittiwakes floating wherever the breeze takes them.

Returning to the mainland, the afternoon is still young. Having experienced something big, now it's time for something small, 50km southeast. St Abb's Head is another seabird colony, this time on the mainland, but your quest is actually a butterfly. The south-facing slopes above Horsecastle Bay, just east of Mire Loch, are strewn with the purple of wild thyme and the yellow of common birdsfoot trefoil.

Nectaring on these flowers or lingering in adjacent long grass are dark-chocolate butterflies called northern brown argus. Unlike examples of this species in northern England, the St Abb's butterflies are of the subspecies *artaxerxes* so display a snowy dot on the central forewing. White is truly the colour of the day.

WHERE TO GO Bass Rock lies in the Firth of Forth, 5km east of North Berwick. Scottish Seabird Centre (♀ NT554857 ✆ tinyurl.com/BassRockGannet) operates cruises around Bass Rock. These depart from North Berwick; some include a half-day landing (recommended). For St Abb's Head (♀ NT913674 ✆ tinyurl.com/StAbbsSNT), park at Northfield Farm nature reserve centre in St Abb's, where the B6438 ends. Follow the cliff path north to Horsecastle Bay.

FLEXIBILITY Cruises: April–October. Northern brown argus: June to early August.

MAKE IT A WEEKEND Go rockpooling at low tide in North Berwick Bay.

ALTERNATIVE LOCATIONS Gannet and fulmar: Bempton Ciffs (*June 3*), Skokholm (Pembrokeshire). Northern brown argus: Bishop Middleham Quarry (*July 17*). Shag: widespread on rocky coasts, including Bempton (*June 3*) and Farnes (*June 22*).

Delicate, subtle, exquisite: the violet helleborine (JL)

August

Harbour seal – ant-lion – whiskered bat – water vole
fen raft spider – harbour porpoise – basking shark
yellow birdsnest – red grouse – osprey – prickly stick-insect
violet helleborine – marsh frog – silver-spotted skipper
edible dormouse – autumn lady's-tresses – clouded yellow

Day 79: August 1

Batfan

WHERE Dumfries & Galloway
TARGETS whiskered bat, brown long-eared bat, noctule bat & Daubenton's bat
ACCESSIBILITY ③
CHILD-FRIENDLINESS ④

Bats are the gulls of the mammal world; frequently subject to undeserved bad press. A crying shame, given that bats pose people not even the slightest risk. Moreover, bats provide a valuable ecological service by munching pests; rather than sucking human blood, bats swallow insects that do, such as mosquitoes and midges. They also provide fantastic wildlife-watching.

The Scottish National Trust has caught on to this latter benefit, launching two dedicated bat trails at its Threave estate, which hosts Scotland's greatest diversity of bat species. The Trust kindly loans visitors bat detectors to enable interpretation of the bats' echolocatory clicks and buzzes. This is key to assigning the flying mammals to individual species. It is also a magical part of the experience to deploy mechanical wizardry that gives you night 'vision' and enables you to enter the bats' world.

> **“Bat detector in hand, wait for soprano pipistrelles to emerge from the visitor centre”**

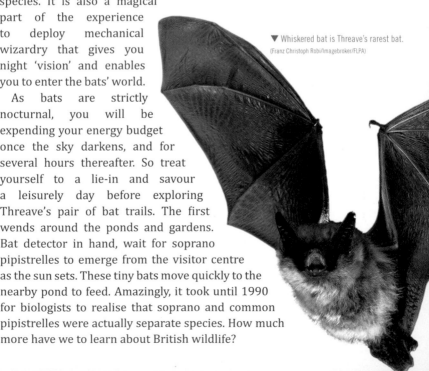

▼ Whiskered bat is Threave's rarest bat.
(Franz Christoph Robi/Imagebroker/FLPA)

As bats are strictly nocturnal, you will be expending your energy budget once the sky darkens, and for several hours thereafter. So treat yourself to a lie-in and savour a leisurely day before exploring Threave's pair of bat trails. The first wends around the ponds and gardens. Bat detector in hand, wait for soprano pipistrelles to emerge from the visitor centre as the sun sets. These tiny bats move quickly to the nearby pond to feed. Amazingly, it took until 1990 for biologists to realise that soprano and common pipistrelles were actually separate species. How much more have we to learn about British wildlife?

▶ Brown long-eared bat hunts close to vegetation.
(Hugh Clark/FLPA)

As you circle the gardens, your detector picks up the rattle of a brown long-eared bat. If the night sky is clear, you may pick out its silhouetted form – long-winged and, of course, long-eared – as it flaps languorously among foliage. Further on, direct the detector upwards at the canopy. This is the feeding height of Threave's rarest nocturnal creature, whiskered bat. Fluttering and fast, these bats beat regular tracks alongside woodland edges.

Relocate a short distance northwest to the nature reserve car park at Kelton Maines. The trail circumscribes Little Wood Hill, taking in the River Dee (which offers watery protection to Threave Castle). Mature ash trees bordering the field provide roost sites for Britain's heftiest and highest-flying bat, the noctule. If you look 30 metres or so upwards, you may glimpse noctules whizzing around – and the detector will certainly be alive with their chatters and pops. Lower down, Natterer's bats dance over the fields, agile and purposeful.

As you reach the River Dee opposite the castle, watch your bat detector for evidence of a rippling drum. This signifies Daubenton's bat, which typically feeds by flying low over water and scooping insects from its surface. After a night like this, you may not be Batman, but you will surely be a Batfan.

WHERE TO GO Threave estate (🖱 tinyurl.com/BatThreave) is 2km southwest of Castle Douglas, just off the A75. Park at the visitor centre for the bat trail around the gardens (♀ NX754605). For the woodland and river bat trail, use the Castle car park at Kelton Mains (♀ NX746616). Visitor centre staff loan bat detectors.
FLEXIBILITY April–October is good for bats, with June–August optimum.
MAKE IT A WEEKEND Try Dalbeattie Forest, 10km east of Castle Douglas, for red squirrel.
ALTERNATIVE LOCATIONS Good places to go bat-watching include London Wetland Centre (*August 19*). The Bat Conservation Trust website (🖱 www.bats.org.uk) often publicises guided walks; there are 100 local bat groups. Alternatively, with your own bat detector, you can find bats almost anywhere.

Day 80: August 2

The British lions

WHERE Suffolk
TARGETS ant-lion, bee-wolf, painted lady, hummingbird hawkmoth &
wood sandpiper
ACCESSIBILITY ⑤
CHILD-FRIENDLINESS ⑤

Lions have long been part of British life and national identity. Cave lions once prowled Britain, King Henry II's coat of arms featured a lion, and motifs of lions feature prominently among British sporting insignia. Today, however, is about a rather different lion.

Seeing an ant-lion arguably represents the apex of insect-watching. Granted, adults are benign-looking creatures, resembling slender damselflies. The larva, however, is a beast unto its own: a formidable, scary-looking predatory insect that sets a deadly trap to sate its voracious appetite.

Ant-lions are recent arrivals in Britain. They were only discovered here in the mid-1990s – indeed, right here at the RSPB's flagship reserve of Minsmere. Amazingly, the best place to see them is typically at the foot of the visitor centre wall. Look for small conical depressions in the ground, as if grains of sand were being sucked into a central vortex.

> **❝Seeing an ant-lion arguably represents the apex of mini-beasting❞**

And not just sand. An unwitting woodlouse, ambling leggily along, reaches the steep-sided pit. The ant-lion larva flicks sand upwards, dislodging the woodlouse which tumbles into the funnel. Resistance is futile. There is no escape. Two gigantic mandibles reach out and grab the victim, whisking it underground, never to be seen again. Eat your heart out, Serengeti; British lions rule.

Even those of formidable constitution may need to recover with a calming cuppa in Minsmere's café. Afterwards, explore the reserve's less terrifying wonders. The Scrape – a muddy, island-filled lagoon – is alive with shorebirds. Waders pausing their southwards odyssey include dunlin, ruff and greenshank. Young avocets shimmy past a wood

▶ The amazing, terrifying ant-lion larva (RN)

Buddleia plants are manna from heaven for hummingbird hawkmoth. (JL)

sandpiper teetering nervously in a quiet channel. A flock of little gulls wafts over the Scrape, feeding acrobatically over the water surface, and a little tern flicks in for its daily ablutions.

Flowering buddleia bushes between the visitor centre and North Bushes seduce a paroxysm of butterflies. Red admirals, peacocks and small tortoiseshells abound; a painted lady graces you with her presence. Out of nowhere, a hummingbird hawkmoth zips in, hovering frenetically as it laps nectar with a preposterously long tongue.

Minsmere excels for family wildlife activities, particularly during the school holidays. Depending on the day of your visit, you could join in with pond-dipping (target: great silver diving beetle – unless the local water vole makes an appearance). Or you might watch a bird-ringing demonstration, where the contenders for cutest bird include long-tailed tit and bearded tit. Or you could indulge in some further insect-searching. Somehow the highlight along the North Wall, a predatory wasp called bee-wolf, no longer seems quite so scary...

WHERE TO GO RSPB Minsmere (♀ TM473672 📱 tinyurl.com/RSPBMinsmere): is signposted from the A12. Leave Westleton east and follow signs.
FLEXIBILITY Ant-lion: June–July for larvae, July–August for adults. Other insects: June–August. Wood sandpiper: July–August.
MAKE IT A WEEKEND Spend another full day around Minsmere. Look for otter and bittern from Island Mere hide and stone-curlew from North Wall. Wander around Dunwich Heath for Dartford warbler and woodlark.
ALTERNATIVE LOCATIONS Ant-lion: only on adjacent Dunwich Heath. Bee-wolf: widespread in English and Welsh sand dunes. Painted lady and hummingbird hawkmoth: potentially anywhere. Wood sandpiper: any muddy-fringed freshwater could hold passage birds including Rutland Water (*August 12*).

Get to the Point!

WHERE Norfolk
TARGETS harbour seal, spoonbill, devil's-bit scabious, chalkhill blue
& clouded yellow
ACCESSIBILITY ④
CHILD-FRIENDLINESS ⑤

The boatman proffers his arm as you step from Morston's wooden jetty into the boat. Taking your seat on wooden benches alongside a score of others, you spy a little egret bouncing along a saltmarsh creek, looking as jaunty as you feel. The boatman throttles sideways then forwards, and you're off. Within minutes Morston's boat-lined channel becomes yacht-dotted Blakeney Harbour.

The outward journey may be short – at 15 minutes or so – but still provides time to relax and enjoy the journey. To the north the muddy shore morphs into a shingle bank that drifts west to become Blakeney Point.

> **"A little egret bounces along a saltmarsh creek, looking as jaunty as you feel"**

Terns flap urgently overhead: Sandwich terns mostly, but look for the tiny, whippy-winged little tern. All will likely be breeding birds from the Point or from Scolt Head Island further west.

A selection of shorebirds dribble past the boat, notably oystercatchers, with their eyecatching carrot of a bill. Another bird with an impressive bill wings overhead, intent yet arthritic. This spoonbill will undoubtedly be a member of Britain's only breeding colony, a short flight west on Holkham Freshmarsh.

Lolling and lounging: Blakeney Point's harbour seals. (JL)

All too soon the boat gets to the Point. The engine eases back, as you track parallel to Blakeney's sandy protrusion. On the sand loaf scores of harbour seals; in the water loll dozens more, some revealing only a whiskered snout or lazy flipper. The pups should be several weeks old, savvy enough to plead at you with liquid eyes. Several of Britain's harbour seal populations have halved this century. The Norfolk population, fortunately, appears stable.

Juvenile spoonbills are once again a feature of English wetlands. (OS)

Within an hour of departure, you disembark back at Morston Quay. Now head west and inland to Warham Camp, an Iron Age fort. Chalk-based grassland covers the concentric circles of the camp's earthworks. An abundance of flora – including such splendid blooms as devil's-bit scabious, knapweed, common rock rose and harebell – provides ample nectaring opportunities for a riot of butterflies and day-flying moths.

Crimson and black cinnabar moths winnow into the air, mini-extra terrestrials. A clouded yellow dazzles; so too a painted lady; at this time of year they could be either locally bred or continental migrants. But it is for a butterfly-confetti of pale silvery-blue – the colour of Manchester City football shirts – that Warham has become locally famous. Chalkhill blues were introduced here illicitly around 2007, but how they have thrived! If the sun is shining in Norfolk's big blue sky, expect counts nearing four figures. This is truly a day of plenty.

WHERE TO GO To see the seals at Blakeney Point (📱 tinyurl.com/BlakeneyP), take a boat from Morston Quay (📍 TG005444). Operators include Bean's and Temple's. For Warham Camp, park on roadside verge 700m south of Warham village (📍 TF946411). Walk 200m south then follow footpath west to the fort.
FLEXIBILITY Harbour seal: May–September best. Spoonbills: March–September. Chalkhill blue: July–August. Devil's-bit scabious: July–November. Clouded yellow: July–September.
MAKE IT A WEEKEND Look for dune tiger-beetle and dune chafer at Thornham (*July 1*).
ALTERNATIVE LOCATIONS Harbour seal: Teesmouth (County Durham), Chanonry Point (Moray). Chalkhill blue: Devil's Dyke (*July 5*), Denbies Hillside (*August 20*). Brownsea (*July 13*). Scabious: widespread on chalk downland, including Ballard Down (*July 6*) and Greenham Common (*August 21*). Yellow: can occur anywhere, including Norwich (*August 22*).

Day 82: August 4
Cathedrals and castles

WHERE Sussex
TARGETS peregrine & water vole
ACCESSIBILITY ⑤
CHILD-FRIENDLINESS ④

The spire strains upwards, contracting towards its tip. Some way down Chichester cathedral's cone, an indentation. Perched there, a peregrine. Solid, robust, motionless: a feathered, winged gargoyle. Then something, somewhere, sears the falcon's retina. A pigeon, perhaps. A movement, for sure. Enough, in any case, to prompt the new lord of our urban skies to slip its ledge and angle away on swift, potent wingbeats.

From its DDT-inflicted nadir of the 1950s and 1960s, when 80% of peregrines succumbed, the falcon's subsequent recovery is barely less than miraculous. Prayers to the church of conservation have been answered. Britain's population of the world's speediest flier has quadrupled. More than 100 pairs now breed on man-made structures, half holding territories in city centres. Pay homage to this remarkable turnaround by spending late afternoon watching the falcon's aerial mastery as the cathedral's family returns to roost.

> **❝The new lord of our urban skies angles away on swift, potent wingbeats❞**

Depending on your viewing angle and the peregrines' inclination, the falcons shape-shift between anchors, fighter planes and broad-shouldered bodybuilders. Females are larger than males, youngsters browner than the deep blue adults. All ages and sexes are fabulous to watch.

The educational opportunities offered by apex predators inhabiting city centres have not been lost on conservationists. There are public viewpoints or webcams in cities from Exeter to Norwich and Bath to Derby. Chichester's peregrines are TV stars, having been filmed for the BBC's *Springwatch*, *Countryfile* and *The One Show*.

You arrived at the cathedral following a visit

◀ Peregrine: the new Lord of urban skies (Ignacio Yufera/FLPA)

▲ Water voles frequent the moat at Arundel Castle. (IHL)

to a castle. A restored medieval fortification, Arundel Castle stands proud: another impressive backdrop for a special wildlife experience. The local water vole population was bumpstarted through a 2005 introduction at the nearby Wildfowl and Wetlands Trust reserve. The best place to see them is the castle moat. Quiet, shady and well vegetated, the moat borders Mill Road, east of the castle and north of the River Arun.

Britain's water vole population leapt off a near-vertical cliff during the 1990s, plummeting by a terrifying 90%. Gradually this cute, frequently confiding mammal is returning to selected waterways. Seeing voles is always a treat – so much so that the RSPB regularly organises viewing events during the school holidays. Not wishing to disappoint visitors, RSPB staff scatter chunks of apple and carrot on a floating platform. This nutritious reward coaxes voles from vegetated seclusion into the limelight.

If no event is in operation, you may have the moat to yourself. Increase your chances of locating your quarry by turning wildlife detective. Look for latrines with scattered droppings, 'lawns' of nibbled grass marking burrow entrances, and funnels through dense understorey. To see voles – unlike cathedral-dwelling peregrines – it pays to look down.

WHERE TO GO Chichester Cathedral (♥ SU859046 ☗ www.chichestercathedral.org.uk) is in the city centre, south of West Street. Use city-centre car parks. For details on peregrines see ☗ www.chichesterperegrines.co.uk. Arundel Castle (☗ www.arundelcastle.org) is north of the A27; use the car park south of the River Arun. The moat is along Mill Road (♥ TQ019075). For details of RSPB events at both sites, see ☗ tinyurl.com/EventsRSPB.
FLEXIBILITY Peregrine: April–August (May–July best). Water vole: resident.
MAKE IT A WEEKEND Watch migrant waders at Pagham Harbour or take a boat trip around WWT Arundel reserve to see more water voles.
ALTERNATIVE LOCATIONS Urban peregrines can be seen in Bath, Derby, Exeter, London, Norwich (*August 22*) and Sheffield. Water vole: Rainham Marshes (*August 19*), Titchfield Haven (Hampshire).

Fen raft spiders are surging back thanks to a successful reintroduction programme. (JL)

Rafts of gulls

WHERE Norfolk & Suffolk
TARGETS Mediterranean gull & fen raft spider
ACCESSIBILITY ⑤
CHILD-FRIENDLINESS ⑤

Every summer, sometime between late July and mid-August, Norfolk birdwatchers wake up to a momentous arrival. Breydon Water is a well-known and well-watched estuary that incises Great Yarmouth. Normally the only Mediterranean gulls in the area are a handful on the beach. Then, overnight, perhaps 500 appear – typically in a single jaw-dropping flock.

I am hardly ancient, but even in my birdwatching lifetime, Mediterranean gulls have undergone a demographic revolution. As a teenager, it was a red-letter day when I saw a 'Med'. Nowadays, the British breeding population exceeds 1,000 pairs.

> **❝Fen raft spider has subsequently gained eight firm toeholds at Carlton Marshes❞**

The Breydon birds, however, are not locally bred. Diligent reading of metal rings snapped around gulls' legs by researchers reveals that most emanate from Belgium's ever-burgeoning colonies. After a hectic nesting season, they spend several weeks in Suffolk. Seeing these classy, bandit-masked creatures in such numbers is a revelation.

► Black, white and scarlet: the simple beauty of an adult Mediterranean gull (IHL)

Given that you are peering across the estuary to count the Meds, scan through the waders that also frequent the sheeny mudflats. In late summer, numbers may be low yet diversity high. Among curlews lazing around there should be the odd whimbrel. Grey, golden and ringed plovers forage close to each other; scurry, peck, stop... scurry, peck, stop. You may discern a greenshank or spotted redshank loping alongside the more numerous common redshanks. Keep checking... and you might just pull something rarer out of the bag.

When you've had your fill, retreat southwards to Carlton and Oulton marshes, home to a ground-breaking conservation project that has staved off national extinction in a globally threatened invertebrate. Since 2011, hundreds of baby fen raft spiders ('spiderlings'; bless) have been released here as part of a recovery programme masterminded by Helen Smith of the British Arachnological Society.

Fen raft spider has subsequently gained eight firm toeholds at Carlton. Amazingly, it is now easier to see here than at any of the very few native sites, which include one up the River Waveney at Redgrave and Lopham Fen.

This is Britain's largest spider, a ferocious predator capable of catching small fish. Spotting one as it poses motionless, head down on a frond of water soldier, may be disconcerting but – for the avoidance of doubt – the species is utterly harmless to humans.

To see spiders – and see them you must, for they are wondrous – walk west from the reserve car park. At either dipping platform in the first marsh, scan aquatic vegetation carefully. The spiders' silvery stripes provide camouflage, meaning that they can be trickier to spot than their 7cm-stretch might suggest. Fortunately, the nursery webs (dense silky affairs) easily catch the eye – and an attentive, protective female is usually nearby. Even spiders have mothers, remember...

WHERE TO GO Breydon Water lies west of Great Yarmouth. View from North Wall by using the Asda car park (♥ TG516083) then walking northwest. Or view from South Wall, using the rugby club car park (♥ TG513075). Carlton and Oulton marshes (📷 tinyurl.com/CarltonM) is west of Lowestoft. Leave the A146 midway between Oulton and Carlton Colville roundabouts, heading northwest to the reserve car park (♥ TG508921). Walk west onto the first marsh.
FLEXIBILITY Gulls: late July to early October. Passage waders: July–September. Fen raft spider: May–September.
MAKE IT A WEEKEND Spend time at Minsmere for ant-lion and more (*August 2*).
ALTERNATIVE LOCATIONS Gulls and waders: widespread. Spider: Redgrave and Lopham Fen (Suffolk), Pant y Sais Fen (Glamorgan). RSPB may offer private safaris to off-limits areas of Cantley reserve (Norfolk) where reintroduced spiders thrive (📷 tinyurl.com/StrumpEvents).

Day 84: August 6
Lundy, Fastnet, Irish Sea

WHERE Devon
TARGETS Lundy cabbage, Lundy cabbage-weevil, grey seal & basking shark
ACCESSIBILITY ②
CHILD-FRIENDLINESS ⑤

I slands are otherly: never precisely the same as the adjacent mainland. Lundy, plugged into the Bristol Channel and marginally nearer England than Wales, radiates otherness. Five kilometres long and thumb-shaped, this granite outcrop disdains trees and hedgerows. A score of human residents 'delight in difference,' writes Patrick Barkham in *Coastlines*, his symphony celebrating National Trust landholdings.

> **66** Remarkably, the yellow-flowered Lundy cabbage occurs nowhere else in the world **99**

The island's name is Norse for 'puffin'. The relationship between place and seabird is long and complicated. During Victorian times, Lundy's puffins were so plundered that 20,000 could be killed for their feathers during a single summer. The arrival of black and brown rats, stowaways aboard ships, wrought further havoc. By 2003, surviving puffins could be counted on a single hand.

Over the subsequent decade, a concerted rat-eradication programme has reaped rewards, with 80 puffins summering in 2014. Manx shearwaters have

The dramatic island of Lundy, with the endemic Lundy cabbage in the foreground (DL & SL)

also benefited hugely, numbers increasing ten-fold to 3,400 pairs. Look for both species in the air and on the water, plus other seabirds such as kittiwake and guillemot, as the MV *Oldenburg* transports you to this steep-sided, seemingly floating, island.

Once ashore, choose between various scintillating opportunities. Non-native mammals, transported to Lundy by a previous landowner, may quickly catch your eye on the soggy plateau. Sika deer and Soay sheep now serve as lawnmowers for the island's sward.

Lundy's eastern slopes, notably along the beach road, are rich in Lundy cabbage; a few may still be in bloom. Remarkably, this yellow-flowered brassica occurs nowhere else in the world. Even more singularly, tiny insects have evolved to co-exist solely with the cabbage, lending credence to claims that Lundy is Britain's invertebrate Galapagos. To see Lundy cabbage-weevil and bronze or blue Lundy cabbage flea-beetles (what names!), place a tray on the ground. Then gently shake a plant so that insects fall onto it.

Millcombe Valley is a good place to try. It is also an outstanding area for lichens, which flourish in the wind-cleansed air. An amazing 350 species have been identified on Lundy, of which 120 encrust Millcombe's trees and 45 are Nationally Scarce. Golden hair lichen is a notable speciality.

Lundy's status as a Marine Conservation Zone makes for exciting wildlife-watching below the waves. Ever-curious grey seals accompany wetsuited-and-booted snorkellers on the sheltered east coast, even playing tag, nibbling at fins and 'kissing'! Exploring the kelp forests – comprising enchantingly named species such as oarweed, furbellows and dabberlocks – is great fun. Expect to see wrasse darting about or blennies peering out of fissures. You may even strike it super-lucky, encountering one of the basking sharks that regularly frequent Lundy's eastern flank during late summer. Most islands excite, but Lundy exhilarates.

▶ Close-up of Lundy cabbage (MT)

WHERE TO GO Lundy Island is in the Bristol Channel off north Devon (🐚 www.lundy.org.uk 🐚 www.landmarktrust.org.uk/Lundyisland). Travel with the MV *Oldenburg*, which sails several times per week from Bideford or Ilfracombe (April–October). Once on the island, explore on foot or by flipper.
FLEXIBILITY Lundy cabbage: flowers best during May–July. Weevil: May–September. Grey seal: resident. Basking shark: July–August.
MAKE IT A WEEKEND Stay on the island. There is so much to do!
ALTERNATIVE LOCATIONS None for the cabbage or weevil. Grey seal: widespread, including Penzance (*August 7*) and Whitby (*August 8*). Basking shark: western coasts, including Penzance, Coll (*August 10*) and Skye (*August 14*).

Feathered friends

I can't remember a time when I haven't watched birds. My father reckons the starting point was on a country lane, hemmed by towering hedges, near our family home in south Devon. I was three, still toddling but nevertheless clearly observant. A big bird appeared in the sky, so my dad's tale continues, prompting little Lowen to ask what it was. 'A crow,' my father grumped. 'No it's not. It's too big,' insisted the precocious fledgling birdwatcher.

A few days later, identification guide purchased, the bird was identified as a common buzzard. In those days, back in the 1970s, buzzards were almost exclusively the property of southwest England. Forty years on, they have spread north and east throughout Britain: a rare success story in a broadcast otherwise dominated by declines and extinctions.

> **❝Birds form the backdrop to your summer of wildlife, and regularly take centre stage as well❞**

Birds have riffed through my life ever since. I cannot recall a single day when I have not seen at least one bird — even if it were just a glimpse of gull or pigeon above the concrete jungle of my hometown. Other creatures you need to look for — but birds you simply bump into, wherever and whenever. Birds form the backdrop to your summer of wildlife, and regularly take centre stage as well.

Perhaps 220 species of bird breed in Britain in any one year with others passing through either side of summer. Seeing them all takes considerable commitment, yet seeing many of them demands remarkably little effort. With a score of diligently planned trips you can rack up impressive quality and quantity.

Deafening seabird colonies, skyscrapers built of rock and windowed with auks, fulmars and kittiwakes. A woodland before dawn, light seeping downward and inward while the air fills with birdsong. A red-throated diver calling forlornly on a remote Scottish loch. A coastal lagoon whirring with the white and black wings of avocets. A bittern blowing over the neck of a reedbed beer bottle. And a common buzzard soaring free over the fields near my home. Birdwatching is — and always will be — magical.

Puffins are iconic and widely known but also under very real threat of extinction with European populations estimated and projected to decline by at least half between 2000 and 2065. (DT)

Day 85: August 7

Sunfish, sea, sand

WHERE Cornwall
TARGETS ocean sunfish, harbour porpoise, short-beaked common dolphin & grey seal
ACCESSIBILITY ④
CHILD-FRIENDLINESS ⑤

T he face stares out of the sea at you. Bloated, eerily pale and beady-eyed, with a pinched mouth. It is as if a malevolent cartoon Mr Moon has fallen from the sky and been trapped beneath the waves. Towards the blunt, rounded rear of the 'face', two narrow pointed 'arms' stretch out in opposite directions. Then you click. Ocean sunfish!

Of all the fish in Britain's sea, this is one of the strangest looking. Laterally compressed, the metre-long sunfish floats on its side. One eye looks down, plumbing the depths. The other looks up, towards the sea surface and beyond. The 'arms' are fins, which flop lazily either side of the elemental divide: splish, splash. As its name suggests, the sunfish is a true oceanic wanderer, but summer coaxes the animals close inshore in western Britain. Mount's Bay, cosseting the Cornish town of Penzance, is one of the species's favoured destinations.

Harbour porpoise in Mount's Bay, with a backdrop of St Michael's Mount (HJ)

To peer at sunfish you need to join an offshore excursion. Travelling by catamaran is ideal: silent and wind-powered, it minimises both disturbance and pollution. You could see half a dozen sunfish, and much else besides. Harbour porpoise is a local speciality; day-counts sometimes reach three figures. Britain's smallest cetacean is stumpy-bodied and round-finned. It is also undemonstrative, rolling though the swell with near-monotonous regularity before disappearing mysteriously as if it has slipped into another world. Seeing it, repeatedly and at close range, is to be cherished.

Contrastingly in-your-face are short-beaked common dolphins. Pods roam around Cornish coasts and regularly enter the bay. If you are

Leaping wonders: adult and calf short-beaked common dolphins

lucky, you may also encounter Risso's dolphin, a larger, stockier animal with a blunt melon of a head. Risso's tall dorsal fin arches back sharply towards its tip, and the animal's grey coat is often scarred white. Occasionally – but sufficiently frequently for you to harbour hope of seeing one – humpback and minke whales enter the bay. Keep alert, keep scanning and keep the faith.

There is a chance of basking shark, although this giant has been scarce of late, and a plausible prospect of blue shark. But it is better to rely on seeing grey seal and seabirds. The seals are abundant, and a typical first view is of a heavy-nostrilled snout sticking out of the water. Of the birds, gannets and fulmars are standard fare,

> **❝Ocean sunfish is a true oceanic wanderer, but summer coaxes animals close inshore❞**

with other candidates ranging from European storm-petrel to great skua, whilst shearwaters include Manx, Balearic and sooty. Have cameras at the ready...

As you coast back to Penzance quay, another pale face squints up at you from just below the foamy surface. The sight is no longer disquieting, but peaceful. No longer a moon, but a sun.

WHERE TO GO Explore Mounts Bay with marine companies that operate from Penzance quay. A recommended operator is Marine Discovery (🖰 www.marinediscovery.co.uk; see ad page 241), which uses a catamaran and collects data on the various species's presence and numbers.
FLEXIBILITY June–October for all targets, but exact timing varies each year.
MAKE IT A WEEKEND Snorkel with basking or blue sharks off Penzance (🖰 www.charleshood.com), enjoy flowering Cornish heath on the Lizard Peninsula (*May 31*) or take the MV *Scillonian* to the Isles of Scilly (*August 18*).
ALTERNATIVE LOCATIONS Sunfish and dolphin: from aboard the MV *Scillonian* can be good. Porpoise: Chanonry Point (*May 20*), Dungeness (*June 16*), Coll (*August 10*), Skye (*August 14*). Seal: widespread including Lundy (*August 6*), Whitby (*August 8*).

The steeply arched back and slender pointed dorsal fin identify this as a minke whale. (AS)

Whale of a time

WHERE North Yorkshire
TARGETS minke whale, humpback whale, harbour porpoise &
white-beaked dolphin
ACCESSIBILITY ④
CHILD-FRIENDLINESS ④

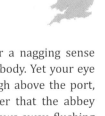

As you step carefully from quay to boat, you suffer a nagging sense that someone is watching you. You turn, but see nobody. Yet your eye is magnetised towards Whitby Abbey. Teetering high above the port, these Gothic ruins are undeniably haunting. Little wonder that the abbey inspired Bram Stoker's creation of Dracula. As the boat draws away, flushing turnstones from a jetty glistening with discarded fish entrails, a sigh of relief escapes your body.

> **66 Feeding minkes arch sleekly above the sea surface before continuing the parabola underwater 99**

You look up; clouds motor purposefully out to sea. You look ahead; that sea stretches infinitely. You look closer. A shadow flickers in the swell. Trompe l'œil or... porpoise! A brief roll of a dark back convinces you that this is indeed the day's first harbour porpoise. A positive omen.

As the boat ploughs the North Sea, its occupants' eyes scan for seabird flocks. Where gannets, kittiwakes and gulls wheel in excitement and plunge with urgency, there will surely be fish below. And where those shoals are forced upwards towards the surface, there will surely be gaping-mouthed leviathans below.

Since the turn of the Millennium, Whitby fishermen have been returning to port with tales of whales. Rising North Sea populations of herring and sardines have coaxed giant cetaceans south and east of their normal British range. On the

What a result this would be! A 'fluking' humpback whale, off Yorkshire! □□

back of this discovery, enterprising locals now offer whale-watching trips... such as yours, today.

The principal target is minke whale. A typical trip encounters small groups of feeding minkes, each arching sleekly above the sea surface before continuing the parabola underwater, out of sight. To see creatures of the deep with a backdrop of the Yorkshire coast snatches your breath away. Were you to encounter fin or humpback whales, as happens on occasion each summer, you might cease breathing entirely.

More likely, the support cast will be smaller marine mammals. Further harbour porpoises, for sure: mini-beasts in comparison to the minkes. White-beaked dolphins, probably: with their stately dorsal fin, these northern creatures recall orca. Add to the saline broth some hefty grey seals and you have a recipe for an excellent excursion.

Returning to shore, pause for thought. Two centuries back, steaming offshore from Whitby would have involved hunting whales rather than watching them; the town's economy was premised on its whaling industry. Once docked, pay homage to this evolution in our environmental attitudes by visiting the whaling exhibit at Whitby Museum. Then hike up to Whitby Abbey and continue whale-watching from the cliffs. There's nothing to fear now; it was merely the ghosts of whalers past that were observing your morning departure.

WHERE TO GO Half-day whale-watching trips depart daily from the Brewery Steps at Whitby harbour (🖰 www.whitbywhalewatching.co.uk; see ad, page 243), with longer trips at the start and end of the season. Advance booking is recommended. Seawatch from the cliff north of Whitby Abbey off Abbey Lane.

FLEXIBILITY Cetacean-watching trips run May–October, best July–September.

MAKE IT A WEEKEND Head for the North York Moors for red grouse ahead of the open season, which starts August 12, or for honey-buzzard, goshawk, common lizard and adder (*July 28*).

ALTERNATIVE LOCATIONS Minke whale: off Northumberland (*July 17*), Coll (*August 10*), Skye (*August 14*). Harbour porpoise: Mounts Bay (*August 7*), Coll, Skye. White-beaked dolphin: off Northumberland. Humpbacks: occasional animals elsewhere in the North Sea or around Penzance (*August 7*).

Day 87: August 9

Black on black

WHERE Anglesey
TARGETS raven, corkwing wrasse, yellow birdsnest, grass-of-Parnassus
& red squirrel
ACCESSIBILITY ③
CHILD-FRIENDLINESS ③

The Corsican pines, slender of trunk and neatly cylindrical of crown, stand in file like giant military pipecleaners. Atop undulating sand dunes, their black silhouettes encircle you, straining towards an ever-darker sky. Dusk is falling on Newborough Warren at the southern extremity of Britain's fifth-largest island, Anglesey.

Failing light serves as conductor's baton for a special corvid choir. Ravens roost communally in Newborough's pinewood, black upon black. Our heftiest crow heralds its arrival with grunts, basal guffaws and the deepest of caws. Whilst numbers are not what they were (the roost formerly topped 2,000 birds), seeing scores of ravens together is a revelation. What a climax to an unforgettable day.

Anglesey is a remarkable island, its diverse terrestrial landscapes encompassing sea-cliff and sand dune, mountain and marsh. There is plenty here for several days of wildlife-watching. Having started at the day's end, let's wind back. Late afternoon is a good time to look for Newborough's red squirrels. Following removal of invasive grey squirrels, Anglesey's reds are again thriving – even spreading back across the Menai Straits into mainland Gwynedd.

Make time to wander in Newborough's dune slacks, a rare habitat. Scarce, specialised plants are the main interest. Find clumps of creeping willow then search for the nodding spikes of the bizarre, chlorophyll-free yellow

Corkwing wrasse: a stunning resident of our rocky coasts (Steve Trewhella/FLPA)

"Our heftiest crow heralds its arrival with grunts, basal guffaws and the deepest of caws"

Ravens roost in large numbers at Newborough Warren. (IHL)

birdnest plus tardy marsh and even dune helleborines. Look too for grass-of-Parnassus, an exquisite flower with heart-shaped basal leaves and delicately veined white petals. Among butterflies is the grayling, though it takes sharp eyes to spot this master of camouflage.

Spend the morning on Holy Island, west of Holyhead. Breeding seabirds may have departed South Stack's wave-lashed cliffs, but the land retains much of interest. Adders regularly bask in the grasslands, and common lizards scurry along the path connecting the car park and Ellin's Tower. Silver-studded blues may still flit amongst vibrantly purple heathland, whilst choughs jeer as a warm-up to the evening's corvid star. Offshore a group of harbour porpoises rotates through the metallic swell, a reminder that islands are about water as well as land.

And so back further, to the day's very beginning. Given the dawn high tide, snorkel before breakfast. The stand-out destination is Porth Castell. Swim through the inlet to explore underwater chambers bejewelled with sea squirts. Sheer walls are studded with sponges and anemones. Squat lobsters, shannies and tompot blennies mooch under rock ledges. Mini-chasms harbour dogfish, whilst corkwing wrasse flash cyan and chestnut. Enjoy their coloured kaleidoscope now, for your raven-rich, pine-scented dusk will be unequivocally black on black.

WHERE TO GO For the raven roost at Newborough Warren (🍎 tinyurl.com/NewboroW), use Malltreath car park (♀ SH410670). Follow the main track southwest towards Llanddwyn until just beyond the track heading right to the estuary. RSPB South Stack (car park ♀ SH211818 🍎 tinyurl.com/RSPBSouthStack) is at the northwest tip of Holyhead island. Walk west to Ellin's Tower. Porth Castell (♀ SH251781): drive towards Ravens Point; park at the dive centre. High tides are best.
FLEXIBILITY Raven: year-round but numbers higher September–March. Yellow birdsnest: July–September. Grass-of-Parnassus: July–October. Wrasse, squirrel: year-round.
MAKE IT A WEEKEND Stay on Anglesey: visit Cemlyn for terns and autumn lady's-tresses, or snorkel at Craig-y-Mor.
ALTERNATIVE LOCATIONS Raven: widespread, including Snowdonia (*May 30*). Wrasse: Kimmeridge Bay (*July 23*). Birdsnest: Warburg Nature Reserve (*July 30*). Squirrel: widespread including Abernethy Forest (*June 5*). Birdnest: Bix (*July 30*), Davenport Wood (Buckinghamshire). Wrasse: Kimmeridge (*July 23*).

Day 88: August 10

Preparing to swim with a basking shark (SW)

Basking in glory

WHERE Argyll & Bute
TARGETS basking shark, minke whale, harbour porpoise &
white-tailed eagle
ACCESSIBILITY ③
CHILD-FRIENDLINESS ③

You are, to coin a phrase, tooled up. Fins, snorkel, mask: check. Wetsuit and GoPro underwater camera: check. Biggest fish in the sea... check!

You perch on the boat's gunwale. The sea off the Hebridean island of Coll was gurgling this morning, but is calmer now. Hand over mask, you fall gently backwards into the water. The rush of cold slams into you despite the Gulf Stream's fairest efforts and your neoprene layers. You bob up to the surface, a human cork. Then you peer underwater at the largest creature you have ever swum with.

Seen from the air above, a basking shark is simple geometry. An equilateral triangle (the dorsal fin) and an isosceles triangle (the tail fin) are its sole visible components. Seen from within the shark's own substrate, however, this is a beast. A gentle giant, for sure, filtering tiny plankton from the water – but a behemoth nevertheless.

Cruising leisurely a metre below the swell, the basker is indifferent to your presence. Relative to its own five-metre bulk, you are trifling. The width of its gaping mouth exceeds the length of your legs. But then you splash – a schoolboy error – and the shark flicks its isosceles and sinews into the murk.

Spluttering with excitement, the icy water forgotten, you surface and pull yourself back into the boat. The skipper squeezes the throttle and you are away in search of further marine fare.

More basking sharks follow, but none stick around long enough for you to join them. Several pods of harbour porpoise arc along. A distant group of short-beaked common dolphin teases you by shifting trajectory towards the boat, before thinking better of it and reverting to course. Then – after shark, after dolphin – whale! A minke rolls a few times, its small, sharp dorsal fin pricking your interest before it submerges and disappears. Minkes plan the dive, then dive the plan. You won't see it again.

Just as you surmise that you must have exhausted wildlife possibilities between Coll and the nearby island of Mull, the Western Isles' avian star flaps into view. The white-tailed eagle was driven to national extinction in 1918. Thanks to a determined reintroduction programme, the world's fourth-largest eagle is once again a fixture in Scottish skies. Even better, its presence brings £5 million of tourist spend flooding into Mull's coffers each year, supporting an extra hundred jobs on the island. Economy and environment working in tandem: another reason to bask in Mull's glory.

Close encounters with a basking shark (SW)

❝Peer underwater at the largest creature you have ever swam with❞

Britain's moorland beauty: red grouse (AB)

Cry freedom

WHERE Derbyshire
TARGETS red grouse
ACCESSIBILITY ②
CHILD-FRIENDLINESS ②

'Go back! Go back!' An anthromorphic interpetation, for sure, of the red grouse's call, but particularly poignant today of all days. When tomorrow comes, it will be open season on a gamebird that occurs exclusively in Britain – and thus we hold sole responsibility for its survival. Today, celebrate the grouse's final 24 hours of freedom before the clock ticks over into what the shooting industry calls the 'Glorious Twelfth'.

The moorlands for which red grouse is the poster-boy are painted vigorously magenta: the bell heather is in ostentatious bloom. Yet for four months from tomorrow, too many of these uplands – spanning northern England, Wales and Scotland – will echo with hunters' barrages as grouse plummet, lifeless, from the skies. *Inglorious* is an apt name for conservationist-turned-commentator Mark Avery's book about this upland conflict.

Avery argues the case for banning driven grouse-shooting. Whilst accepting the industry's economic importance (the Moorland Association computes that it adds £67 million to upland England's coffers), he berates the associated illegal killing of predators, notably hen harriers (see 🖱 www.henharrierday. org), and damage to moorland ecology. On his blog, Avery concludes that grouse moor-management 'is an anti-social practice, carried out for the benefit of the few at the expense of the many.'

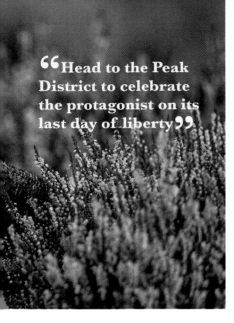

"Head to the Peak District to celebrate the protagonist on its last day of liberty"

But enough already of the conflict, of the class-politics. Head to the Peak District to celebrate the protagonist on its last day of liberty. The chestnut-coloured, feathery-footed and crimson-eyebrowed grouse occurs widely across the Dark Peak's moorland, although some sub-populations are faring better than others. Simply by driving the A57 north of Glossop you should see a few whirr across the road like airborne clockwork toys.

Arguably the finest site is Derwent Edge, which braids the peaty moorland plateau that towers above Ladybower Reservoir. From Cutthroat Bridge on the A57, the footpath snakes through heather and burnished grassland, upwards to the millstone-grit escarpment.

Under a sky bleached of individuality, you should soon hear grouse uttering their evocative call. The higher you ascend, the greater the chance you will see them. Look for grit feeders put out for the grouse – albeit with mixed emotions, given *why* those grouse are being offered supplementary nutrition. Should you arrive early in the day, you may even chance upon grouse surveying their domain from atop rocky protrusions such as Wheel Stones and Back Tor.

After a few hours communing with this unique creature, it is time for you to *go back!* Descend the bare tracks to the main road, listening for the fluting of skylarks and watching for the parachuting of meadow pipits. In the knowledge of what tomorrow will bring, these avian serenades now feel somewhat melancholy.

WHERE TO GO The Peak District National Park (🖰 www.peakdistrict.gov.uk) is centred on Derbyshire. For Derwent Edge, follow the A57 15km west from Sheffield. Use the car park just east of Cutthroat Bridge (📍 SK217875). Follow the footpath west to ascend the Edge.
FLEXIBILITY Red grouse are resident, but the grouse-shooting season lasts four months from August 12.
MAKE IT A WEEKEND Stay in the Peaks. Head to Snake Pass (📍 SK088928) and walk north along the Pennine Way for mountain hare and the odd lingering dunlin or golden plover.
ALTERNATIVE LOCATIONS In the Peaks, look for red grouse around Kinder Scout, above the Goy Valley and at Danebower Quarries. Elsewhere, the North York Moors excel (*July 28*).

Day 90: August 12
Osprey!

WHERE Rutland
TARGETS osprey, wood sandpiper, Roesel's bush-cricket & violet helleborine... & the Birdfair
ACCESSIBILITY ⑤
CHILD-FRIENDLINESS ⑤

Sometime in the early 1980s, I saved up sufficient pocket money to buy my first-ever computer game for the family Acorn Electron. *Osprey!* called upon players to save Loch Garten's famous fish-munching raptors from the cumulative vagaries of weather, low fish stocks and nest-raiding by simulating the impact of the player's management decisions. Developed in association with the RSPB, the game's buzz derived from the osprey's extreme rarity as a British breeder.

Fast forward 30-plus years: how the osprey's world has changed. Nearly 200 pairs now breed in Britain – and not only in Scotland. Thanks to translocation programmes and natural colonisation, sites in England and Wales now proudly host nesting ospreys.

> **In 2015, Rutland Water's hundredth osprey chick spread its wings**

The most successful site is England's largest artificial waterbody, Rutland Water. Ospreys have bred around the reservoir since 2001 (🖱 www.ospreys.org.uk). In 2015, the site's hundredth chick spread its wings.

Mark this conservation milestone with an early-morning boat trip. The *Rutland Belle* visits the ospreys' favoured hunting waters. Even with eight pairs breeding in 2015, there are plenty of fish-rich bays and channels to go round. Views should be spectacular as these striking raptors plunge talons first into the water, emerging with a writhing fish.

A cruise ticket offers discounted entry to the reservoir's Egleton and Lyndon reserves; it would be rude not to. The scissoring of Roesel's bush-crickets accompanies your stroll between the reserves' hides. Cup hands over ears to track down this now quintessential summer sound, and admire this attractive orthopteran which is rapidly expanding its range from southeast England.

◀ A young osprey, preparing for its autumn flight south. (JL)

Roesel's bush-cricket is spreading northwards through England. (JL)

From Egleton's hides, you should spot various migrant waders. Scan the muddy shorelines for common, green and even wood sandpipers. With its bold silvery 'eyebrow' and glittering upperparts, the latter is a smart bird indeed.

In August, Rutland Water is synonymous with the British Birdwatching Fair, the country's biggest wildlife love-in. If your visit coincides with the Birdfair, explore the growing flock of marquees. Stands sell everything a wildlife enthusiast could want. Should you want for nothing, you could chat to numerous conservation bodies or enjoy lectures by experts (typically including yours truly).

Should your trip be a Birdfair-free day, head instead to Great Merrible Wood in nearby Uppingham. Beneath a canopy of ash and pedunculate oak grows the sumptuous violet helleborine. Delicately purple of stem and lightly lilac of flower, this delectable orchid should be in peak condition. The same is true of Rutland's next generation of ospreys, each youngster stretching its wings ahead of a testing migration southwards to Iberia or west Africa.

WHERE TO GO Rutland Water (🌐 www.rutlandwater.org.uk) is east of Oakham. The *Rutland Belle* departs from Whitwell car park (📍 SK925082 🌐 www.rutlandwatercruises.com) off the A606. Egleton Reserve is on the west shore (📍 SK877072 🌐 tinyurl.com/EgletonRes), Lyndon on the south (📍 SK894056). Great Merrible Wood (📍 SP834962 🌐 tinyurl.com/GreatMerribleW) is 4km southwest of Uppingham. Park on Horninghold–Great Easton minor road at 📍 SP831958. Cross the gate then walk east through two fields to the wood. The northeast corner is best for helleborines.
FLEXIBILITY Osprey: April–September. Bush-cricket: July–October. Helleborine: late July to late August. The Birdfair (🌐 www.birdfair.org.uk): typically third week of August. Sandpiper: May or July–September.
MAKE IT A WEEKEND Chambers Farm Wood (*August 13*) for brown hairstreak.
ALTERNATIVE LOCATIONS Osprey: Abernethy Forest (*June 5*), Cors Dyfi (*August 17*). Bush-cricket: widespread in southern England. Helleborine: Warburg Nature Reserve (*July 30*). Sandpiper: widespread on passage, including Minsmere (*August 2*).

Day 91: August 13

Summer's golden days

WHERE Lincolnshire
TARGETS brown hairstreak, purple hairstreak & hazel dormouse
ACCESSIBILITY ⑤
CHILD-FRIENDLINESS ④

D eep in the Lincolnshire Limewoods, famed and named for small-leaved lime trees, you join a handful of amateur conservationists. The group is one of dozens across England and Wales that dedicate time to helping our cutest and most elusive small mammal: hazel dormouse.

This golden, furry-tailed creature – best known for prodigious naps (it hibernates from October to May) – is in trouble in Britain. The combination of its rarity, nocturnal habits and arboreal habitat makes seeing hazel dormouse challenging. Almost the only viable option is to join a survey of specially designed dormouse-nestboxes. Hence today's gathering in Chambers Farm Wood.

> **"Cue unanimous sighs of fondness at the hazel dormouse's inimitable charm"**

Although dormice are doing well here, there is no guarantee of success; low expectations and patience are key. Individuals licensed to handle dormice climb ladders to check nestboxes. Almost all will be empty, most showing no sign of mammalian occupation. Should a box be occupied, the dormouse is brought to ground level for weighing and admiration. Cue unanimous sighs of fondness at the mammal's inimitable charm.

The dormouse is one of two golden stars you are seeking in Chambers Farm Wood today. Managed by the Forestry Commission, this site is one of Britain's finest for our latest-emerging butterfly, brown hairstreak. Don't be deterred by the banal-sounding moniker. Formerly named golden hairstreak, this is one of our most exquisite butterflies. Hairstreaks rest and feed with their wings raised,

◀ A rare encounter with an open-winged brown hairstreak (IHL)

allowing admiration of their golden-bronze underwing with its broad orange stripe and cheeky tail-like protrusions from the hindwing.

These little stunners are hard to track down. Brown hairstreaks occur only locally, and populations have crashed by 40% since the 1970s. They typically remain out of sight, tucked away in the canopy of tall trees, descending only when whim takes them or the lure of nectar is overriding.

Fortunately, Chambers Farm Wood offers plenty of sugary attractions, and most visitors succeed in finding a couple of hairstreaks. The best areas are the stands of blackthorn at the Five Ways corner of the main ride, and the triangular meadow ('Minting Triangle') a little way east.

Hazel dormouse in a specially provided box (JL)

Keep your eye out for other butterflies too, particularly those with 'purple' in their name. Purple hairstreaks will still be flying, and this is the Lincolnshire Wolds' best site for purple emperor, which sometimes persist well into August here. Again, the Five-Ways area is best. Finish the day with a visit to the Butterfly Conservation butterfly garden – and learn how having green fingers can help our favourite winged insects.

WHERE TO GO Chambers Farm Wood (📍 TF147740 📱 www.forestry.gov.uk/chambersfarmwood) is 15km east of Lincoln, east of the B1202. Five Ways is 1km northeast of the car park, at the junction between Five Rides. Disturbing dormice is illegal without a licence: no checking nestboxes yourself.

FLEXIBILITY Brown hairstreak flies early August to late September. Purple hairstreak: July–August. Lincolnshire Dormouse Group usually offers opportunities to see dormice each August (contact e anne.goodall@esl-lincoln.co.uk).

MAKE IT A WEEKEND Call in at Frampton Marsh (Lincolnshire) where the RSPB has created a fantastic new habitat for breeding and migrant waders.

ALTERNATIVE LOCATIONS Dormouse: Briddlesford Woods (Isle of Wight). Brown hairstreak: Alners Gorse (Dorset), Whitecross Green Wood (Oxfordshire/Buckinghamshire), Grafton Wood (Worcestershire) and Shipton Bellinger (Hampshire/Wiltshire). Hairstreak: widespread, including Fermyn Woods (*June 30*) and Knepp (*July 11*).

▼ White-tailed eagle, master of Skye's skies (IHL)

The eagle has landed... again

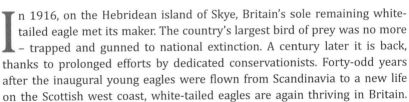

WHERE Western Isles
TARGETS white-tailed eagle, golden eagle, harbour seal & otter
ACCESSIBILITY ④
CHILD-FRIENDLINESS ⑤

In 1916, on the Hebridean island of Skye, Britain's sole remaining white-tailed eagle met its maker. The country's largest bird of prey was no more – trapped and gunned to national extinction. A century later it is back, thanks to prolonged efforts by dedicated conservationists. Forty-odd years after the inaugural young eagles were flown from Scandinavia to a new life on the Scottish west coast, white-tailed eagles are again thriving in Britain.

> **❝The white-tailed eagle is a flying barn door that would smash urban speed limits❞**

How apposite to celebrate that particular success by watching *erne* on Skye itself.

About 20 pairs of white-tailed eagles now hold territories in the home of Talisker malt, so you could bump into one anywhere. If you are in pilgrimage mode, however, head to Portree where pastel-coloured blocks of houses nuzzle the quay. Join one of several boats departing Portree harbour to explore the rocky coast towards the Sound of Raasay.

Early-morning trips are best for one very simple reason. Hunger. After a night slumbering rather than feeding, eagles are famished. Boat skippers have cottoned on to this, hurling fish into the water to encourage scavenging eagles

Scan rocky, seaweed-strewn bays for otter. (IHL)

to offer clients jaw-dropping views and fill up their camera memory cards.

Nothing, but nothing, prepares you for the sheer size and pure speed of a plunging white-tail. This is a flying barn door that would smash urban speed limits. The fish should be thankful that it is already dead...

Once the eagle has powered off to enjoy breakfast alone, the boat rounds the wee island of Raasay. You should come across harbour porpoise swimming with metronome regularity. You may spot black guillemots (aka 'tysties') lazing on the water, harbour seals lounging on rocky shorelines or an otter frolicking in the kelp. In deep water, you may even chance upon a minke whale going about its business. Great encounters all, but that breathtaking eagle nevertheless stands (flies?) proudly as the day's unsurpassable highlight.

So why not make it two species of eagle in a day? Skye may be best known for its white-tails, but 30 pairs of golden eagles also call this island home. For the best chance of seeing them, lace up your walking boots and hike up the Cuillins. Should that seem like hard work, alternatives include scanning the skies above the car park near Strathaird Farm and taking the ferry to Raasay, where two pairs breed. Whatever your approach, your chances are Skye high: here the *eagles* (plural) have definitely landed.

WHERE TO GO On Skye, boats leave Portree harbour (♀ NG485435). Recommended operators are Stardust (♨ www.skyeboat-trips.co.uk) and Brigadoon (♨ www.portree-boat-trips.co.uk). Access to the Cuillins is from Sligachan and Glen Brittle. Strathaird Farm (♀ NG541171) car park is on the B8083 near Elgol.
FLEXIBILITY Eagles: resident. Seal and otter: best May–September.
MAKE IT A WEEKEND Stay on Skye. Search quiet seaweed-rich bays for otters. Visit the harbour seal colony at Dunvegan Castle. Explore the Cuillins for ptarmigan or red deer. Seawatch from Rubha Hunish, Waternish or Neist Point for minke whale, short-beaked common dolphin and basking shark.
ALTERNATIVE LOCATIONS White-tailed eagle: Coll (*August 10*). Golden eagle: Findhorn Valley (Highland). Harbour seal: Chanonry Point (*May 20*), Blakeney Point (*August 3*). Otter: widespread, including Stackpole (*May 27*) and Avalon Marshes (*June 25*).

Rainham is brilliant for bug-hunting: bryony ladybirds are a speciality. (JL)

Mini-beast magic

WHERE Essex
TARGETS bryony ladybird, shrill carder bee, wasp spider, water vole & marsh frog
ACCESSIBILITY ⑤
CHILD-FRIENDLINESS ⑤

It's time to release your inner child. If it helps, bring one along with you. Mini-beast adventures are treasure hunts; Rainham Marshes' bounty is copious and glittering. Since expanding its public face from birds pure and simple to nature in myriad forms, the RSPB has embraced the richness of its reserves to captivate allcomers.

Mini-beasts are integral to the attraction. Join an organised excursion to search flowering plants, peer under leaves, and swish sweep-nets through grass. Even if you've got obvious insects nailed – butterflies, dragonflies and moths, say – your eyes will expand into saucers when you start spotting and 'potting' manifold beetles, shieldbugs, ladybirds and arachnids.

Head anti-clockwise from the modernist visitor centre. Shrill carder bee, an extreme national rarity, favours flowering plants near the first bench. This bumblebee is well named: listen carefully to discern its high-pitched buzzing. Along the eastern flank of the cordite store, bryony ladybird is a jewel worth seeking. Unknown in Britain before 1997, it is amber-orange with 11 black spots.

The store itself is a sheltered suntrap, perfect for insects. You may spot horehound longhorn, a glittering micro-moth with unfeasibly long antennae, basking on leaves. Hoverflies are everywhere, suspended in mid-air before accelerating away or sprawling over leaves. Two large wasp or hornet mimics – *Volucella zonaria* and *inanis* – consider themselves invulnerable to predators. Clouds of marmalade hoverflies are complemented by the hairy-eyed *Syrphus torvus*. Male *Eristalis intricarius*, furry bee-mimics, defend their territory like jump-jets.

The mini-beast list has legs yet. A fencepost jumping spider keeps multiple watchful eyes on you before springing away. Wandering along the boardwalk hemming ditches, you soon spy water ladybird (small, yellow and boldly dotted). Emerging from scrubby carr into open grassland, you reach the domain of Rainham's most striking spider. Here female wasp spiders – so-named for their exclamatory warning stripes – weave zigzag webs. Helpful signposts save you stumbling into them blithely. Drop to ground level and examine these beautiful, grasshopper-munching invertebrates at close range.

Fellow mini-beast searchers may have turned back by now, but you should continue. August is a brilliant month to watch two of Rainham's larger specialities. You will have no problem spotting marsh frogs as they sprawl at the soggy intersection between water and land.

> **66 Hoverflies are everywhere, suspended in mid-air before accelerating away or sprawling over leaves 99**

Save the best for the end. If their breeding season has been successful, Rainham's water voles should be plentiful. Where channels cut through the reeds, approach quietly. Scan the edges and listen for nibbling. At Rainham, where the wind cossets willows and more, Ratty is easier to see than you might think. My personal best here is 20 individuals in an hour. Can you beat it?

WHERE TO GO RSPB Rainham Marshes (♀ TQ552792 🎣 tinyurl.com/RSPBRainham) is just west of the M25, south of the A13/A1306 junction. Check the events page of the website for dates of mini-beast searches, pond-dipping and other events.

FLEXIBILITY Mini-beasts: May–September. Wasp spider: August–September. Shrill carder bee: July–September. Water vole: resident but August–September ideal. Frog: May–September.

MAKE IT A WEEKEND Spend another day at Rainham but target birds and dragonflies, including willow emerald damselfly. Or Wat Tyler Country Park (Essex) for dragonflies including possible blue-eyed hawker.

ALTERNATIVE LOCATIONS Wasp spider: local in southern England grasslands, including London Wetland Centre (*August 19*). Shrill carder bee: Wat Tyler (*June 11*), Newport Wetlands (Gwent). Water vole: London Wetland Centre (*August 19*) and Arundel Castle (*August 4*). Ladybird: best here. Frog: Dungeness (*June 16*), London Wetland Centre.

Day 94: August 16

Creatures of the night

WHERE Suffolk
TARGETS stone-curlew, Reeve's muntjac & badger
ACCESSIBILITY ④
CHILD-FRIENDLINESS ⑤

Early morning at Cavenham Heath, where the sandy heathland is necklaced with diamonds. Spider webs – in unanticipated, magical abundance – shimmer with the legacy of a clear night and autumn-boding temperatures. Beneath the watery jewellery, the bristly ling shades the scene mauve. Sheep graze, with cows further back. Distant squeals from Suffolk's famed porcines drift on the breeze. In the foreground is a jaw-dropping, hundred-strong flock of wailing 'heath chickens'.

> **❝Goggle-eyed and gawky, stone-curlew is a rare old bird❞**

Despite their livestock neighbours, these are not poultry, but Britain's sole nocturnal shorebird. A shorebird that shuns contact with shores, breeding in the country's most arid terrain. Goggle-eyed and gawky, stone-curlew is a rare old bird. Just 350 pairs nest in Britain, and the combination of scarcity, night-time activity and day-time camouflage makes it inadvisable to search for stone-curlews on breeding grounds.

Birds of a feather flock together: in this case, stone-curlew. (JL)

Far better to await the close of the breeding season, when stone-curlews assemble by the score, gathering themselves ahead of migrating southwards into Africa. Breckland's Cavenham Heath is one of just a handful of sites where post-breeding flocks gather – and it would be a poor day if you saw fewer than 50 birds. The record count tops 150! Even better, once liberated from the secrecy demanded by raising offspring, stone-curlews turn extrovert, opening their lives to unconstrained inspection. The views are remarkable, so watch them for a good few hours.

There is plenty of other wildlife too. A hobby angles past, sharp and intent. Its quarry, swallows doing laps low over the sandy grassland, are themselves alert for airborne prey. A tree pipit flies over, calling breathlessly. Stonechats chide your passage, while flirting with fencepost and heathery summit. One drops to the ground to nab an orthopteran: probably a field grasshopper but Roesel's bush-cricket is common here too.

Along the 'wetland trail', flanking an enchanting chalk stream, dragonflies such as migrant hawker and common darter flaunt themselves. A Reeve's muntjac feeds sedately in undergrowth; Breckland offers excellent views of this non-native deer. A few migrant warblers – common whitethroat, chiffchaff and willow warbler – scrounge insects, occasionally breaking into half-hearted song.

Given the early start, grant yourself some respite then regroup at a Suffolk Wildlife Trust site near Ipswich as the sky starts to darken. You can never do too much badger-watching, and booking a berth in the comfy Margaret Grimwade Hide enables you to do so in style. The stage is floodlit, and the 'actors' encouraged to perform with a generous sprinkling of peanuts. All being well, you should enjoy prolonged views of several snuffling badgers with only a windowpane stopping you from being within an arm's length of the day's second creature of the night.

WHERE TO GO Cavenham Heath National Nature Reserve (tinyurl.com/CavenhamHeath) is 5km southeast of Mildenhall. In Tuddenham, leave High Street at the telephone box (TL736715) and drive 1km northeast along a rough track (Icknield Way Trail) to the car park. View stone-curlews from post 9 on Heathland Trail. Margaret Grimwade Badger Hide near Ipswich is managed by Suffolk Wildlife Trust (www.suffolkwildlifetrust.org/badger_hide); its location will be revealed upon booking (01473 890089).
FLEXIBILITY Stone-curlews flock here early August to mid-October. Muntjac: year-round. Badger: hide opens three evenings per week, April–September.
MAKE IT A WEEKEND Redgrave and Lopham Fen (Suffolk   tinyurl.com/RedgraveLophamFen) has fen raft spider.
ALTERNATIVE LOCATIONS Stone-curlews flock at Winterbourne Downs (Wiltshire   tinyurl.com/WinterbourneDowns). Badgers: widespread (for viewing facilities see   tinyurl.com/BadgerSites). Muntjac: widespread, including Holkham (Norfolk).

A seething mass of Manx shearwaters and gannets off Borth (JB)

Birds of a feather

WHERE Ceredigion
TARGETS Manx shearwater, gannet & osprey
ACCESSIBILITY ⑤
CHILD-FRIENDLINESS ④

Watching flocks of birds provides some of Britain's most exhilarating wildlife experiences. Most, however, occur at seasons other than summer: think swirling waders on estuaries, shape-shifting starling murmurations and giant gaggles of geese. Most, but not all. Which is why you are standing at the apex of Cardigan Bay, poised on the beach fronting Borth village, waiting for the wind to drop, the tide to rise and the show to begin.

> **"Some Manxies come stupidly close, barely beyond the shoreline and even over the beach"**

With the naked eye, the gossamer bay is fraying. Either that or a dense cloud of mosquitoes is dusting its surface. Neither are plausible – but nor is the reality particularly credible. A hundred metres offshore, the water is dense with an immense raft of Manx shearwaters, Britain's answer to the albatross.

There are thousands, nay *tens* of thousands of them: shear madness. By some estimates perhaps one in every ten Manx shearwaters *in the world* gathers here in late summer to feast upon shoals of whitebait, clupeid and sandeel. Pairs of long, slender wings – black above, white below – flicker constantly like on-off switches as birds heave up from the feathered swell to flutter a few score metres before flopping back into the water.

It is not only 'Manxies' in the melée. An invitation to Borth's banquet is hardly one to be declined by other seabirds. Gannets – huge white crucifixes

WHERE TO GO Watch seabirds from the beach west of the B4353 between Borth
(📍 SN607890) and Ynyslas (📍 SN606925). Cors Dyfi (📍 SN701985 📖 www.montwt.
co.uk/reserves/cors-dyfi) is 5.5km southwest of Machynlleth on the A487. Follow
updates on the osprey blog (📖 www.dyfiospreyproject.com).
FLEXIBILITY Seabirds: late July to mid-August; light, onshore winds, early mornings
and high tides are best. Osprey: April–September.
MAKE IT A WEEKEND Pond-dipping at RSPB Ynys-hir can produce giant diving
beetle and more, plus a wander in meadows and woodlands.
ALTERNATIVE LOCATIONS Nowhere else hosts such a gathering of feeding Manx
shearwaters, but waters around Skomer (or on adjacent mainland from Jacks Sound
into St Bride's Bay) can hold big numbers. Osprey: Abernethy Forest
(*June 5*). Gannet: breeding colonies include Bempton (*June 3*), Bass Rock (*July 31*)
and Grassholm (Pembrokeshire).

with black tips to the wings – are numerous and active. Some tussle amongst the throng; others plunge into the water from a few metres up. Sharp eyes may pick out a sooty shearwater or Balearic shearwater, both scarce visitors from seas further south. The scissory wings of Sandwich and Arctic terns look delicate in comparison, but these seabirds are no less deadly predators.

As the tide rises yet further, so the fish are shunted ever closer to shore. With them comes the throng of famished winged predators. Time to whip out your camera. Some Manxies come stupidly close, barely beyond the shoreline and occasionally even over the beach. Take the opportunity to admire their slender black bills with prominent nostrils encased by tubes (hence 'tubenoses', the collective name for shearwaters, petrels, albatrosses and their ilk).

As the tide cedes to the moon's gravitational pull, so the shoals and their seabird attendants retreat. The curtain is falling on Borth's spectacle. Yet the day is still young. So head over to Cors Dyfi Reserve, and admire another piscivore: Wales's most famous ospreys. Assuming they have bred successfully, the pair's youngsters should have fledged and be fattening up for their first southwards migration. Wish them – and the similarly migratory Manx shearwaters – luck.

A successful hunt for this gannet (OS)

Day 96: August 18
Pelagic wanderers

WHERE Cornwall & the Isles of Scilly
TARGETS Cory's & great shearwaters, short-beaked common dolphin, lesser white-toothed shrew & prickly stick-insect
ACCESSIBILITY ③
CHILD-FRIENDLINESS ③

As its engines hum, shudder then roar, the MV *Scillonian* sidles away from Penzance dock and bids farewell to mainland Britain. In the bay to the east, the wooded islet of St Michael's Mount stands proud, shimmering and elusive. The sky echoes the colour of old bone that has endured the elements. The sea gleams like molten mercury and – fortunately, given two days of southwesterlies hurtling across the Atlantic – is as flat as the proverbial *crêpe*.

This bodes well. The wind's legacy should push ocean-soaring seabirds the ship's way, yet the crossing to the Isles of Scilly will be calm enough for you to spy your ocean-dwelling quarry. Moreover, your breakfast is unlikely to make an unwanted reappearance – something for which the maritime journey to this remote archipelago is renowned.

So sip coffee on deck whilst scanning for shapes contorting ripples, piercing the surface or adding quavers to the sky. Two triangles protruding upwards betray four-plus metres of basking shark. A shape-and-splash, then another, then another... surely... yes! A pod of short-beaked common dolphins angle towards the ship to become the *Scillonian*'s outriders.

> **"Scan for shapes contorting ripples, piercing the surface or adding quavers to the sky"**

The search is on for seabirds: fulmars, gannets, kittiwakes. A flicker and flutter of a tiny European storm-petrel, visible for seconds, hidden thereafter. Manx shearwaters for sure, tilting black and white over the swell. And, if those southwesterlies have 'worked', bigger fare. Perhaps Balearic shearwater, a Critically Endangered species with the colours of a chocolate digestive. Hopefully great shearwater, sooty-capped breeder

▶ Cory's shearwaters are blown towards Britain by southwesterly winds. (OS)

In Britain, lesser white-toothed shrew occurs only on Scilly. (HL)

of remote South Atlantic islands. Or Cory's shearwater, all stiff-winged nonchalance. Your coffee goes cold, undrunk.

Arriving in Hugh Town around midday, make good use of the four-ish hours until the *Scillonian* returns. Either hop aboard an inter-island service to visit Tresco or Bryher, St Agnes or St Martins, or stay on St Mary's. Personally, I favour Bryher, with its twisting tracks and changing vistas. But 'Mary's' is undoubtedly convenient, with ample wildlife to keep you occupied.

Try Old Town cemetery for prickly stick-insect, which arrived with imported plants but is now embedded here. Adjacent Old Town beach is the best place for lesser white-toothed shrew, a speciality that resides nowhere else in Britain. Overturn rocks along the foreshore, or check the path to Peninnis Head. Visit Porth Hellick Pool or Lower Moors for migrant waders such as green sandpiper (wouldn't a pectoral sandpiper be nice?). And then return to MV *Scillonian* for round two of marine wildlife-watching. And coffee.

WHERE TO GO Travel to the Isles of Scilly (🖱 www.visitislesofscilly.com) is by sea or air; choose the former for marine wildlife-watching. Bar Sundays, MV *Scillonian* sails daily from Penzance (🖱 www.islesofscilly-travel.co.uk).
FLEXIBILITY Marine wildlife: July–October. Stick-insect and shrew: resident but easiest to see June–October.
MAKE IT A WEEKEND Stay on the Scillies to do an evening pelagic trip or cruise Penzance Bay for harbour porpoise and other cetaceans (*August 7*).
ALTERNATIVE LOCATIONS Shrew and stick-insect: none. Shearwaters: Cornish headlands such as Porthgwarra and Pendeen. Dolphin: Penzance (*July 20*), Bude (*August 18*), Coll (*August 10*).

A capital day

WHERE London
TARGETS Aesculapian snake, autumn squill, water vole, noctule bat
& wasp spider
ACCESSIBILITY ③
CHILD-FRIENDLINESS ④

Despite being safely enclosed in nearby London Zoo, the roaring lion is somewhat disconcerting. It nevertheless adds atmosphere to your day of capital wildlife-watching. It even fits with the tropical temperatures and humidity of the London Underground – the legacy of a sultry night.

Such conditions bode well for the morning's target, as the 'Camden creature' stays resolutely hidden underground unless the air temperature exceeds 20ºC.

The Camden creature is no mythical beast, but nor should it be here. Perhaps 30 Aesculapian snakes call Regent's Canal home, and today's first mission is to track one down. Nobody knows exactly how these harmless, mud-green European serpents reached London, but some fingers point towards the adjacent zoo. To see this clandestine non-native, walk the canal's

> **"The Camden creature is no mythical beast, but nor should it be here"**

northern towpath either side of the Snowdon aviary, looking patiently in sheltered, sunny areas of the wall and slope above.

From north London to the capital's southwest. If time is on your side, head to Hampton Court. Stunning as its palace may be, your quarry is botanical. On Home Park's short turf, atop the Thames' alluvial floodplain, grows a delicate, lilac and Nationally Scarce flower that is otherwise pretty much restricted to southwest England's coastline. The presence of autumn squill here is anomalous, if less mystifying than Aesculapian snake.

Spend the remainder of the day at the WWT London Wetland Centre in Barnes. This is Britain's showcase urban reserve, with wetlands,

A female wasp spider in its frizzy orb (JL)

▲ A rarely seen Aesculapian snake, curving through Camden's leaf litter. (JL)

reedbeds and carr created from the carcasses of defunct reservoirs. Sir David Attenborough, resident of nearby Richmond, described it as 'the ideal model for how humankind and the natural world may live side by side in the 21st century.'

Start with a walk on the Wildside, as the reserve's northwest corner is known. Keep your ears pricked for the chomping teeth of a water vole: introduced in 2001, the population has swollen to 350 individuals. Dragonflies zip and cruise: common darter, black-tailed skimmer and small red-eyed damselfly among them. Between Wildside gate and the reedbeds look for common lizard, particularly around bridges. Along the 'south route' search for wasp spider in its foamy web. This stunning arachnid is garbed in red, black, yellow and white.

As chucking-out time approaches, relax. You've chosen today specifically to join one of the centre's after-hours bat walks. These nocturnal safaris are a treat. Visitors split into groups, each equipped with a bat-detector that enables you to 'listen' to the bats' echolocation clicks. This allows you to confidently identify bats to species. Noctule bats hawk high in the sky, Daubenton's low over the water, with three species of pipistrelle (including the rare Nathusius's) in between. Top stuff. Indeed, capital.

WHERE TO GO Regent's Canal is between Primrose Hill and Regent's Park. Walk the canal's north bank west from Prince Albert Road/Albert Terrace junction, to beyond Snowdon aviary (♥ TQ282837). East of Hampton Court Palace, enter Home Park (♥ TQ162677 ♻ tinyurl.com/HomeParkMap) through Jubilee Gate on Barge Walk. London Wetland Centre (♥ TQ225767 ♻ www.wwt.org.uk/visit/london) is 100m east of the A306/A3003 junction in Barnes. Check the website for bat walk dates.
FLEXIBILITY Aesculapian snake: warm days, May–September. Autumn squill: August. Wasp spider: August–September. Bats: June–September. Water vole: year-round.
MAKE IT A WEEKEND Rainham Marshes (*August 15*) for mini-beasts and more.
ALTERNATIVE LOCATIONS Autumn squill: Avon Gorge (Gloucestershire), south Devon coast. Water vole: widespread, including Rainham (also wasp spider) and Arundel (*August 4*). Local bat groups organise walks (♻ tinyurl.com/LocalBat). Snake: only Colwyn Bay (Conwy).

Day 98: August 20
Silver and gold

WHERE Surrey
TARGETS silver-spotted skipper, chalkhill blue, lace border,
Roman snail & autumn gentian
ACCESSIBILITY ①
CHILD-FRIENDLINESS ③

Chalk paths vein the otherwise lusciously green surface of Denbies Hillside. The view towards Leith Hill would command your attention were you not fixated on a tiny, fiery butterfly at your feet. Common across southern and central European limestone, the silver-spotted skipper barely scrapes into southeast England. Even in Britain's sunniest and driest region, the skipper demands warm south-facing downlands that enable the sun to pulse blood through the capillaries of its wings.

The silver-spotted is the rarest of Britain's five 'golden skippers', and the latest flying. This tiny butterfly has a rapid, buzzy flight that makes it hard to track. Pursuing butterflies up and down steep escarpments is a non-runner. The best tactics are to stake out sheltered chalk scree on tracks that cleave the hillside or to wait by lilac-flowered plants such as dwarf thistle and greater knapweed.

> **"If you were to sketch a cartoon butterfly, this would be it"**

All skippers are cute, but the silver-spotted tops polls. If you were to sketch a cartoon butterfly, this would be it. Eyes as big, liquid and black as a baby grey seal. The fluffiness of a teddy bear. And a body so plump that it seems impossible for tiny wings to sustain flight. Cracking.

The enormous Roman snail, a chalk downland speciality

◀ Silver-spotted skipper in a rare moment of repose (IHL)

Now change colour scheme. Look for blue butterflies and yellow flowers, specifically blue butterflies atop yellow flowers. Where you encounter sloughs of kidney vetch, you should spot Adonis and chalkhill blues, both exquisite late-summer insects. The blue tone of the males differs between the species. Adonis opts for the blue of an intense Mediterranean summer sky. Chalkhill is a leached silvery-blue, the hue of early morning in an English spring.

As you clamber upslope or scramble downhill, you will doubtless spy other butterflies and day-flying moths. Brown argus, common blue and gatekeeper for sure. Marbled white, clouded yellow and large skipper, possibly. Moths should include the stunning clouded buff, but the gossamer-winged lace border – a Nationally Scarce downland specialist – would ascribe today to red-letter status.

Track down other invertebrates. Hummocks mark the mounds of yellow meadow ants. If the morning started damp, enormous Roman snails venture out to feed. In long grass, a female wasp spider may wait, patient but alert, in her frizzy orb.

There are exciting plants too. Clustered bellflower and autumn gentian are the chalk downland stars, but search at the foot of the hill for common dodder, a parasitic plant that necklaces around its unfortunate host. Finally, keep alert for reptiles. Adders may lounge in quiet suntraps, and you could bump into a slowworm or a scurrying common lizard. Bounteous nature is the lifeblood of this amazing Surrey hillside.

WHERE TO GO For Denbies Hillside (🖱 www.nationaltrust.org.uk/denbies-hillside), leave the M25 at junction 9. Go south on the A24 to Dorking, then west on the A2003 then take Ranmore Road. Use Ranmore Common car park (♀ TQ141504) then follow tracks down- and cross-slope.
FLEXIBILITY Silver-spotted skipper: mid-July to early September. Chalkhill blue: mid-July to early September. Lace border: May–June and August–September. Roman snail: April–September. Autumn gentian: August–September.
MAKE IT A WEEKEND Bookham Common has brown hairstreak; try blackthorn over the railway bridge from the car park. Chobham Common is good for grayling and possible sand lizard.
ALTERNATIVE LOCATIONS Silver-spotted skipper, autumn gentian: Aston Rowant (Oxfordshire), Newtimber Hill (Sussex). Chalkhill blue: Devil's Dyke (*July 5*), Warham Camp (*August 3*). Roman snail: Fackenden Down (Kent).

Reptiles and amphibians

In the midst of a book celebrating the spectrum of British wildlife, I hate to confess to something so single-minded, so exclusive, so otherness-rejecting as an obsession. But if there is one animal featured in this book that gets my heart pounding and juices flowing like no other, it is the adder. Britain's sole venomous snake, a string of diamonds chaining its length and a devilish vertical papercut of a pupil, bewitches me beyond all else.

No class of animals evokes more trepidation than snakes, lizards and their *compadres*. Even that most heinous of human crimes, murder 'in cold blood', invokes these ectothermic creatures, which are guilty of no more than an inability to generate their own body heat. Our fear has become manifest in reptilian beasts of lore: dragons duelled with St George and served as guard in *Shrek*; basilisks slither from Greek mythology to Harry Potter's chamber of secrets.

That reptiles rarely command good press is fundamental to the attraction. I never tire of watching adders bask, writhe or slither across the ground in front of me: on my 42nd birthday, I saw 42 across two local sites.

I see Britain's two other native snakes much less frequently. Grass snakes are common for sure, but are harder to predict. You are likely to bump into one somewhere during your summer of wildlife, but where is a hard question to answer. Smooth snakes are the ultimate, of course; a true rarity in Britain. Instead, in this book, I offer you Britain's clandestine fourth serpent: Aesculapian snake, the Camden creature that sneaks along the banks of London's Regent's Canal.

> **❝I never tire of watching adders bask, writhe or slither across the ground❞**

Our lizards feature prominently on summer days out. Common lizards at several sites, the gloriously green sand lizards at a couple, and even the potentially indigenous common wall lizard at one location. Amphibians appear too, but sporadically. To be frank, summer is sub-optimal for seeing creatures that breathe through their skin. The breeding season for common frog and common toad, and for all three newts, is over. Fortunately, however, that for our most local amphibian – natterjack toad – is in its full throes, and the churring of a choir of males is a perfect end to selected summer evenings.

If there is one British creature to which I am addicted above all others, it is our only venomous snake: the adder. (JL)

Day 99: August 21
Greenham Common ladies

WHERE Berkshire & Buckinghamshire
TARGETS autumn lady's-tresses, autumn gentian, grayling, starfruit & edible dormouse
ACCESSIBILITY ③
CHILD-FRIENDLINESS ②

Greenham Common: symbolic homeland of the struggle against nuclear warfare. Greenham Common: restored heathland where the summer's final orchid flourishes. After 19 years of non-violent protest against cruise missiles, Greenham Common Women's Peace Camp may have been disbanded in 2000, but Greenham Common's ladies live on.

Autumn lady's-tresses is a delicate, slender orchid, the last of its summer kind. Individual plants are beautiful at close range, with snow-coloured tubular flowers twirling around a maypole of a stem. But Greenham Common is all about collectives, so it should not surprise that the short, dry turf is spiked with thousands of floral stunners.

Given such numbers, seeing the lady's-tresses is harder than you might think. Greyish-green stems blend into the cropped grass, meaning that spotting them from head height is a hit-and-miss affair. Better to walk to the best area (100m east of the car park by the control tower), then lie down carefully on the ground and look at finger height above its surface for the base of the floral swirl. You will soon spy clusters, groups and crowds: a botanical peace camp.

> **"Autumn lady's-tresses is a delicate, slender orchid, the last of its summer kind"**

As you search, you may flush another cryptic entity. Grayling is a superbly camouflaged butterfly that blends in with bare ground. Easier to see should be brown argus, a square of dark chocolate with chilli flakes. Among other

▶ Peaceful, respectful, subtly beautiful: autumn lady's-tresses (JL)

236

plants, common centaury, devil's-bit scabious and dwarf thistle punctuate the grassed-over runway. Then wave goodbye to the common's memories of protesting women and its swathes of floral ladies.

An hour's drive east, pause at Black Park Country Park. A scruffy overgrown pond seems an unlikely site for one of Britain's rarest plants. Starfruit – named on account of its six-pronged fruit – has been introduced here as part of a careful conservation programme. Seeing it involves shunning Harry Potter's Forbidden Forest (the real-world location of it, anyway) to traverse the heathland, navigating your way to Black Park pond and scouring its muddy edges.

As evening threatens, drive north to Wendover Woods for a mammalian

Bright-eyed and bushy-tailed, the edible dormouse (JL)

treat. Yews arch over you, accelerating the rush of night. The boughs above soon resonate with whickering and grunting. Flick on your torch to illuminate the bulging eyes, horseshoe ears and fluffy tail of an edible dormouse. Then another... and another. The yews are crawling with the Chilterns' cuddliest creature. Seeing it should require no struggle.

WHERE TO GO Greenham Common (🐭 www.greenham-common.org.uk) is 3km southeast of Newbury. Use the control tower car park (📍 SU499651); walk 100m east. Black Park Country Park (📍 TQ006829 🐭 tinyurl.com/BlackParkCP) is off the A412, 4km northeast of Slough. Starfruit pond is on heathland north of 'Five Points'. Wendover Woods is off the B4009 Tring–Wendover road. Use Mansion Hill car park (📍 SP884099). Look here or 100m southeast.

FLEXIBILITY Lady's-tresses and gentian: August–September. Grayling: end June to August. Starfruit: June–August. Dormouse: June–September.

MAKE IT A WEEKEND Visit Aston Rowant (Oxfordshire) for silver-spotted skipper and Chiltern gentian.

ALTERNATIVE LOCATIONS Lady's-tresses: Wilverley Plain (Hampshire), St Aldhelm's Head (Dorset). Gentian: widespread, including Denbies Hillside (*August 20*). Grayling: widespread including Minsmere (*August 2*). Dormouse: none. Starfruit: best here.

Day 100: August 22

Dewy damselflies

WHERE Norfolk
TARGETS small red-eyed damselfly, willow emerald damselfly, clouded yellow & peregrine
ACCESSIBILITY ⑤
CHILD-FRIENDLINESS ④

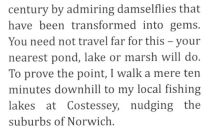

Every August there comes a morning when you notice that summer has changed. You perceive a crispy edge to the air, a touch of bronze in the green. The background hum of hoverflies and sawing of grasshoppers is a notch less intense. Summer has not ceased; autumn has not stolen its place. But, irredeemably, the season has turned.

If last night's skies were clear, your garden lawn will be sparkling. Seize this first dewy dawn of post-summer. Celebrate reaching your wildlife-watching century by admiring damselflies that have been transformed into gems. You need not travel far for this – your nearest pond, lake or marsh will do. To prove the point, I walk a mere ten minutes downhill to my local fishing lakes at Costessey, nudging the suburbs of Norwich.

Glittering jewel: a dew-encased small red-eyed damselfly (JL)

Arrive at dawn, before the sun has awoken and whilst the air is spikily chilled. Search vegetation, high or low, for roosting damselflies. The species is immaterial; any will do. In my case there are two: blue-tailed and small red-eyed damselflies. The former is common and widespread, the latter spreading urgently across England following its arrival in the late 1990s.

When you spot a damselfly, look closely. It glitters. Decorated with tiny water droplets, the damselfly conceives no prospect of flight.

> **"Find another damselfly. Its baubles will differ. Each glitters with individuality. Love them"**

A young peregrine on Norwich Cathedral (RC)

It freezes, crystalline and wondrous. Admire it. Then find another damselfly. Its baubles will differ. Each glitters with individuality. Love them.

Then leave them. As the morning thaws, so the jewelled damsels dry out and wing away. Spend the rest of day 100 honouring your local late-summer wildlife.

For me, in Norwich – and for you too, should you wish to join me – this means checking a sunny glade at Queen's Hills housing estate nearby. A hummingbird hawkmoth buzzes me, and a slowworm curves away at my footfall. Clouded yellows that arrived in early summer have bred, and the new generation of this migrant butterfly has emerged. Their apple-green eyes bulge as much as the powerful veins stoking their wings.

Then I weave through suburbs to reach the River Yare at Eaton. I am back on damselflies. Willows in the car park, brambles nearby or sedges caressing the chalk-stream bank hold the latest damsel to have taken Britain by storm. Willow emerald damselflies have come out of nowhere to conquer southern England. They pose on branches, alert for errant insects to devour.

And then to central Norwich, to its cathedral. I look upwards until I spot a young peregrine, motionless, sentry-like. As I marvel at the affinity that the world's fastest bird now shows for our cities, I close my summer of British wildlife. Where will you end yours?

WHERE TO GO If you follow my itinerary: Costessey Pits are off Norwich Road south of Old Costessey (♀ TG185112). For Queen's Hills, drive through Old Costessey towards Ringland; park in the layby by the storm pond (♀ TG156128). Walk 150m south through woods to a sunny glade by Poethlyn Drive. At Eaton, park immediately east of the River Yare bridge (♀ TG201060). Use city centre car parks for Norwich Cathedral (♀ TG235089).

FLEXIBILITY Mid-August onwards for crisp post-summer dawns. Small red-eyed damselfly: July–September. Willow emerald damselfly: late July to October. Yellow: July–September. Peregrine: resident but best March–August.

MAKE IT A WEEKEND Head for Blakeney Point for harbour seal and Warham Camp for chalkhill blue (*August 3*). Holt Country Park (Norfolk) for silver-washed fritillary and adder.

ALTERNATIVE LOCATIONS Dewy damselflies: a pond near you! Willow emerald damselfly: Strumpshaw Fen (Norfolk), Marshside (Kent), Alderson Lake (Suffolk). Urban peregrines: various, see *August 4*. Yellow: can occur anywhere, including Warham Camp (*August 3*).

241

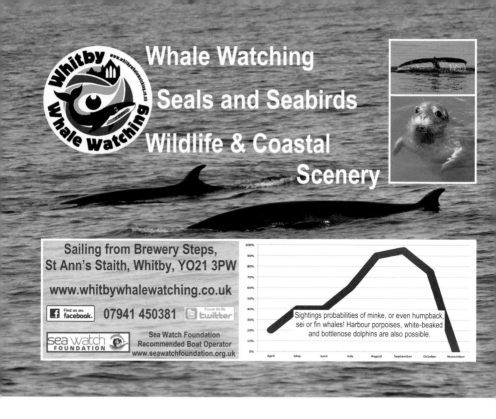

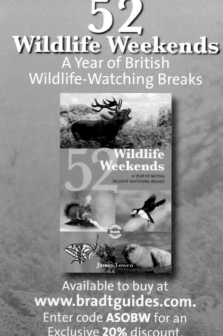

Further Information

Books

Here is a personal selection of books to accompany *A Summer of British Wildlife*. These focus on identification and locations for wildife-watching, but also include some of the inspirational nature narratives which I have referenced.

General nature

52 Wildlife Weekends: A Year of British Wildlife-Watching Breaks. James Lowen, Bradt Travel Guides 2013.
Coastlines: The Story Of Our Shore. Patrick Barkham, Granta 2015.
The Old Ways: A Journey On Foot. Robert Macfarlane, Penguin 2013.
Few And Far Between: On The Trail of Britain's Rarest Animals. Charlie Elder, Bloomsbury 2015.

Habitats

Britain's Habitats: A Guide to the Wildlife Habitats of Britain and Ireland. Sophie Lake and Durwyn Liley, Princeton WILDGuides 2014.

Mammals

Where to Watch Mammals in Britain and Ireland. Richard Moores, A&C Black 2007.
Britain's Sea Mammals: Whales, Dolphins, Porpoises and Seals, and Where to Find Them. Jon Dunn, Robert Still and Hugh Harrop, Princeton WILDGuides 2012.

Reptiles and amphibians

Britain's Reptiles and Amphibians. Howard Inns, Princeton WILDGuides 2009.

Birds

Where to Watch Birds in Britain. Simon Harrap and Nigel Redman, Helm 2010.
Collins Bird Guide. Lars Svensson, Killian Mullarney and Dan Zetterström, Collins 2009.

Dragonflies

Britain's Dragonflies. Dave Smallshire and Andy Swash, Princeton WILDGuides 2014.
Dragonflight. Marianne Taylor, Bloomsbury 2013.

Butterflies and moths

Discover Butterflies in Britain. David Newland, Princeton WILDGuides 2006.
Britain's Butterflies. David Newland, Rob Still and David Tomlinson, Princeton WILDGuides 2014.
Concise Guide to the Moths of Great Britain and Ireland. Martin Townsend and Paul Waring, British Wildlife Publishing 2007.
The Butterfly Isles. Patrick Barkham, Granta 2011.

Other invertebrates

Collins Complete Guide to British Insects. Michael Chinery, Collins 2009.
Britain's Hoverflies. Stuart Ball and Roger Morris, Princeton WILDGuides 2015.
Field Guide to the Bees of Great Britain and Ireland. Steven Falk and Richard Lewington, British Wildlife Publishing 2015.
Grasshoppers and Crickets. Ted Benton, Collins 2012.

Underwater life

RSPB Handbook of the Seashore. Maya Plass, Bloomsbury 2013.
Seasearch Observer's Guide to Marine Life of Britain and Ireland. Chris Wood, Marine Conservation Society 2007.

Plants

Orchids of Britain and Ireland: A Field and Site Guide. Simon and Annie Harrap, A&C Black 2009.
Harrap's Wild Flowers. Simon Harrap, Bloomsbury 2013.
Britain's Rare Flowers. Peter Marren, T & AD Poyser 2005.
Meadows. George Peterken, British Wildlife Publishing 2013.

Apps

High-quality wildlife identification apps for smartphones are gradually hitting the market. I routinely use the following:

Collins Bird Guide. Touchpress.
Bumblebees of Britain and Ireland. Natureguides.
iRecord Grasshoppers and Crickets. Field Studies Council.
Dragonflies of Britain and Ireland. Birdguides and WILDGuides.
Moths of Britain and Ireland. Bloomsbury and Natureguides.

Useful websites

In addition to websites mentioned in the *Practicalities* section of each of the 100 days, keep your eye on:

 www.xcweather.co.uk Arguably the most complete weather site.
 www.tidetimes.org.uk For checking tide times before visiting estuaries.
 www.atropos.info/flightarrivals News of migrant insects.
 www.birdguides.com Up-to-the-minute information on interesting birds.
 www.british-dragonflies.org.uk Website of the British Dragonfly Society.
 www.ukdragonflies.com Forum for dragonfly observations.
 www.ukbutterflies.co.uk Forum for butterfly observations.
 www.ukbms.org An online database of butterfly sites and records.
 www.birdforum.net A community of wildlife-watchers (well beyond birds).

Index of Sites

Geopolitical areas (eg: counties in England) are *italicised*; sites are in plain type; photographs of locations are marked in **bold** type. Only the first mention of each entry in the main text for each day is specified. We have omitted from site names both protected area status (eg: 'National Nature Reserve') and site management (eg: RSPB), which are both mentioned in the *Practicalities* boxes accompanying each day.

Index of advertisers

Index of wildlife targets

This index relates solely to 'target wildlife', ie: the highlights given at the start of each day. Scientific names follow each species in parentheses. After each scientific name is a simple descriptor of the 'type' of creature involved (eg: bird, moth, plant) where this is not evident from its name.

Page numbers in plain type indicate the first mention (only) of the species during a particular day; those in **bold** type indicate that the species is one of the 'targets' for the day; and those in *italic* relate to photographs. The index does not extend to mentions of species other than in the body text for each day (eg: not to the *Practicalities* boxes or double-page articles).

First edition published March 2016
Bradt Travel Guides Ltd
IDC House, The Vale, Chalfont St Peter, Bucks SL9 9RZ, England
www.bradtguides.com
Print edition published in the USA by The Globe Pequot Press Inc,
PO Box 480, Guilford, Connecticut 06437-0480

Text copyright © 2016 James Lowen
Maps copyright © 2016 Bradt Travel Guides
Photographs copyright © 2016 Individual photographers (see below)
Project Manager: Anna Moores
Cover research: Anna Moores & Ian Spick

ISBN: 978 1 78477 009 9 (print)
e-ISBN: 978 1 78477 154 6 (e-pub)
e-ISBN: 978 1 78477 254 3 (mobi)

British Library Cataloguing in Publication Data
A catalogue record for this book is available from the British Library

Photographs Janet Baxter (JB), Dr Tristan Bantock (TB), Andy Butler (AB), Robin Chittenden/ Harlequin Pictures (RC), John Dixon (JD), www.FLPA-images.co.uk (individual photographers credited alongside image), James Hanlon (JH), Hannah Jones/Marine Discovery Penzance (HJ), Martin Kitching/Northern Experience Wildlife Tours (MK/NEWT), Hannah Lawson (HL), Iain H Leach (IHL), Durwyn Liley & Sophie Lake/Footprint Ecology (DL & SL), James Lowen/jameslowen.com (JL), Ben Locke (BL), Peter Moore (PM), Rebecca Nason (RN), Robert Petley-Jones (RP-J), Shutterstock. com (individual photographers credited alongside images), Alick Simmons (AS), Oliver Smart/ SmartImages (OS), Andy & Gill Swash/worldwildleimages.com (A&GS), Mark Telfer (MT), David Tipling (DT), Shane Wasik/Basking Shark Scotland (SW)

Front cover Top, left to right: Small tortoiseshell butterfly (JL), Adder (Jules Cox/FLPA), 'Wasp' orchid (JL); Main image: Puffin (Johan Siggesson/Nature in Stock/FLPA)
Author photo, page 2 by Amy Lowen
Title page Gannet is Britain's largest seabird (OS)
Back cover Top: red squirrel (IHL), bottom: elephant hawkmoth (JL)

Maps David McCutcheon FBCart.S and Ian Spick

Typeset and designed by Ian Spick, Bradt Travel Guides Ltd
Production managed by Jellyfish Print Solutions; printed in the UK
Digital conversion by www.dataworks.co.in